Straitjacket Sexualities

ASIAN AMERICA
A series edited by Gordon H. Chang

The increasing size and diversity of the Asian American population, its growing significance in American society and culture, and the expanded appreciation, both popular and scholarly, of the importance of Asian Americans in the country's present and past—all these developments have converged to stimulate wide interest in scholarly work on topics related to the Asian American experience. The general recognition of the pivotal role that race and ethnicity have played in American life, and in relations between the United States and other countries, has also fostered the heightened attention.

Although Asian Americans were a subject of serious inquiry in the late nineteenth and early twentieth centuries, they were subsequently ignored by the mainstream scholarly community for several decades. In recent years, however, this neglect has ended, with an increasing number of writers examining a good many aspects of Asian American life and culture. Moreover, many students of American society are recognizing that the study of issues related to Asian America speak to, and may be essential for, many current discussions on the part of the informed public and various scholarly communities.

The Stanford series on Asian America seeks to address these interests. The series will include works from the humanities and social sciences, including history, anthropology, political science, American studies, law, literary criticism, sociology, and interdisciplinary and policy studies.

A full list of titles in the Asian America series can be found online at www.sup.org/asianamerica

Straitjacket Sexualities

UNBINDING ASIAN AMERICAN
MANHOODS IN THE MOVIES

Celine Parreñas Shimizu

STANFORD UNIVERSITY PRESS
STANFORD, CALIFORNIA

Stanford University Press
Stanford, California

Published with the assistance of the Edgar M. Kahn Memorial Fund.

Library of Congress Cataloging-in-Publication Data

Shimizu, Celine Parreñas, author.
  Straitjacket sexualities : unbinding Asian American manhoods in the
movies / Celine Parreñas Shimizu.
      pages cm
  Includes bibliographical references and index.
  ISBN 978-0-8047-7300-3 (cloth : alk. paper) -- ISBN 978-0-8047-7301-0
(pbk. : alk. paper)
  1. Asian American men in motion pictures. 2. Masculinity in motion
pictures. 3. Sex in motion pictures. 4. Motion pictures--United States--
History. I. Title.
  PN1995.9.A77A795 2012
  791.43'65211--dc23
                         2011049005

Typeset by Bruce Lundquist in 11/14 Adobe Garamond

For my sons, Bayan and Lakas, with love

Contents

Acknowledgments

While I bear all responsibility for this work, Juliana Chang, Stephen Sohn, and Jerry Miller enabled me to write with the most demanding audience in mind. Thank you for reading and responding to every chapter in the best writing group ever. Rhacel Salazar Parreñas and Juno Parreñas generously shared close sisterly company in the scholarly life as the book took shape and got done. Shelley Lee and Stephanie Batiste read parts of the manuscript and significantly deepened my study. My series editor, Gordon Chang, provided essential advice I used to open and close this book. With their unflagging faith Harry Elam, David Palumbo-Liu, Purnima Mankekar, Constance Penley, Helen Lee, and Jon Cruz energized my work. Anitra Grisales copyedited the manuscript with humbling commitment.

The Departments of Asian American Studies, Film and Media Studies, and Feminist Studies at the University of California at Santa Barbara provided a home for me as I embarked on this project. I thank my colleagues Lalaie Ameeriar, Diane Fujino, Ambi Harsha, erin Khuê Ninh, Sameer Pandya, John Park, Jeff Sheng, Xiaojian Zhao, Tania Israel, Stephanie LeMenager, Laury Oaks, Mireille Miller-Young, Eileen Boris, Rudy Busto, Pat Cohen, Anna Everett, Ingrid Banks, Kum-Kum Bhavnani, Zaveeni Khan-Marcus, Sarah Fenstermaker, Maria Herrera-Sobek, Shirley Lim, Leila Rupp, Beth Schneider, and Dean Melvin Oliver for helping me more than they know. I value Arlene Phillips, Elizabeth Guerrero, and Gary Colmenar for their steadfast support. The Institute for Social, Behavioral, and Economic Research and the Academic Senate Committee on Research at UCSB provided grants that enabled my work at the University of Southern California Warner Brothers Archive, the UCLA Film and Television Archive, and the Library of Congress. I thank IHC's Holly Unruh, ISBER's Barbara Walker, and the Academic Senate's Connie Howard for their support. Thanks to my wonderful colleagues beyond UCSB—Gilberto Blasini, David Eng, Peter X, Feng, Bakirathi Mani, Konrad Ng, Viet Nguyen, Chon Noriega, Eve Oishi, Hung Thai, and Tristan Taormino for supporting my work.

The Research Institute of Comparative Studies in Race and Ethnicity (CCSRE) at Stanford University provided fellowship support that freed me to focus on this project. I am thankful to Matt Snipp, Hazel Marcus, Shelley Fisher Fishkin, Anthony Lising Antonio, Yvonne Yarbro Bejarano, and Michele Elam. Great appreciation goes to Elizabeth Wahl, Chris Queen, and Heidi M. Lopez, who aided my work. Cindy Ng at the Asian American Activities Center and Monica Moore and Jan Hafner in the Program in Modern Thought and Literature enriched my return to the farm. In CCSRE, Tania Mitchell and Sarah Gamino and in the Department of Art History, Zoe Luhtala and Art Librarian Roy C. Viado as well as Joe Legette in Media Services facilitated my teaching and research at Stanford. I bonded with my cohort of CCSRE Fellows, especially Lori Flores and Melissa Michelson, during the fellowship and beyond.

My students at UCSB and Stanford helped me tremendously as I articulated my thinking. My research assistants Pauline M. Vo, Vanessa L. Triplett, and Kalene Asato helped me in important aspects of my work from research to production—I appreciate your abilities, esteem your talents, and thank you immensely for working closely with me and supporting my work in these past years.

I wholeheartedly thank Greg Pak, John Castro, Gene Cajayon, Justin Lin, Ernesto Foronda, Chi-Hui Yang, and Jason Scott Lee for the interview/conversations that helped me to understand better the work of Asian American men in the movies. I am grateful to Abe Ferrer, David Magdael, Keo Woolford, and Quentin Lee for sharing their references with me.

With the editorial guidance of Alex Cho of Flowtv.org and Huping Ling of the *Journal of Asian American Studies*, parts of earlier versions of this work enjoyed publication. I appreciate the audiences at the Asian American Activities Center, the CCSRE Fellows' Forum and the Department of

Comparative Literature at Stanford, the Center for Race and Gender at UC Berkeley, the Department of American Civilization at Brown University, and the School for Social Transformation at Arizona State University and the Society for Cinema and Media Studies, the American Studies Association, and the Association for Asian American Studies. The anonymous readers improved this book with their enthusiastic engagement and keen insights. I am thrilled with the fearless and visionary Stacy Wagner, my editor at Stanford University Press. My gratitude also goes to editorial assistant Jessica Walsh, who shepherded this book's production, and to Judith Hibbard, Richard Gunde, and David Luljak for taking it to the finish. I collaborated with the brilliant photographer Jeff Sheng who generously shares his work.

Outside of the academy, Sylvia Argenal, Monica Salamy, Rachel Carlson and Rachel Gold made possible the time and space to work. The friendship of Sachi Thompson, Emily Kenner, Su-Mien Chong, and Paksy Plackis-Cheng directly aided me in writing this book. I cherish my clan for giving me fortitude: my parents, my brother and my six sisters and their partners—Rolf and Sharon, Rhacel and Ben, Rhanee and Claudio, Cerissa and Ian, Juno and Noah, Aari and Mahal and Sid. The Shimizu/Risk/McCobb families—Robert and Judy, Gerald and Jenny, and Susie and Philip—nourished me as I completed this book in their company, in the round room of my own. My nephews and nieces Ronin, Nolan, Matthew, Daniel, Javi, Bea, Zoe, Pablo, and Diego brought fun and laughter as I wrote. My husband, Dan Parreñas Shimizu, shares his life with me and astonishes me everyday. To live and love with you gives me the joy to create. My brilliant and beautiful sons inspire and fuel these pages. This book is a gift of love to Bayan and Lakas, for now and the future, as you make your own way.

Straitjacket Sexualities

Ethics and Responsibility

The Sexual Problems of
Asian American Men in the Movies

The April 2004 edition of *Details*, the popular U.S. men's life and style magazine, features a photo of an everyday Asian American man-on-the-street, albeit one with a "man-purse." The caption professes to convey a light-hearted ribbing that ultimately conflates and makes mutually exclusive the differences and similarities between Asian American and gay men: "One cruises for chicken; the other takes it General Tso–style. Whether you're into shrimp balls or shaved balls, entering the dragon requires imperial tastes."[1] Asian Americans protested the image on a national scale with a massive internet campaign that included tens of thousands of signatures demanding an apology from *Details*.[2] In the *Harvard Crimson*, Jacquelyn Chou '07, a student involved in the protests quickly organized outside the magazine's offices in New York City, critiques the image as one that "stereotyped Asian men, stereotyped gay men, and it also stereotyped our concepts of masculinity. . . . In a nation where we are composed of so many different types of people, we should work on being inclusive rather than exclusive."[3] Chou identifies how Asianness, gayness, and manhood are all denigrated in this stereotype—what Homi Bhabha defines as "arrested representations."[4] Indeed, the *Details* image ridicules not only the looks but attributes, behaviors, acts, and practices of gays and Asians and reduces them to uniform and static identities. In evaluating this image, however, Chou recognizes differences within gay and Asian America and refuses to fear the queer or keep racial identity straitjacketed. In this we can see how the *Details* spread presents an opportunity for scholars, critics, and activists to re-image Asian American manhood as not simply counter to feminism or complicit in homophobia.

When we acknowledge that the *Details* image also fits into a longer tradition in Hollywood movies of iconic portrayals of Asian American men, we identify a persistent problem: the rapacious and brutal (Sessue Hayakawa in *The Cheat*, 1915), pedophilic (Richard Barthelmess in yellowface in *Broken Blossoms*, 1922), masochistic (again Barthelmess, in *Son of the Gods*, 1932), criminal (the Fu Manchu series), treacherous and also romantic (Philip Ahn in *They Met in Bombay*, 1941, *Daughter of Shanghai*, 1937, and *King of Chinatown*, 1939), and quaint (Charlie Chan and Mr. Moto). Sexuality and gender act as forces in the racialization of Asian American men in these early representations. A crisis of masculinity forms when Asian American men fall short, i.e., they are problematically represented in movies as veering away from the norm. But this crisis must not lead to solutions that actually deepen and reemphasize Asian American masculinity as lacking, such that the presumed and unstated racial problem is really the queer and the feminine. We need to beware that the representation and criticism of Asian American men in the movies can also be straitjacketed into a narrowly circumscribed vision of masculinity, informed by a reactionary claim to male power and privilege. The solution to the problematic representation of Asian American men in the movies is not to add the phallus, which ultimately reproduces sexual heteronormativity and gender hierarchy, but to identify new criteria that dodge the crosshairs of victimization with an accounting of male power and privilege.

Hypersexual Asian American Women and Asexual/Effeminate/Queer Asian American Men

Touring my first book, *The Hypersexuality of Race: Performing Asian/American Women On Screen and Scene* (2007) for two years, I described how Asian American women use their ascription as pathologically hypersexual on screen and scene to articulate as political their own desires and sexualities. I identified hypersexuality—or the excessive proclivity for sex deemed as natural to Asian American women—as a disciplining and productive force. A persistent question popped up coast to coast: If Asian American women are hypersexual, what do you have to say about Asian American men as asexual, effeminate, and gay? There is a lot of pain surrounding this perception of Asian American male emasculation on screen, but in answering it, we must be careful not to inflict harm. Too often, the perception of asexuality, effeminacy, and queerness as racial emasculation is met with a demonization of difference and the valorization of severely constrained genders and sexualities. The understanding of Asian American female hypersexuality as companion to Asian American male hyposexuality would describe the female as the one in an empowered position over the disadvantaged Asian American male. This logic holds up only if we subscribe to a normative sexuality that uses criteria that both Asian American women and men ultimately fail to fulfill—for racial reasons. My response, then, is to look at historic and contemporary engagements of Asian American masculinity in U.S. industry movies in order to dispel the easy and inaccurate assessment of asexuality, effeminacy, and homosexuality as emasculation—what I call straitjacket sexuality—ascribed to them in U.S. popular culture.

Rather than present a sequel that pits Asian American female excess against Asian American male lack, I emphasize the differing situations of power that inform male and female representations. Asian American men need to account for the opportunity of power they face. Mark Anthony Neal critiques the concept of the "'Strong Black Man' which can be faulted for championing a stunted, conservative, one-dimensional, and stridently heterosexual vision of black masculinity that has little to do with the vibrant, virile and visceral masculinities that are lived in the real world."[5] Where's the flexibility versus the rigidity of black manhood? he asks.[6] While African and Asian American masculinities differ in their contexts, they share some concerns in the assignation of hypersexuality to black men and hyposexuality to Asian American men in popular culture. Both deviate from the norm—into what I see as places of possibility rather than closure or fixity.

The crux of my argument is to recommend an acknowledgment of the special position Asian American men occupy as an ethical event, what Richard A. Cohen calls "the event of ethics— . . . the absolute alterity of the other person encountered in the immediacy of the face-to-face."[7] In paying attention to how films use the power of facial expression and bodily gestures, acts and movements to express what the self desires—especially in relation to another—I consider the cinematic space between people rich with the desire for connection and ripe for instantiating new relations. Encounters in representations—between filmmakers and spectators or within their diegesis—act as discrete sites for the forging of ethical relations because they are where and when we see subjects articulate their desires, hopes, and wants. And in exposing themselves, subjects come to recognize their own limits and possibilities in seeing how they may affect the other as the other affects them. The direction this recognition goes from here can entrench relations of inequality or break them open. This for me is the power of cinema—its ability to introduce new ways of relating and offering solutions to problems of unequal relations.

In a kernel, I am interested in cinematic representations as an accounting of power. In exploring film, I ask whether its contribution to the discourse of Asian American manhood accounts for male abilities to oppress and be oppressed—as part of my goal of understanding film relations as comprising ethical acts. Here I present ethics as an important structure for viewing Asian American masculinity especially when the normalizing maneuver in response to sexual problems in representation is especially pressing in the case of men. That is, alternatives for Asian American masculinity in representation risk the unethical because of their structural location in wielding power and receiving discipline. Indeed, contemporary Asian American male filmmakers and actors see the Asian American male body as a site of racial wounding, gender grief, and sexual problems in ways haunted by the framework of falling short of the norm—where the identification of castration becomes a rally cry for changing and protesting hurtful images that lead to, when unwatched, seduction by patriarchy and heteronormativity. Rather than hurt others, unfasten the straps of Asian American manhood to expose the boundless dramas and pleasures of how Asian American men live at the crossroads of power. Asserting the presence of both vulnerability and strength, they forge manhoods that care for others. They invest in the most rewarding of relations beyond propping up the self.

Responsibility, then, is consciousness of how one takes and gives lashes as a man, within a society that hierarchizes and privileges by race, gender, and sexuality. As Michel Foucault contends, we cannot argue for freedom of sexual expression for we need to be aware of the importance of choice in sexual relations.[8] I extend this argument to the accounting of gender power for Asian American men in the context of the romanticization of male victimization by race and sexuality and the vilification of queerness as a further constraining of sexuality. Thus the problem particular to Asian American men that I address in this book is the expression of freedom that can curtail others'.

The expression of Asian American masculine sexuality in representation, unlike that of Asian American women in possessing gender power over others, instantiates an ethical struggle worth pursuing. In *The Hypersexuality of Race*, for example, I commend experimental filmmaker Machiko Saito's *Premenstrual Spotting* (1999) for exposing the ramifications of incest on Asian American female subjectivity. The critique of her artistic irresponsibility regarding the airing of dirty laundry requires the silencing of her female subjection by sexuality. When I talk about ethics and responsibility, thus, I am talking about how one's self-expression should not curtail those of others.

A focus on gender liberation in terms of sexual power—wherein the appearance of a man must mean the arrival of power in the sense of domination—gets us in trouble; it's a discourse that fetishizes inadequacy against the norm. Whether in assessing the absence of representation or measuring masculine success in terms of what R. W. Connell calls "hegemonic" manhood—or the traditional scripts of masculinity that require a gender hierarchy of men over women and the binary logic of straight versus gay—we remain trapped in a framework that hierarchizes race and defines sexuality and gender within a kind of fixity.[9]

How a man experiences gender need not be measured by whether he beats up other men or conquers women to lick his wounds but whether his experiences make others feel as well. To engage images of Asian American men in the movies may actually mean that we need to explore new and better terms for organizing our definitions of manhood—especially when we see Asian American men in the movies risk themselves for the sake of others.

Rather than vilify asexuality, effeminacy, and homosexuality, my book focuses on the ethical manhoods Asian American men carve through gender and sexuality in the movies. Using the conceptualization of ethical relations by Emmanuel Levinas, I show the exposure of both strength and vulnerability by men in intimate relations with others as a crucial expression of responsibility—in acknowledging one's ability to oppress and at the same time experience subjugation, as well as generate pleasure and good feeling. By recognizing the importance of caring for the well-being of others beyond bolstering the self, I highlight a sensibility of empathizing with others who occupy structural locations different from one's own. What we can ultimately learn from moments of tenderness and force—so often intertwined—by Asian American men on screen is not only the wider range of male experience but how the idea of the penis and the phallus likely informs our understanding of masculinity. That is, the phallus represents male power as exemplified in conquest and the submission of others to brutality and the naturalized propensity for violence and physical power. The problem, too often, is the conflation of the literal male penis with the symbolic power of the phallus. Instead of understanding the penis as representing male phallic power absolutely, let us consider how the penis hardens temporarily. In always threatening to soften, its vulnerability to castration becomes even more prominent. Thus, to make a distinction between the penis and the phallus then allows for us to identify what is undesirable in aspiring to dominate others. Doing so reveals the crucial role of vulnerability in envisioning manhood, especially for those who attempt to lay a claim to power where little is usually accorded.

In claiming power responsibly, we must find a place in ourselves for the simultaneity of powerlessness. According to Leo Bersani, jouissance risks the shattering of the self and identifies the phenomenon of powerlessness in sex.[10] That is, orgasm shows surrender in overwhelming the body. Vulnerability to the other in the exposure of the self critiques our most accepted structures of relationality across race, gender, and sexuality, such as the nature of viable masculinity for men who fall outside normative sexual relations. Because of the effectiveness of cinema in presenting dramas of power, we see how Asian American men present masculinities that embrace asexuality, effeminacy, queerness, and multitudinous other sexual formations—in short, plural masculinities. As such, *Straitjacket Sexualities* identifies a number of ethical moments in the movies wherein masculinity is figured anew and in unexpected ways that challenge and exceed straitjacket assessments.

Straitjacket Sexualities shows the many manhoods represented in Hollywood and Asian American cinema in the post–Civil Rights era. I begin with the premiere documentary *The Slanted Screen* (2006) and the problematic identification of racial emasculation on the screen. What happens when we diagnose the representation of emasculated men as a misrepresentation of an entire community? I then engage how two experimental films draw two very different relations to cinema in forging their recommendations of manhood for Asian American men. From here, in Chapter One I rewind to 1966–1972 when Asian American manhood burst into the national and international scene with the on- and off-screen sexuality of martial arts action hero Bruce Lee, who epitomized gender power as an antidote to those suffering with the pathology of male lack. I then move in

Chapters Two and Three to the 1980s/1990s and Hollywood figures such as Long Duk Dong to the range of manhoods found in independent films today such as the model minorities gone awry in *Better Luck Tomorrow* (2003) as well as anxiety-ridden men in *Charlotte Sometimes* (2002). Chapter Four studies recent pornography that has drawn national attention to the sexual problems of Asian American men in sexual representation. By looking at various representations of explicit sex that range from political pornography to experimental film, I illustrate the problem of celebrating heterosexual male privilege that does not account for its injury to others. Then, in Chapter Five, I call back from the archives of cinematic history the work of James Shigeta and Jason Scott Lee so as to correct the amnesia regarding the absence of Asian American male romantic leads in U.S. industry cinemas and to highlight the manhoods they present in history. The Epilogue reflects on *Gran Torino* (2008), where a young Hmong American man claims the power of lack in ways that teach an old white man to become more ethical, in caring for others beyond the self.

Straitjacket Sexualities examines the powerful ways both heteronormative sexuality and gender hierarchy organize the perceptions, projections, and imaginings of Asian American manhoods in Hollywood movies and their interlocutors in Asian American independent film practices. I direct my critique to both sites of movie production and draw my counter-critique from both sites as well. Rather than lack, I evaluate what is presented in films by and about Asian American men and analyze those images that upend the meaning of access to normative gender and sexual power. The stories told about Asian American men in Hollywood movies and independent Asian American film can and do go beyond the assessment of asexuality/effeminacy/queerness to deeper questions about how to establish oneself as a man within sexual, gendered, and racial orders. By attending to the sexuality and gender of race within these screen worlds, I examine the creative ways Asian American male filmmakers and actors attempt to formulate their masculinities in, through, and beyond straitjacket sexualities.

A History of Sexuality for Asian American Men

I am specifically concerned about representations of Asian American men engaging desire, love, romance, and sex in composing their manhoods. For

Asian American communities, erotic relations are historically intertwined with the politics of reproduction as part of national belonging. Asian American men have been racially targeted through sexual exclusions that created bachelor societies and prevented them from participating in heterosexual institutions and practices such as marriage and sex.[11] We can see in the selection of my films that the sexual implications of the historical exclusions inform and exceed the content of the films available about Asian American men. Compounding this problem of male sexual victimization is the perception that Asian American women benefit from their sexualization by popular culture in a way that contributes to the asexuality/effeminacy/queerness ascribed to Asian American men. This negative rendering of different sexualities and genders for men organizes racial critiques of representation as well as the priorities of Asian American cultural production. Racial critique too often comes from a male understanding of gender and sexuality; or, racial lenses take priority in a way that leaves different experiences of sexuality and gender inaccurately and inadequately addressed. Manhood, race, sexuality, and representation need particular analysis of how privilege and power tensely intersect with subjugation and pain.

Straightjacket Sexualities is the first full-length study of sexuality and gender as they define the racialization of Asian American men in Hollywood films in the years 1959–2009. It argues that the attribution of asexual, effeminate, and queer as lacking that characterizes discourses of Asian American masculinity inadequately captures how Asian American men wield power as well as experience its disciplining force. Oft-repeated, the assessment of lack secures gayness, asexuality, or feminine masculinity as wrong and undesirable—as if these identities are themselves not wonderful, rewarding, and viable. Forsaken by the diagnosis of lack are the rich and revealing processes of coming to manhood by Asian American men as part of a more expansive repertoire of voices and visions that make racial masculinities on screen and in history fascinating. Relevant to American culture—past, present, and future—Asian American intimacies on screen, especially those that engage these marginalized qualities, capture the dramas and processes of becoming a man within unjust and unequal social terms and conditions. In this process, Asian American men formulate an ethic that captures the dilemmas of power over others, by others, and of the self through their performances in film.

Ethical Manhoods and Cinema as Technology of Ethics

Straitjacket Sexualities intends to transform our perception toward a mutable understanding of manhood that finds definition in the very acts, forms, gestures, and practices of Asian American men in their intimate engagements with others in the movies. I attend not only to *masculinity*—the characteristics, traits, and qualities that describe how one is gendered male—but also to *manhood*—the inner life of being, becoming, and performing maleness. What makes a man a man is not only his ability to be virile, have an erection, and copulate, but his being as a self, his formation as a subject, and his development as an agent or an actional being in relation to others. My formulation of ethical manhood attends to how the self holds the potentiality of becoming aware of one's position in a network of power relations and of acting responsibly in wielding and enduring power. By looking at intimate relations on screen, I redefine our understanding of power beyond the phallus embodied in the erect penis and exemplified in the predominance of brute masculinity, or macho, to acknowledge the presence of vulnerability. By analyzing how events of intimacy and sexuality are scenes for the formulation of ethical manhoods, I hope to deliver us from an assessment of inadequacy and lack to one that accounts for the lashes men give as well as take in their various relations with others. I ultimately advocate an ethical manhood that recognizes its power not only to hurt others, *but to remap what is valued in our society*.

I closely study what kind of manhoods Asian American men formulate when they encounter others and how they specifically engage the larger field of social relations that place them in a certain position in our society, especially as lacking the qualities that make men viable subjects. In their relations, I ask if they acknowledge their subjugation and their power and if they account for the impact of their behavior—their acts and gestures—upon others. In this way, *Straitjacket Sexualities* looks to cinema as a technology of ethics. Cinema enables us to see subjects engage intimately with others—through close-ups of the expressions of the face, the impact of touch not only on skin but psyche, and the uniqueness of desire and its expression for each character. For the philosopher Emmanuel Levinas, the ethical event is in the recognition of intimacy as involving someone else—totally separate from you, but for whom you have the possibility of intertwining not only bodies but lives. What enables this connection, this investment in the other, is a kind of open exposure to the self as vulnerable. I understand this surrender of the self, as affected by another, as strength—in a way that may be counterintuitive to those who valorize the notion of absolute strength as the ultimate form of manhood. Richard A. Cohen describes ethics as powerful "not because it opposes power with more power . . . with a bigger army, more guns . . . but rather because it opposes power with what appears to be weakness and vulnerability but is responsibility."[12] Responsibility is the highest form of relating for it involves accountability to the other, but also a laying bare of oneself in the hope of recognizing one's investment in the other.

My focus on ethical relations, thus, prioritizes the importance of the broader field of social relations so as to expand our criteria of manhood beyond benefiting oneself to include accountability to others. I benefit from studies that situate the production of masculinity within a web of social relations—American cultural histories, racialized masculinities, feminist approaches, and recent studies of queer masculinities—and bring them to relevance in my particular study of cinema.[13] I show how U.S. industry films that include Hollywood and Asian American independent films dramatize racial, sexual, and gender encounters as engagements of power and privilege that are important to individual ethical formations of manhood, in practices that we see both in private and public. That is, *Straitjacket Sexualities* identifies the sexual and gender formations of racialized subjects as we see them in movies, and reads their undoing of sex and gender constraints as significant beyond their interpellation as less than human, primitive, and belonging outside civilization. As such, *Straitjacket Sexualities* makes central the ethical dilemmas that racialized characters undergo in their personal entanglements as socially significant beyond themselves.

As I have analyzed in regard to screening African American masculinity within cross-racial desire, the cinematically constructed intimate scenes of love, desire, seduction, and erotic relations prove worthy of assessing the processes of manhood for racialized men.[14] Films and performance open the door to intense dramas of power in the typically private realms of love, friendship, desire, romance, and sexuality, enabling us to interrogate how subjects relate to each other as complexes of emotional, psychic, sexual, and physical attachments. These scenes destabilize gender and sexual restrictions of race by showing the pluralities of desires and the diversity of sexual acts and identities that exceed the gender and sex of racial identity categorizations. Through film, filmmakers and actors attempt to carve subjectivities and selves in the intricate commingling of public and social forces and private and individual desires and pleasures. The book is concerned with forwarding manhoods and masculinities that emphasize how subjectivities and relations are determined by the ethics of one's actions and the structures that limit one's choices. By studying individual developments of the self in terms of their intimate, intense, and private enactments within and against the social definitions of masculinities for Asian American men, we can change the criteria for evaluating viable manhoods not only for Asian American men but for other men as well.

If the task is, to use Judith Butler's words, to "[find] a way of appropriating [norms], taking them on, and establishing a living relation to them," my concern is not just to remedy the lack of desirable images for racialized men, but to better analyze and theorize actual representations of race and masculinity.[15] Identifying the dynamics of power, privilege, and the politics of pleasure in producing and consuming these images of manhood is crucial to formulating viable masculinities—beyond just the correction of stereotypes or the attempt to gain equal access to patriarchy. By framing Asian American masculinity in terms of the struggle to form an ethical self, we critique the straitjacketed ways we assess gender and sexuality in racial scenes and subjectivities.

Following Butler, I find implicit the presence of race in philosophical inquiry usually seen as unmarked by social difference. Thus, I insert the particularities and specificities of sexual scenes of racial subjection into seemingly abstract philosophies scrutinized for the absence of race in order to produce theory that explicitly addresses race. In "Signification and Sense," Levinas describes "signify(ing) from the 'world' and from the position of the one who is looking."[16] Here, relations between others are situated and expressions of the self need an "embodied subject" not only to receive meaning but to act upon it (15). Thus not only is the self as a producer of cultural objects important, for these "paintings, poems, melodies . . . express or illuminate an era" (15), but also the expression of meaning is only possible in how the other makes one conscientious of a wider world of meaning. In this way, Levinas prioritizes not only relationality but alterity—radical otherness—in the articulation of the self, in ways useful to studies of social meanings of representation, including that of race and racism. Scholars like Crystal Parikh and Haiyan Lee similarly utilize Levinas in their study of racialized subjects. Parikh's book on the political practices of betrayal and the figure of the traitor in Asian American and Chicano literature, presents "ethical critique as a mode for following the minority subject as it wrestles with the implications of its own existence."[17] Lee devises a political theory of female subjectivity that she calls "contingent transcendence," which locates everyday social encounters as moments and locations where ethical relations may be formed. In her study of the film *Lust, Caution* (2007), Lee discusses sex scenes as sites for disrupting the mind/body split for the female lead character, a spy who uses her body and sexuality to seduce a military officer on behalf of the nationalist revolution. The cathartic experience of how "desire opens the self up for the ethical encounter with the other and entangles the social and the political"[18] ultimately defies patriarchal nationalism when she identifies her own agency through sex.

I build from here to focus on what is possible across relations of difference in the cinema. For example, in *Time and the Other*, Levinas says, if "the pathos of love consists to the contrary of (love as a fusion), an insurmountable duality of beings; it is a relationship with what forever slips away."[19] I assume no universality in this description but apply its specific language to a scene that is common between us—the movies, whose meanings we fulfill, as Teshome Gabriel argues, depending on our social locations and our commitment to learning about the other rather than imposing our own traditions and "domesticating" cultures of an "alien" text.[20] Representations of love, desire, sex and romance, or eros, dramatize our responses to otherness. Encounters with another involve mystery—as that which constantly remains elusive despite the deepest proximity. Cinema in particular allows for us to name that elusive mystery when we see the concrete dialogue, and the facial and bodily expressions that comprise moments of intensity between particular subjects. For Levinas, eros needs attending to in its "communication" beyond "possession and power" as "neither a struggle, nor a fusion, nor a knowledge. One must recognize its exceptional place among relations. It is the relationship with alterity, with mystery" (68) that is most promising precisely because of the ethical opportunities it introduces. Not only do we discover more about our own potentials and possibilities in how we rise to meet the other, but it is in the process of interpreting what we see in the faces and gestures of people that we can see how subjects have the opportunity to make ethical choices that affect others.

Cinematic representations of intimacy between others holds such power—in the ripe possibility of catharsis or cataclysm risked in reaching out to touch, to speak, and to look. Cinema captures these attempts to cross the chasms between people, who chance finding out if the other invests in one's well-being too. This is an ethical relation for it seeks mutual acknowledgment of one's need for the other. The language of Levinas thus enables me to articulate that the exposure of one's vulnerability hopefully gives rise to caring for the other. To assume responsibility for the other in this way, according to Levinas in *Otherwise Than Being*, is powerful for it puts into question one's own being and in doing so, testifies to the possibilities of connection with another.[21] So, to express liability and dependability is a testament to the worthiness of investing in future relations yet unmade and uncharted. Missing from assessments of straitjacket sexuality then is the simultaneity of vulnerability and strength composing ethical manhoods, detectable on screen in the plunge to commit oneself to another without the guarantee of reciprocity.

The Method of Intimate Literacies: Touch, Look, and Speech

Straitjacket Sexualities looks at the ways Asian American men in the movies compose their manhoods through a reading method informed by the philosophy of Emmanuel Levinas, specifically the theorization of relations between subjects and the physical space between them that concretizes the distance between people in spite of proximity. Rather than the fusion of two within intimate relations, touch can make the other even more elusive so that they render possession futile and maintain mystery, and so remain interesting. My focus on acts of touch, the looks characters deploy, and the speech they deliver during privileged interactions with others comprises a method I call "intimate literacies." In these moments, I work to provide a vocabulary that identifies precisely how Asian American men compose their racialized manhoods in terms of their concrete actions while relating to others on screen. Noting how these forms and gestures comply with and critique the established criteria for a manhood of regard includes how their look compels a gaze upon which we recognize some kind of important stature or how others regard their physical presence in terms of comfort, arousal, attraction or repulsion. In terms of emotions, I look to how they expose themselves as vulnerable to and expressive of their wants. Certain or not, they risk their emotions as being unmet; how do they then cope with that rejection? In the outward expressions of desire, I note if their kisses inspire fires of desire or if their speech compels others to listen—or not. I interpret how others regard what they say and how they speak but also the impact of their bodily presence on screen in their physical comportment such as roostering about or bowing their heads in deference to others. Using the representation of senses such as touch, sight, and smell, I find how Asian American men establish their presence so the looks they confer, what they say, and how they touch others mean something substantial beyond their own possession of feeling. I intend to answer the questions of how others respond to their expressions of desire and how they negotiate the position of disprized subject within a larger field of social relations. Therefore, I read the scenes of Asian American men's intimate relations on screen for the potential of illuminating how power circulates and works on and off screen. It is not enough to see Asian American men and women represented; we must also see and analyze how they are constructed and what they are concretely doing in these representations against their typical attributions as lacking. I look to films as the opportunity to isolate how each encounter with others in distinct social fields affords a reassembly of what we use to compose the kinds of manhood we celebrate and know. We will see how Asian Americans engage the imposition of the framework of lack, as it is composed by stigma, shame, guilt, and anxiety and go from there to fashion more promising relations with others.

My close reading of scenes of intimacy involving Asian American men in the movies then does not merely look to identify moments of asexuality, effeminacy, or essential queerness. The method I follow indeed builds from my first book, *The Hypersexuality of Race*, but rather than presenting a sequel that idealizes Asian American male hypermasculinity as the logical companion to Asian American female hypersexuality, I explode this diagnosis. *Straitjacket Sexualities* highlights the opportunity to promote different criteria for evaluating manhood. I emphasize the subject position of Asian American men as close to risking the unethical when crafting alternatives to patriarchy and heterosexism because of their particular structural location at the crossroads of possessing patriarchal power.

While Eve Sedgwick argues there are dynamics between men that deserve their own analysis, feminism must not be forsaken by movements to center male subjectivity.[22] We must always account for our power and subjugation. Whether they undergo a conscious psychic process or unconsciously engage social scripts and roles, Asian American men possess power to choose specific performances, gestures, and acts. These acts do not occur outside the racializations of their sexualities and genders. Specifically, the method of intimate literacy attends to the ways in which Asian American men negotiate the pressures of heteronormativity (the aspiration to the normal for those excluded by it) and patriarchy (the value-based hierarchy of gender) in scenes where the self is exposed to another. An ethical approach requires contextualizing these acts within the psychic drama told in the film and the discourses of masculinity of the specific era as well.

So, rather than approach racial, sexual, and gendered representations to classify identities or verify stereotypical roles,[23] I introduce the importance of mapping through intimate literacies the sexual, emotional, psychic, and bodily compositions of Asian American men in the concrete scenes of their representations so as to make them available for men as they make their way across their cinematic legacies. This allows us to discover the challenges that characters, their creators, and critics face beyond straitjacket sexualities to move to the more compelling realm of how they establish manhoods that reveal the intricate commingling of public and social forces and private and individual desires and pleasures. In analyzing the transformations that occur through gender and sexual labor that Asian American men perform in intimate relations on screen, I show how they engage asexuality/effeminacy/queerness as part of a larger wrestling with ethical questions of masculine subject formation. As such, I analyze the representations of Asian American men to recognize other manhoods available beyond the disprized and castrated versus the macho and heroic.

Asian American Macho, Its Champions, and Its Critics

"Unnormal" gender and sexuality dominate the discourses of Asian American masculinity. I use the word "unnormal" to describe the distorted asexuality/effeminacy/queerness assignation that is a condemnation of lack and not so much a clinical abnormality. I name this assessment of lack "straitjacket sexuality" so as to capture Asian American men's strange distance from acceptable and traditionally white masculinity, especially through racial and sexual difference in the movies. The discursive terrain that sets the scene for a new take on Asian American manhoods includes cultural production by Asian American men, queers of color, and feminists as well as Hollywood productions. In terms of cultural production, prominent Asian American men exacerbate the position of racial victimization by lack, or straitjacket sexuality—accepting it and reacting to it in unconstructive ways, such as in writer David Mura's attribution of his sexual promiscuity to racial discrimination, justifying a certain misogyny; Darrell Hamamoto's attempts to reinscribe Asian American male sexual fulfillment via yellow pornography, as I will argue, at the expense of women; and Frank Chin's privileging of heteronormativity and gender hierarchy in defining the Asian American cowboy. Vulnerability, compared to the centrality of victimization and bravado, remains offstage.

Well-known and highly regarded critical studies of Asian American manhoods are few, but all enable my work in their confrontation of the attribution of gayness as synonymous with Asianness in the U.S. and beyond. Book-length studies of Asian American masculinities include David Eng's *Racial Castration*, Daniel Kim's *Writing Manhood in Black and Yellow*, Jachinson Chan's *Chinese American Masculinities*, and Brian Locke's *Racial Stigma on the Hollywood Screen*—all of which call for a queer and feminist reading of Asian American manhoods. However, none provide a sustained critique of the moving-image production of Asian American men in terms of what secures their image as lacking in the last fifty years, such as what Asian American actors and filmmakers do to wrestle with and respond to the assignation of straitjacket sexuality. In terms of articles, Richard Fung's search for the Asian/North American penis, Hoang Nguyen's evaluation of Brandon Lee's pornographic presence, Joon Oluchi Lee's "joy of the castrated boy," Tasha Oren's recommendation of a shocking aesthetic to dislodge entrenched ideas about Asian American manhood, and Viet Nguyen's nuanced conceptualization of "remasculinization" acknowledge and engage the concept of lack in Asian American male discourses of sexuality in ways that I build upon.[24]

Asian Americanist and feminist literary scholars have assessed the persistent diagnosis of effeminacy and asexuality of Asian American men since the founding of Asian American studies, describing how this diagnosis characterizes a masculinist understanding of race politics.[25] These critics argue that genders and sexualities of Asian American men are widely targeted by racist regimes, which subsequently authorizes a platform that privileges male subjectivity and makes claims for Asian Americans wholly, without accounting for gendered variations in the racial experience. Along that line of argument, *Straightjacket Sexualities* is the first book to focus on the U.S. cinema industry's representations of Asian American men in order to strip off straitjacket sexualities as a framework and as a practice that curbs the imagination in envisioning other manhoods.

I now move on to analyze the film *The Slanted Screen* (2006), a documentary dealing directly with issues of representation for Asian American men as a problem in Hollywood cinema. Through analysis of this documentary, I identify the specific problematization of race, masculinity, and sexuality in terms of valorizing or resisting macho, one constricted version of straitjacket sexuality. As an illustration of the varying ethical approaches to the sexual and gendered problems of Asian American men in the movies, I then evaluate two short and widely screened independent films that employ the strategy of speaking through and back to Hollywood films while addressing their own Asian American male subjectivities as products of interracial sex acts. Both Kip Fulbeck's *Some Questions for 28 Kisses* (1994) and Stuart Gaffney's *Transgressions* (2002) illustrate the importance of film and sexuality in envisioning forms of just filmmaking and just manhoods. Both of these two short experimental documentaries make use of the power of cinematic representations of sexuality. While using similar devices as *The Slanted Screen*, of speaking back to images of Hollywood films, they come up with different definitions of power, representation, and manhood. I ask if these films offer inclusive and expansive visions or remain in the realm of straitjacket sexuality for Asian American men. I open the book with this documentary and these two experimental films to map the particular problem of representation for Asian American men, critique existing solutions as insufficient to our thinking of new ways to define masculinity and race and to argue for envisioning ethics as useful to understanding manhood.

Problems with Power in *The Slanted Screen*

In addressing the misrepresentations of Asian American men as gendered and racialized subjects, Jeff Adachi's *Slanted Screen* functions as the male counterpart of the widely taught and female-focused documentary *Slaying the Dragon* (1988) by Deborah Gee. Both of these films invite viewers to understand the power of representation for the creation and maintenance of stereotypes in the repeated oversimplification of racial and gender identities in U.S. cinemas. By citing Hollywood films, they argue that such misrepresentations shape perceptions and thus affect real lives so that there is a direct relation between representation and reality. Representations inflict racial wounds, pathologize gender, and construct an abnormal sexuality that's either brutal, unavailable, or absent for Asian American men. Especially harmful, according to the films, is the curbing of Asian American aspirations. This follows Loni Ding, who theorizes that representations validate Asian Americans in giving worth to their histories and presences in the United States.[26] Films like *Slaying the Dragon* and *The Slanted Screen* thus emphasize the importance of working within and against the industry and using media to change misconceptions to improve Asian American lives. A dynamic contribution, both works address the situation of actors and filmmakers who must work within an industry drenched in whiteness and, though the films don't explicitly say it, heteronormative sexuality, where Asian American women are hyperfeminine and Asian American men are straitjacketed as if asexuality/effeminacy/queerness equals lack.

The Slanted Screen begins with what now seems like an incredulous event: the existence of an immensely popular Asian American male matinee idol, Sessue Hayakawa, the early Hollywood star who enjoyed his status as a fashionable party maven, film director, and producer with his own production company. In early Hollywood, this Asian American man was one of the most highly paid and recognizable stars.[27] He eventually starred in over ninety films and, as *The Slanted Screen* mentions, even with white female leads. The contemporary working actors interviewed in the film relate to Hayakawa's legacy. Unlike Hayakawa, who "overpowered" white women, Asian American actors, even those who demonstrate masculine gender prowess (such as Jet Li, in Andrzej Bartkowiak's 2000 film *Romeo Must Die*), are little legible as sex symbols today.

But the problem is actually larger than sex. In interviews featured in *The Slanted Screen*, Asian American male filmmakers one after another describe how Asian Americans have no viability in Hollywood as the bearers of the story. Director Justin Lin, regarded as the Asian American Spike Lee and director of the popular *The Fast and the Furious* Hollywood action franchise, brought us the movie that changed the industry's perception of Asian American directors and film. In talking about raising funds for the seminal film *Better Luck Tomorrow*, he describes countless predictions about the impossibility of the film's success and receiving suggestions to change the characters to white ones, which made no sense considering the film is about the pressures of model minority expectations and racialization on primarily Asian American male teens.

In *The Slanted Screen*, the actor Jason Scott Lee describes the pain he expresses in his face when performing the role of Bruce Lee in *Dragon* (1993). In the scene, he views Mickey Rooney portraying a derogatory yellowface character in *Breakfast at Tiffany's* (1961). Here, representation wounds even powerful icons of the screen, so that we understand even more why Bruce Lee is lauded by so many actors interviewed in the documentary. In *The Slanted Screen*, to see Bruce Lee is to "hold your head high" in playing the lead role in a new genre and to access a powerful and fearsome masculinity within the existing gender order. For many in this film, Bruce Lee, as someone who beat up other men, compensates for the effeminacy of characters in Hollywood films such as *Broken Blossoms* in 1919 and *Reflections In a Golden Eye* in 1957, or even the oversimplified and caricatured yellowface characters Fu Manchu and Charlie Chan. As mentioned in the interviews of *The Slanted Screen*, these two caricatures possess "Satanic" qualities, hold a "preternatural preference for white women," and use "Oriental mind tricks" and other devious devices to dominate the world or solve crimes using the wisdom of Oriental mysticism and fortune cookies. When a film offers only racially focused solutions that do not ultimately account for sexual and gender difference or the ways Asian American men and women's representations may require different solutions, it emasculates Asian American men.

Ultimately, *The Slanted Screen* argues that the problem with racial representation is gendered male; in other words, racial wounding is masculine wounding. For example, toward the end of the film, a childhood expert testifies that children are sensitive to media, and that not seeing diversity on screen communicates a certain lack of social worth. It argues for the need for role models to instill a sense of one's value in society, to alleviate racial self-hate, and to unleash the imagination so that Asian Americans may aspire to roles other than the limited ones we see on screen. That is, although *The Slanted Screen* recognizes the power of the media to racialize groups negatively, it fails to recognize that the different ascriptions men and women face in their racialized representations—such as the hypervisibility of hypersexuality for Asian American women—require different solutions. We see hints in *The Slanted Screen*, however, in the words of two actors who provide unexpected solutions to the problem of straitjacketed sex for Asian

American men. The actor Cary Hiroyuki Tagawa, who is cast in villainous roles, recognizes that he will never play the hero, so he sets out to portray the "baddest" possible villain, with excessive virility and power. Bobby Lee advocates a comedic approach to ethnic issues—describing how John Cho, Margaret Cho, and he all have big network deals—testifying to how networks want them on television. "This would not be possible five years ago," he says. "Just imagine, twenty years from now . . . I'll be old (laughter) . . . hope I get a chance to see [what happens]." In line with Tasha Oren's recommendation to use unexpected strategies to counter Asian American male lack, he uses humor. The film ends with an overall optimism, saying new filmmakers are making images of Asian American men "in their own terms." As Oren says, these terms should be surprising and thus, game-changing. *The Slanted Screen* calls for new heroes as well as excellent filmmaking and performance that will accustom the public to thinking of Asian Americans—on screen and off—in new ways, eventually leading, according to Justin Lin, to a more level playing field. The future should be open for a multitude of representations of Asian Americans as a whole, *The Slanted Screen* contends, as it concludes with a question: What are the strategies for overcoming the harm done by of stereotypes? However, I argue that what actually needs to be addressed is racial representation as a problem of gender, one requiring careful navigation of the structural location of Asian American men who, at one extreme, compete with women in meekly submitting to oppression, and at the other extreme, lash out in anger. A specific gender and sex analysis more concretely addresses the problem of racial representation: for example, the concept of hero can refer to a desire for access to gender normalcy that renders women as derivative of men.

Because the solutions can also fall within the straps of straitjacket sexuality, I ask how the anxiety generated by attempts to access normal, heterosexist, and patriarchal masculinity hierarchizes masculine subjectivities. In looking at this documentary to open the book, I provide the context for the chapters that follow. Specifically, when the film identifies a gendered problem but falls short of providing gendered solutions, my task is to change the very identification of the problem of race, masculinity, and sexuality from victimization and its attendant solution of overcompensation to an ethical dilemma about *privilege and possibility that depends upon how Asian American act and do their masculinity.* In *Straitjacket Sexualities*, Asian American male engagements and entanglements with Hollywood films go beyond a critique of the lack of access to patriarchy and heteronormativity, to render more accurately the richer dramatic terrains of masculinity, sexuality, and race. Diagnoses of male lack subscribe to limited ideas of gender and sexuality; they do not serve our understanding of Asian American masculinities and manhoods as simultaneously complex and constricted. Our critical interventions need to capture better the gender and sex of race as Asian American men wrestle with the ethics of masculinity, engage questions about friendship, romance, violence, shame, guilt, and other dilemmas of love, sex, and race through the power of the moving image. When the gendered male problem becomes generalized as racial, the implications are to ignore male privilege and to further entrench us in the binary of asexual, effeminate, and homosexual men and hyperheterosexual women in Asian American representations. I will now show how problems of racial representation are gendered and sexualized differently in two experimental documentaries: one accuses women and further entrenches gender hierarchy in Asian American cultural politics, and the other shows the formulation of an ethical manhood that accounts for how race permeates gender and sexuality in terms of power.

Kip Fulbeck and Stuart Gaffney: Self as the Site of Change

In two short films—*Some Questions for 28 Kisses* (1994) and *Transgressions* (2002)—the self is the primary site of investigation for understanding the facticity of Asian American men in U.S. industry cinemas. When the self is constricted into a position of lack, it cannot become the site of change, but must remain trapped and submerged in straitjacket sexuality. The videotape *Some Questions for 28 Kisses* by Kip Fulbeck has been praised by the Hawaii International Film Festival as a "terrific, intense, multimedia experience—deconstructing Hollywood's images of Asian Americans—it ought to be seen by Asian American women."[28] Not only does the blurb follow *The Slanted Screen*'s understanding of male images as representing all Asian Americans, the perspective shows an understanding of Asian American females as privileged over men. Problematic indeed is the understanding of Asian American women as holding power over Asian American men through their representations as desirable to white men. This is an effect of the straitjacketed framework that lauds hypersexuality as a desirable representation and asexuality as an undesirable one—in a constricted definition of sexuality as a technology of achieving freedom by dominating others.

The narration by filmmaker Fulbeck begins with "This video gets people angry." The video, which edits together footage of Hollywood films featuring Asian women kissing white men, analyzes neither the images nor the way they trouble the self in relation to these images but blames Asian women for their hypersexualization in U.S. industry cinema. When the film marries scenes from Asian female–white male pairings and individual audio testimonies from Asian women and white men regarding their sexual and romantic desires and practices, an equation of representation with reality emerges. For example, one voiceover features a letter from an Asian female to an editor: "Dear Editor: As a 22-year-old Asian American woman, who has experienced many relationships with Asian men, I have to conclude that Asian men DEFINITELY have an inferiority complex and this is why I have given up dating them. I have been dating Asian men, particularly Chinese men, for the last four years, hoping and working to build a stable and loving relationship, but all the Asian men I have dated resembled the stereotypical characters that has supposedly plagued them for years." Another track of personal ads by white men seeking Asian women accompanies her voiceover: "Caucasian gentleman is proposing an intimate relationship with a self-assured Asian female, exotically stunning in stature, while exuding an unequivocal sensual feminine aura. Prerequisites: affinity for champagne, caviar and a belief in Amerasia. . . . Professional single white man, slender, intelligent and nice-looking seeks well-educated, warm-hearted, slender Japanese female with an attractive smile." Rather than evaluate the dynamics of gender and race in these sexual representations carefully, the film gives us a blanket assessment that simply links "real" testimony to representation. By establishing that the hypersexuality of Asian American women on screen leads to the hyposexuality of Asian American men on scene, the complexity of representation is untouched. The video equates Asian American women's sexual choices in lives to these Hollywood images.

From here, what emerges is an argument about the effects of these representations on men, rather than women. When we see a shot of an Asian American woman relating to a white man in an intense scene of intimacy, an intertitle text pops up to ask: Are Asian men socially inept? The male voice inserts himself as agitated by this scene and demands a shift in our attention. The voiceovers present the mutually desiring pairing of Asian women and white men as occurring at the expense of Asian men. The Asian American women are presented as seduced by power, such as in scenes where the white men wink at the audience in their encounter with these "Other" women. An Asian woman in a bikini approaches the actor Rob Lowe and sits in the adjacent lounger while waving back her large and long hair. He looks directly at the camera with a smug smirk. Sean Penn grunts with pleasure as he is attended to by an adoring Asian woman in bed. Sylvester Stallone sweats all over an Asian woman with stunning hazel eyes as she dies in his arms while asking him not to forget her. Ralph Macchio is overwhelmed by a Japanese American woman's geisha-clad dance in *Karate Kid II* (1986). John Lennon sits next to Yoko Ono in an interview as filmmaker Kip Fulbeck's narration expresses a deep anxiety about Asian female–white male sexual relations. Textual interjections address the gender imbalance of sexual representations of Asian Americans in Hollywood. "How many times have you seen an Asian man kiss on TV" scrolls across the screen while we see a display of white men kissing Asian women. By phrasing the text in this way, Fulbeck incorrectly attributes a choice to Asian women on and off screen. A more appropriate question would be: How many white men fabricate a persistent fantasy of Asian women kissing white men?

Against an attack on Asian women, Fulbeck then addresses Asian men as victimized by the media. "Are Asian men socially inept?" is followed by "Are Asian men less sexual? Do they really have small penises?" And all the while, we watch Asian women and white men kissing on screen. He asks: "Was Bruce Lee killed by white America? Brandon Lee?" then, "Why is Maxine Hong Kingston so popular?" The Bruce Lee question is unanswerable, and perhaps Kingston is popular for excellence in her craft. The video attributes a particular power to Asian women and powerlessness to Asian men. White men are curiously approached: "Do you consider talking about this subject a personal attack? Do you know the difference between Asian and Asian American?" The Asian women are accused, while the white men are confused and the Asian man asserts his power to describe their liaisons at costly to his subjectivity. The film concludes with its own confusion—a sort of "I don't know what to make of this mess" statement. Fulbeck ends by asking, "Where are you located in this thing?" while rendering himself as equally "slamming white men, Asian women, and men." In his tone and in the content of his narration we hear accusations for women and white men, and victimizations for Asian men. In terms of a theory of representation, the footage is an indictment of Asian women's complicity rather than their construction. Representation for Fulbeck is a trap that fixes meaning, captures and solidifies identity, and sets the terms of our interpretations. His use of the medium reveals a straitjacketed understanding in terms of a narrowly circumscribed vision of masculinity.

In *Transgressions*, Stuart Gaffney troubles his own biracial positioning in relation to Hollywood representations of sexual relations between the Asian feminine and the Western masculine with a queer and mixed-race critique. Unlike Fulbeck, Gaffney attempts to use existing representation to imagine a different relationship between representation and reality, creating another world entirely. That is, he won't contain his own experiences within existing frameworks of gender hierarchy and heteronormativity but imagines the meanings of representations in new and unexpected ways, rather than as an archive of injury for men and of triumph for women. His experiences as a product of interracial desire cannot be integrated into existing logics but must be evaluated to see what's different.

Resonating with Judith Halberstam's work in *A Queer Time and Place*, Gaffney imagines the possibility of existing in the visual and thus historical record. He exposes the process of looking for oneself in the fissures of representation that usually relegate his subjectivity to the margins. Mostly using footage of John Lone and Jeremy Irons in David Cronenberg's movie adaptation of David Henry Hwang's Tony-award winning play *M. Butterfly*, Gaffney looks for ancestry in the man-in-Oriental-drag and his/her white male lover. In a dynamic use of found footage, he intersperses his monologue of charting a new self. Unlike Fulbeck, Gaffney explores himself rather than hurls judgment against Asian American women for their subjection by white male desire, in a more ethical use of the power of filmmaking.

The video *Transgressions* begins with the carefully coiffed John Lone as Song Liling, his/her long hair fanning a dress with high neckline. She/he plays a high-class performer in female drag serving tea to a suited French diplomat played by Jeremy Irons. She/he serves him demurely, head and eyes directed downward, avoiding his gaze while he reaches for the cup in his/her hands. Here, we see an Asian man performing the production of an Asian woman as a voiceover attributes ancestry in these scenes for the filmmaker. "I am a product of interracial desire," continues the solemn voice. "Transgressive love is in my genes. To touch someone of another race, to see the different color, the different texture of skin. To sense so much difference in what is familiar: how do we resist it, how do we stand it?" The speech personalizes the scene of intense attraction and sexual desire while revealing the complex ways spectators make their own meanings as significant to their subjectivities. Jeremy Irons as Rene Gallimard gazes upon John Lone's Song Liling with an outpouring of desire; he wants him/her and casts a look upon him/her that exposes his feelings of vulnerability to the power of his emotions. The white man and the Asian man playing an Asian woman affect each other powerfully. Attraction for each other overwhelms them individually. She/he gets up, and holds on to the wall, turning away from him, as if she/he cannot bear to see the exposure of these feelings or risk his/hers.

The film of course is based on a play about the deception of a white Frenchman by a Chinese spy, a man posing as a woman, in a love affair that lasted a generation. How can such duplicity be possible, asks Hwang? He argues that the fantasy of the compliant Oriental embodied in an Asian woman powerfully provides a narrative that enables a white man to exercise his fantasy on the body of an Asian man. What is really revealed is the homosocial relation between white men and Asian men as sexual, in ways that engage fantasies and enactments of power. Gaffney instead stages his own story through this appropriated footage so as to articulate his own becoming as a queer biracial Asian American man. He does this by recasting the footage of Song Liling and Rene Gallimard, feeling the impact of each other's touch upon their bodies, which secures their purchase of the emotional truth of what is, on the surface, a deceitful relationship.

Jeremy Irons as Rene Gallimard approaches John Lone as Song Liling and upon reaching him/her, places his hand upon his/her shoulder and closes his eyes to appreciate the contact. Here we see Gaffney's use of the cinema to convey the shattering power of touch between lovers. He/she closes his/her eyes as well—then she/he turns to face him, still unable to look up, following his hand on his/her body with his/her eyes. She/he performs an attempt to resist accompanied by a commitment not to move away, as he now gently frames his/her face with his hands, then rubs his face against his/hers softly, without moving away. He smells his/her face and follows closely the essence emanating from the skin of his/her whole body. She/he becomes aroused, opens his/her mouth then they kiss for the first time, with passion. Gaffney's voiceover links his own conception to this scene. "What did my parents think touching each other for the first time? Could they have thought as they saw their different hues against each other, of what shades they might produce in their children, could they have thought that their transgressive love could produce another transgressive love in me? Could they have thought of transgression at all?" In the intensity of the coming together of two others in passion and sexual heat, he asks if they use the knowledge of crossing cultural barriers to fuel their actions—especially in surrendering to pleasure. The footage shows a kind of succumbing to the power of touch and the way the taste and smell of the other create a change in the heightening of one's senses. Gaffney's voiceover continues, "Is this my parents on screen? Is this the document of their desire, my primal scene, the moment of my creation?" Gaffney recasts the footage to attribute his own conception as both a mixed-race and queer offspring so that a theory and ethics of responsibility emerge in his practice of cinema. In other words, he appropriates existing footage to create his own birth in representation and claim a place in history. Beyond this, the content of his birth is an accounting of individual desire as not outside group ascriptions of identity. These public identities fuel private desire so much so that he feels transgressions shape his own identity as queer and as mixed race and also exceed it in attempting to produce a useful theory of the link between race and sexuality.

Gaffney uses the screen in this way—to create a story not yet there but also to show how these screens are imprinted on our bodies as viewers and bearers of history. When Rene Gallimard and Song Liling picnic at a beautiful vista, we see her caress his/her face before he/she sits down, to serve him food. Dressed demurely, almost severely, in a way that highlights the intense sexual attraction they hold between them, he/she touches him in a way that requires him to close his eyes and absorb its power. He connects himself to him/her so that when he/she moves slightly away, he remains in tune. Gaffney asks here, "Is this my mother? Am I the product of a fetish? I am characterized by ambiguity. I am defined by lack of definition. I am the product of interracial desire, transgressive love is in my genes." We then see running under this monologue the projection of another movie onto Rene Gallimard's face as he sits in the dark. Gaffney says that in our genes we know of people we love, they are imprinted on us physically. While he never knew his parents in love, their sexual coming together produced his being; thus their love is imprinted in him physically. Likewise, these films inform our ideas of our origins, beyond our appropriation of them. Gaffney is the "burning remnant of love. I never knew them to love each other. Somewhere buried in me, I know I am it."

Even his own sexuality as a man who desires other men finds reflection on screen. When John Lone's Song Liling becomes a man in the movie, he approaches Jeremy Irons' character in the holding truck cell, totally naked, covering his genitals and his chest with his hands as in Botticelli's *The Birth of Venus*, gloriously revealed on a shell. "Is this me on screen? Is this the document of my desire? Which one is me, the Anglo or the Asian? Where am I in this picture? Do they try to merge and become one? And if they merged and became one would it be me?" He then meditates on the status of mixed race Asian/white men in the movies where Dean Cain "plays 100% white and Russell Wong plays 100% Asian while both are 100% Eurasian." They are organized by convenient categories in a screen where there are "no Eurasian roles." Gaffney dares to imagine and invest in a future where he not only comes into being on screen with an accounting of his multiple identities but infuses this desire with a futurity in queer and reproductive terms. He describes answering an ad for "hapa sperm by a hapa woman." What would it mean to be a hapa (biracial Asian and white) born of hapas continuing a family line? This is a fantasy in a scenario where one's ancestors do not look like oneself. That is, "I do not look or love like my parents" who are of Asian or white and heterosexual identities. He then uses found footage of what is supposedly the bones of "both Mongolian and European—a mixed type of two races," asking, is this his "long lost mom from a long line of hapas transgressing [their] way across Central Asia?" Gaffney looks to the movies not only for ancestry but for queer futurity. From here he declares that he will always say his race is queer as his sex is queer, offering a theory of identity by engaging the power of cinema to make legible his own identities and concerns, rather than simply accepting its limited terms. Unlike Fulbeck's film, which fails to use the medium of film to see the way manhood is steeped in gender hierarchy and heteronormativity or to engage the complexities of interracial sex and desire beyond a binary understanding of power and powerlessness, Gaffney's tackles rather than accepts the representations that limit our understanding of manhood.

In this Introduction, I show three different accountings of male power in assessing the problem of Asian American male gender and sexuality in moving image representation. We see in *The Slanted Screen* the problem of identification in Asian American men's representations where the solution does not address the phallocentrism that results from diagnosing a shortfall from heteronormativity and gender hierarchy. In *Some Questions for 28 Kisses*, we see the straitjacketed framework for Asian American men and the hyperfemininity and hypersexuality for Asian American women at work—in ways that deepen gender inequality and aggravate male pain. *Transgressions* gives us hope for it charts the forces of gender and sexuality in relation to race but also the power of representation in accounting for and identifying these dynamics. These films teach us to keep in mind that the failure to imagine new terms of gender and sexuality beyond our own victimization can aggravate other inequalities—through our practices, choices, acts, gestures, and forms. To acknowledge one's power can better solve these problems, especially with the language of cinema helping us to imagine the actual ways men can be responsible in accounting for their power and their subjugation in their relations with others.

Mapping Straitjacket Sexualities: Chapters in Brief

Images of racialized and sexualized masculinities in the U.S. cinema industry capture a crisis on and off screen in how Asian American men are excluded from normative definitions of masculinity, and a wider range of representation. However, because of the lack of access to sexual heteronormativity and representational subjectivity in straitjacketed criteria of manhood, the field remains open to the possibility of establishing new terms of masculinity and representation that directly address relations of inequality across gender and race. While my method looks carefully at cinematic history to dethrone the assessment of lack as the primary way we assess Asian American men, I also look for possibilities that do not require domination of another or ignore the problems of established structures of image production in a hero who saves the day. I want to imagine images of Asian American men in the movies who present the possibility of reestablishing a relationship to heteronormative racial and sexual masculinities—which may include presenting lack as power as well. *Straitjacket Sexualities* assesses Asian American manhoods on screen with an eye toward harnessing the multiple possibilities of sexual acts and identities. Thus, the book attends to the archive and contemporary filmmaking to look at particular scenes of sex, desire, eroticism, and romance to ask not only how these are possible in their times but how they perform and produce ethical manhoods or fail to do, even when trying.

Chapter One begins with a star without equal, Bruce Lee, who burst upon the scene in 1966 as Kato in the television show *The Green Hornet*. Soon after, he showed another way of being a leading man in establishing a powerful transnational stardom. This chapter illustrates ethical manhood as comprising intimacy, vulnerability, and even the possibility of a powerful asexuality, as described by feminist critique. I study the transnational fantasies of racial manhood in the desires for and displays of bodily acts by the legendary martial arts film star in *The Big Boss* or *Fists of Fury* (1971), *The Chinese Connection* or *Fist of Fury* (1972), *The Way of the Dragon* (1972), and *Enter the Dragon* (1973). In this chapter, I work against the assessments of Bruce Lee's sexuality and masculinity as an antidote to lack, to argue that while Bruce Lee did have sex in the movies, he did so by expanding our understanding of sexuality beyond the penis and the phallus. In this way, I forward Bruce Lee as formulating an ethical manhood that anticipated the new moving-image representations of men in the 1970s that still resonates today. He provides an important antidote to the pain many Asian American men experience when confronting the diagnoses of asexuality and effeminacy that renders them as victims; he instead invites them to acknowledge both their power and their discipline in composing their manhoods. The practice of caring for self and others in Bruce Lee's image, as well as acceptance and rejection of shame, can be seen in Hollywood films that focus on Asian American masculinity and sexuality.

Chapter Two studies the representation of Asian American men in Wayne Wang's *Eat a Bowl of Tea* (1989), Ang Lee's *Wedding Banquet* (1993), and John Hughes' *Sixteen Candles* (1984) in terms of the shame that is the special experience of the asexuality/effeminacy/homosexuality construct. It shows how a victimized and castrating framework is deeply embedded in the thinking around Asian American male representations in the movies, and then revisits characters previously dismissed as shameful in the project of empowering Asian American men. I understand shame to result from the binding of stereotype to the self, to produce an ongoing struggle with dignity. Thus, straitjacket assignations of falling short of the norm of manhood contribute shame to the being of Asian American men. I identify the practice of acknowledging one's assignation and one's wrestling with that same assignation, especially when repeated over time in representation, in narrative films in the 1980s and 1990s featuring Asian American men so as to show the limits of aspiring to racial pride. That is, I evaluate how shame can provide racial joy. Wayne Wang's *Eat a Bowl of Tea* features a whole community's policing of one man's sexual practices in the post–World War II era, Ang Lee's *Wedding Banquet* focuses on a young gay professional Chinese American, and John Hughes' *Sixteen Candles* includes the foreign exchange student Long Duk Dong to articulate a politics of racialized manhood through sex. I explore the implications of working against and with the images of Asian American men as shamed and debased in their race, sexuality, and gender as a way to expose the limits of criteria that diagnose their failures.

Chapter Three maps the textures and complexities of the watershed films by Asian American men released in the early years of this new century, specifically in terms of the various spaces of manhood between ethical responsibility and heterosexual patriarchy available in these works. We see in these Asian American male-authored films a different kind of romantic story about race, as told through male rivalry over women and the thematic of male aggression in articulating sexual desire. The ideals and struggles of manhood represented here reveal wrestling with a phallocentric formation of manhood. If films are technologies of the ethical—especially in scenes where others relate across romance—we may or may not see the ethical accountability of Asian American men not only to women but to their own subjection as effeminate, asexual, and queer. The chapter focuses on the independent films *Better Luck Tomorrow* (2003), *The Debut* (2000), and *Charlotte Sometimes* (2002) to help chart the ethical ways of life the films recommend to Asian American men in making demands upon themselves and each other. I study these films together to give sense of the wide-ranging future possibilities of Asian American male representations.

Chapter Four addresses the fraught sexuality of Asian American men in the movies, including pornography, and Asian American male authorships of sexually explicit material across a wide range of genres. I look at their attempts to subscribe to or reverse the bolstering of male narcissism, phallic economies, heterosexism, and patriarchy. By evaluating these contrasting engagements in the films of Darrell Hamamoto (*Yellowcaust* and *Skin on Skin*), James Hou (*Masters of the Pillow*), Hoang Nguyen (*Forever Bottom!*), Jeffrey Lei (*Dick Ho*), and Greg Pak (*Asian Pride Porn*), as well as the blog of the celebrated heterosexual porn star Keni Styles, I show how we need to attend to what an ethical, responsible, and attractive masculinity could look like for Asian American men on and off screen and the special ways filmmaking intervenes in this discourse. The problem of Asian American manhood in the movies is defined by Hamamoto and Hou in terms of lack of sex, and they propose solving it by securing phallic power in an ongoing conflation of the penis with the phallus. I frame the phallus/penis distinction so as to chisel away at the concept of dominance defining sexual relations. In this way, I change the discourse of Asian American manhoods to address the confines that constrict complex, ambiguous, and ambivalent sexualities that men demonstrate in the movies then and now. Through close readings, I show how scenes of sex acts are encounters with power that produce the possibility for the shattering of the self and the opportunity for reassembling and assembling the self, rather than reestablishing patriarchy and macho sexuality.

Chapter Five focuses on two Asian American men who in the movies portray intensely romantic and variedly sexual figures and who provide us an archive that breaks apart straitjacket sexuality. I show how the sexuality of pornography discussed in Chapter Four is not the only form of sexuality available to Asian American men, who have been engaging in intimate relations in the movies for more than fifty years. In the 1950s and 1960s, heartthrob James Shigeta starred in films like *The Crimson Kimono* (1959), *Walk Like a Dragon* (1960), *Flower Drum Song* (1961), and *Bridge to the Sun* (1961). Shigeta's films engage the meanings of manhood for Asian American men in direct relation to white manhood and white/Asian womanhood. He is a star who always gets the girl, proving false the claim that Asian American men never do in U.S. movies. But even when Asian Americans do get the girl, as he does in *The Crimson Kimono*, they are not necessarily relieved of their disprized status. In Asian and Asian American settings, James Shigeta's characters endure a questioning of their ethnic and racial background in their emotional and sexual relations. James Shigeta, in his performances as one of the very first Asian American romantic leading men in major Hollywood films, shows us a way of establishing an ethics of racialized manhood that exceeds the recovery of the lost phallus. From here, I conclude with the life and work of the actor Jason Scott Lee. I examine his negotiation with the power of representation. In his case, fantasy roles and characters have countered Asian American men's supposed asexuality, effeminacy, and other racial interpretations of their gender and sexuality on screen. Through an interview with the last Asian American romantic hero we've seen since James Shigeta, and by analyzing his feature films, I present the ways in which his choice of roles has attempted to create new maps of manhood, which we see play out in his living "pono" or a calm ethical life of responsibility and accountability that expands our ideas beyond hierarchal and heteronormative manhood. In screening how Asian American men in desire, love, romance, and sex formulate an ethics of masculinity from their particularity, we capture both their wielding of power over others and their bearing of lashes by others as a special subject position from which a theory of ethical relations may emerge. Finally, in the Epilogue, I evaluate Clint Eastwood's *Gran Torino* (2008) for the lead character Thao's assertion of the power of lack in the face of macho as that which inspires an old white man to change, opening up the possibility for recognizing the different representations Asian American men demand in the movies.

ONE

With Vulnerable Strength

Re-Signifying the Sexual Manhood of Bruce Lee

Iconic images of Bruce Lee, one of the most celebrated martial artists and movie stars from the last century, continue to circulate today, most frequently with clothes falling off his bare chest. Big, black, bushy hair tops his handsome face, with lips pursed together and eyes intent in a confident look as the rippling texture of his torso reveals adherence to a disciplined physical regimen and the chiseled, muscled arms affirm his reputation of brute strength made famous by his one-inch punch. With a body on the verge of exploding in its expression of strength and power, this man seems to exemplify a magnificent exception to the supposed problem of Asian American male lack by possessing traits of hegemonic masculinity of strength and power. In protecting the Green Hornet as Kato on television and in beating multitudes of men to death in films that established a new action genre across the world, his image combated the Hollywood tradition of representing Asian men as weak—but did he kiss, love, or possess sexuality? Is he sexy, or does he have sex? These questions seem crucial to the problem of assessing Asian and Asian American men as entrenched in cinematic lack, far away from masculine power.

Most critics say Bruce Lee possesses gender power while lacking sexual prowess. Jachinson Chan, who claims Lee's sexuality reads ambiguously, asserts we can't tell if he's homosexual or heterosexual since he occupies an alternative masculinity.[1] But such an ambiguity may deepen the image of lack and its attendant lowly stature in male hierarchies when we recall that Richard Fung points to the Asian male's sexual illegibility on screen.[2] David

Henry Hwang celebrates Bruce Lee's refutation of weakness that dominates the history of Asian and Asian American male representations, but questions why Bruce Lee "never appeared in a love scene though it would seem almost obligatory for heroes in the action and adventure genre."[3] What criteria do these critics use to diagnose asexuality? I will argue that the limited definition of male power does not do justice to its subject's struggles with forging an ethical manhood. Along with his work on screen, Bruce Lee's letters and interviews chronicle the formation of an Asian American male subject wrestling with racial stereotypes, attributions of senseless violence and asexuality, as well as a commitment to acting and the thoughtful interrogation of his choices. Most importantly, he expands our measure of both masculinity and sexuality—beyond gender hierarchy and male power over women.

This chapter studies how Bruce Lee expanded our understanding of sexuality beyond the conflation of the penis and the phallus where the on-screen appearance of a biological man needs to signify power over others. Between ferocity and tenderness, vulnerability and strength, and caring not only for the self but others—especially friends, family, and women—Bruce Lee formulates an ethical manhood not aligned with patriarchy alone but with a larger field of social relations. Unlike the literature that emphasizes Bruce Lee's invincibility as one that secures nationalist pride or what Vijay Prashad calls antiracist polyculturalism,[4] I instead highlight his specific theorization of racialized gender and sexuality through performances of violence and sex. I argue that Bruce Lee's expressions of vulnerability disclose the emotional costs of violence, and the performances of intimacy that bookend the explosion of his body in committing violence captures his formation of gender and sex as both exposure of self and confrontation with others. His definition of sexuality in film and beyond is powerful in making legible sexualities beyond sexual intercourse or promiscuity. He expands available standards for recognizing viable masculinity. Bruce Lee's performances of sex and violence are moments for the making of ethical manhoods that acknowledge the power one holds in relation to the power that holds one down—by cultivating a physical power that ultimately prioritizes, through his facial and bodily expressions, the fraught meaning of wielding strength against others toward violent ends as well as the significance of a sexual coming together. My attention to Lee's sexual and intimate interactions restores what has been castrated in the analysis of his work on film: sexuality as larger and more expansive than the limited criteria privileged by hegemonic masculinity.

In assessing Bruce Lee's legacy as such, I underline his vulnerability in displaying his different formulation of manhood. The victim position of asexuality and effeminacy and the emasculated rendering of homosexuality so permeate our measure of manhood that Bruce Lee's major contribution, primarily located in his cinematic visage and in the sinews of his body in accounting for one's power and subjugation, is ignored. In contrast, I evaluate how intimate relations of violence and sexuality that produce the expressions of his face and his physical countenance describe an ethical conundrum of manhood itself.

Bruce Lee's characters deploy violence only when compelled to do so in order to defend self and community. Fighting is an ongoing negotiation where the participants agree to stop, or the one with the upper hand always offers a way out before dealing death to his opponent. When the fight moves toward the taking of a life, the culmination is a glimpse into a great culpability that confesses the steep costs of that brutality—besieging the one who wields death as well. Bruce Lee uses his face and tenses his body to express his ethical struggle with the meaning of violence and as I will show later, the meaning of wielding male privilege in sexual relations.[5]

In terms of violence, Bruce Lee's characters conduct amazing feats that brutalize a tremendous number of men. They perform these acts for a greater good, but still they accept responsibility and punishment for killing and hurting others. In *Love and Arms*, Helen Douglas charts as an ethical dilemma the use and justification of violence against the paradoxical formation of more unjust forms of violence.[6] Unlike contemporaneous action heroes such as those played by Clint Eastwood, who never regret their acts of violence (until later in life, with Eastwood's own films that reflect upon war and violence), Bruce Lee's characters demonstrate a manhood that is ethical in its accountability.[7] Thus, I will show what is so effective about Bruce Lee's expression of emotional intelligence and regret at committing violence that leads to his opponents' deaths. The revelation of consciousness catching up to the body's conducting an injustice shows an ethical manhood aware of the well-being of others and civil society beyond gains for the self. Through Bruce Lee's performance and experience of violence and sexuality as powerful and thus deserving of accountability, we learn how he refuses to celebrate violence in the sense of justifying murderous acts or both structural and individual violence against women—whether in the traffic of groups or individual acts by men toward a single woman.

My readings of Bruce Lee's films go against the grain by instantiating how racial masculinity can be nuanced, especially extending to an ethics that revolves around his characters' relationships to others with less power, such as women or physically less capable, thus weaker men. Moreover, previous criticism shows the tendency to look for the penis or for phallic representation in love scenes as well—when a larger repertoire of sexuality, romance, love, and desire actually transpires. Bruce Lee expands our recognition of sexuality to include forms of courtship, gallantry, romance, kissing, touching, flirtation, and even long-term investment in love and marriage in, for example, *Fist of Fury*, fantasy and sex in *The Big Boss*, and flirtation and camaraderie in *The Way of the Dragon* and *Enter the Dragon*. The struggle for ethical manhood—the need to account for power in addressing injustice—is laid bare as both a psychic and physical struggle in Bruce Lee's performances of sex and violence. Thus, this chapter recasts Bruce Lee not only through a masculinity that relies on his ability to brutalize and physically dominate other men or conquer women, but a very problematization of that violence and sexuality as defining his character and hegemonic manhood itself, which I consider a poor frame for privileging Asian American manhoods on screen. I argue that Lee's manhood is contingent upon a larger field that must account for his ethical relations with male friends, romantic relationships, and his protection of community as well as nation.

I begin my analysis here by giving a sense of the transnational nature of Asian American manhood in the body and work of Bruce Lee. I then evaluate the discursive context that situates Bruce Lee within a racial frame and provides a traditional masculine solution to Asian American male queerness as emasculation, asexuality, and effeminacy in popular culture. I show how the literature that primarily frames Bruce Lee in singularly racial terms attests to the difficulty of identifying heteronormativity and gender hierarchy, or straitjacket sexuality, when reading the screens and scenes of male encounters with others in violence and sex. This difficulty so limits our analysis of representations of Asian American men that we neglect to ask some important questions about the structures of manhood in the movies: How does vulnerability make a scene of violence successful or make a sexual encounter on screen meaningful and significant? Within the context of his own letters and interviews, as well as scholarly writings and popular articles and reviews about Bruce Lee's life and work, I closely read his films in terms of the expressions of his body's vulnerability through violence and the demonstrations of expanded forms of sexualities in his films and his life. That is, vulnerability in violence exceeds the celebration of brutish male power as antiracist and anticolonial redemption and in sexuality goes beyond genital love and phallic power as selfishly and narcissistically prioritizing male pleasure and privilege in sex.

Close readings of Bruce Lee's first three Hong Kong–made films make an argument that he redefines gender not as a certainty but as that which involves uncertainty in the expression of both vulnerability and strength. It's not merely the jumping, flying, and superheroic strength but the explosive emotional vulnerability that precedes and secures each expression of violence as well as the tenderness that he demonstrates in scenes of love, desire, sex, and romance that makes his manhood. I present these readings against the assessment that Bruce Lee did not have sex or that he had ambiguous sex. I show how Bruce Lee's characters definitely demonstrate desire and desirability, as well as romantic and sexual hunger and fulfillment. I then conclude my close readings with the last films of his life. Against the popular interpretations of his sexuality in *Enter the Dragon* (1973), his Hollywood film, as the quintessential illustration of Asian male sexual inadequacy in comparison to normative white and excessive black manhoods, I reframe his acts as a refusal to participate in the patriarchal trafficking of women. I then analyze the casting of a fake Bruce Lee in the posthumously released *Game of Death* (1978) and *Game of Death 2* (1981) to show how the missing emotional exposure of the face reveals the inadequacy of framing Bruce Lee as embodying violence as a solution to Asian American male effeminacy and asexuality in popular representation. Moreover, it is vulnerability and power together, as well as the simultaneity of tenderness and ferocity in his touch, that forms Bruce Lee's manhood on screen. This definition makes his manhood captivating today as we seek viable manhoods, in terms of gender, race, and sexuality, for and beyond Asian American men in representation.

The chapter then links Bruce Lee's films with three other films that comment on, continue, and claim his legacy. The popular film *Dragon: The Bruce Lee Story* (1993) about Bruce Lee's life further mythologizes his manhood as Asian American, but it adds the emotional intimacy of his family as well as his endurance of racism. What's fascinating in *Dragon* is the performance of Jason Scott Lee, whose stardom in the 1990s seemed to promise a response to Asian American male asexuality and effeminacy in the movies. The Justin Lin film *Finishing the Game* (2007) presents the inadequacy of mimesis—the repetition of the same—in imagining Asian American man-hoods on screen. Notable too is Lin's career of producing both independent and Hollywood films that explore and create compelling manhoods for racialized men. The video *JJ Chinois* (2002) is Lynne Chan's transgender appropriation of both Bruce Lee's aesthetic and sexuality. Playfully, it expands the relevance of Lee's male iconicity beyond heteronormative sexuality. These films help me to formulate the significance of ethical manhoods in their accounts of both the flagellations and lacerations of power that men take and give where strength registers as uncertain, where touch is powerful in its susceptibility, and where male power can be responsible and giving.

The Enduring Legacy of Bruce Lee

Early in his career, Bruce Lee was rendered a figure hard to read. Born in the United States, raised in Hong Kong, educated in both Hong Kong and the United States, he became the first Asian American male star of global proportions, from the Golden Age of U.S. television in the 1960s to the box-office-record-smashing kung fu artist and actor in Hong Kong and post-humously, the world—and has remained legendary for more than forty years since his sudden death at age 32 in 1973. In an early article written soon after his return to the United States at age 18 from a childhood spent in Hong Kong, Bruce Lee, "movie star from China," is described as unusual and ambitious. As one writer put it, if a dojo formed in every town, Mike Lee would be "velly happy."[8] The writer for this Seattle newspaper article did not even get Lee's name right and used disparaging Orientalisms and distorted English language throughout the article. And even later in Lee's career, at a retrospective screening of his work in New York in the 1990s, *New York Times* film reviewer Vincent Canby comments on Bruce Lee's audition tape for *The Green Hornet*, saying Bruce Lee seems so American but also so not.[9] Throughout his life and beyond, Bruce Lee has been the subject of an Asian American racialization in the press: unrecognizable and illegible for his experiences as an immigrant and as an Asian American.

Bruce Lee, according to Penny Von Eschen, is a product of globalization in that an exchange of culture enabled his traveling opera singer Chinese father and German and Chinese mother to have him born in the United States.[10] Later, the circulation of his films expanded from Asia to be shown to millions all over the world. "For audiences from Calcutta to Los Angeles and Hong Kong to New York, Lee embodied anti-racist and anti-imperialist yearnings," showing that "while audiences interpret popular culture in their own image, it is also produced, distributed and consumed in unequal and hierarchical relations of power."[11] At the time of his death, Bruce Lee lived a transnational life of shuttling between Hong Kong and Hollywood in a time when these patterns were first possible with the ease of air travel and the rise of mass culture in entertainment—attesting to the transnational structure of image-making in his negotiations with being too exotic or too Western. In one of his later interviews, Bruce Lee said, "sometimes I feel a little schizophrenic about it. When I wake up in the morning, I have to remember which side of the ocean I'm on and whether I'm the super-star or the exotic Oriental support player."[12] Struggling with Hollywood's stereotype assignation, he moved to Hong Kong to make films. He first broke box-office records in Hong Kong before setting new records all over Asia, Europe, Latin America, Australia, and the United States. Unlike other scholars who study Bruce Lee's representations through a primarily racial lens—which sees gender and sexuality through race—I use a sexual and gendered analytic of race in order to assess how Lee's legacy in the movies breaks the racial pride = male pride equation to open up a different measure of manhood.

Twenty-five years after Bruce Lee's shocking death, *Entertainment Weekly* and other popular U.S. magazines commemorated his achievements in significantly transnational terms. Lee was credited for "single-handedly populari[zing] the martial arts genre for Western audiences, paving the way for dozens of successors, from Chuck Norris (who got his break as Lee's op-ponent in *The Way of the Dragon*, also known as *Return of the Dragon*), to Jackie Chan, who worked as a fight-scene stuntman in *Enter the Dragon*."[13] Many others, such as Chow-Yun Fat, Jet Li, and even Bruce Li, capitalized on "Bruceploitation" films in the 1970s and beyond in such movies as *Bruce Lee, The Man, The Myth* (1976) and the recent hit *Legend of the Fist* (2010), starring Donnie Yee. *Publisher's Weekly* describes Bruce Lee's "Elvis-like" popularity and following. In the article, Judith Rosen narrates how Bruce Lee is mentioned by *Premiere Magazine* as the ninth most popular movie actor of all time—even "ahead of George Clooney." And she includes how *Time Magazine* "singled out Lee, along with Mother Theresa and Jackie Robinson, as one of the 20 most courageous people of the last century."[14]

How did a young Asian man enter this country to work as a dishwasher and within six years appear on national television on his way to international stardom—within the context of Asian and Asian American manhood's low place in the gendered hierarchy of U.S. industry representation?

In its issue celebrating the heroes of the last century, *Time Magazine* declares Bruce Lee as one in an otherwise bad "century for the Chinese." Joel Stein writes that although Lee was largely unrecognized in his life—his obituary in *The New York Times* ran eight sentences and included a note from the paper's film critic Vincent Canby saying "movies like *Fist of Fury* 'make the Italian western look like the most solemn and noble achievements of the early Soviet Cinema.'"[15] The critique nonetheless indicates a cross-continental and contemporaneous understanding of cinema in a comparative frame. Twenty-six years later, Joel Stein says that:

> What Canby missed is that it's the moments between the plot points that are worth watching. It was the ballet of precision violence that flew off the screen; every combination you can create in *Mortal Kombat* can be found in a Lee movie. And even with all the special effects money that went into the *Matrix*, no one could make violence beautiful as Lee's.[16]

Here, Stein discusses the introduction of a new genre of filmmaking that exceeds cinema to include the convergence of dance and martial arts, the popular medium of video games that emphasize the body in action, and technology that falls short of the body's power. As such, Stein captures the explosive body and its importance to defining manhood as the thing so mesmerizing about Bruce Lee in his movies.

It's an ambivalent celebration, however, for every compliment is followed by a belittling of Bruce Lee's importance. While Stein praises Lee for using "nothing but his hands, feet and a lot of attitude," he remains a mere "little guy [turned] into a tough guy."

> In 1959 a short, skinny, bespectacled 18-year-old kid from Hong Kong traveled to America and declared himself to be John Wayne, James Dean, Charles Atlas and the guy who kicked your butt in junior high. In an America where the Chinese were still stereotyped as meek house servants and railroad workers, Bruce Lee was all steely sinew, threatening stare and cocky, pointed finger—a Clark Kent who didn't need to change outfits. He was the redeemer, not only for the Chinese, but for all the geeks and dorks and pimpled teenage masses that washed up at the theaters to see his action

movies. He was David, with spin-kicks and flying leaps more captivating than any slingshot.

Although Asian American men are perceived to rank low in the gender hierarchy of manhood, Lee is lauded as the "patron saint of the cult of the body: the almost mystical belief that . . . by force of will, we can sculpt ourselves into demigods." And seemingly, out of nowhere and by virtue of his own individual grit, he establishes a new manhood unlike any available before. No guns, just his very body.

Yet Stein's celebrating and belittling continues: "Lee never looked like Arnold Schwarzenegger or achieved immortality." This might be an appropriate way to frame Lee, considering Hollywood's dismissive treatment of his ferocity. As Stein articulates it, "despite [Lee's] readiness to embrace American individuality and culture, Lee couldn't get Hollywood to embrace him, so he returned to Hong Kong to make films. In these films, Lee chose to represent the little guy, though he was a very cocky little guy." Stein then renders the films made in Hong Kong as "uniform: Lee makes a vow not to fight; people close to Lee are exploited and killed; Lee kills lots of people in retaliation; Lee turns himself in for punishment." While Stein dismisses his craft, this is precisely where Bruce Lee's films make a contribution: his violence punishes not only its recipients but its producer in the moment of delivering force—it is a declaration of responsibility for others despite the cost to the self. Here the question of audience comes into play. In Hong Kong, revenge and cross-ethnic/national tensions are the more accurate motivations for violence and depending on the location of the audience, violence is a response to racial or colonial injustice. In the United States, Lee's films signify a rewriting of manhood on screen.

Yuan Shu describes Bruce Lee's politics as expressed in his racially motivated cinema. Shu considers that violence "allows a certain dignity for the minority protagonist and serves as a form of redressing the problem of social injustice."[17] He celebrates how Lee "allows his body to evolve as the filmic representation of nationalism. He reinvents the Asian masculine body and reinscribes it with political and cultural significance, making his films relevant as an expression of Asian American politics and culture."[18] Shu argues that Frank Chin and others take this masculinist perspective and end up affirming what they intended to critique. Nevertheless, for Shu Bruce Lee's "masculine body" still directly redefines Western assignations of the "soft body" or the Japanese attribution of the Chinese "sick body" to "remasculinize the Asian male body as tough, aggressive and competitive."[19] Thus, Shu's approach still leaves a question: Is masculinity here defined simply in terms of achieving what Asian American men have been deprived of—a hyper-strong Asian male body that can hurt others? I will show that Bruce Lee offers a richer definition of power in relation to manhood as an ethical struggle over the implications of violence.

Violence can be defined as the physical and psychic encounter where we see an exchange of force with the other with whom one struggles for recognition as human and deserving of respect. The violence in the encounter with the other in Bruce Lee's movies involves hand-to-hand combat and thus is very different from the violence of a gun fight. The other lives by way of a physical fight, where one's hands and feet cause the other to stop or die. Unlike in previous films, such as Westerns that feature John Wayne, guns kill people. Though it requires skill, the kind of engagement a street fight or a physical encounter brings up in people is different. David Bordwell describes the special way cinema captures and represents this form of combat.[20] It's also different for the audience—especially in a cinematic shooting style that places viewers in the position of the one getting hit. Indeed, Bruce Lee utilizes the power of the cinema to present a body that contradicts the naming of Chinese manhood by racism. As such, he uses film to rebut, refute, and refuse his assignation as low in the racial hierarchy of men. He uses the qualities considered most recognizably macho: male physical power at the site of an encounter with another—usually a stranger in a life-and-death encounter. Stein describes Lee's power on screen: "He had a cockiness that passed for charisma. And when he whooped like a crane, jumped in the air and simultaneously kicked two bad guys into unconsciousness, all while punching out two others mostly offscreen, you knew the real Lee could do that too. . . . He spent his life turning his small body into large weapon."[21] In that mythical moment, Bruce Lee's character wins. In the symbolic moment, Lee's characters slay racism and colonialism through his performances as a physically superior man against a multinational and multicultural cast of opponents. But this established interpretation of Bruce Lee's manhood in the movies as all power remains incomplete.

Vijay Prashad understands Bruce Lee to offer an antiracist and polycultural critique. Antiracism is the "ethos that destabilizes the pretense of superiority put in place by white supremacy" and polyculturalism, while multiculturalism "accepts the existence of differences in cultural practice, but it forbids us to see culture as static and antiracist critique as impossible."[22] While Lee operated within antiracist polyculturalism, he was met with racism and a shallow understanding of his cultural contributions as irrelevant and uninteresting to American culture. The examples include his own wife's family's resistance to him, along with his particular experience with racism in Hollywood. As cited in Prashad, Bruce Lee "wrote in a Taiwanese newspaper in 1972, 'I am a yellow-faced Chinese, I cannot possibly become an idol for Caucasians.'"[23]

Prashad situates Lee "along the grain" of Asian American filmmaking in its "desire to confront the cultural injury of white supremacy with the salve of a plural heritage."[24] Notably, he cites Bruce Lee saying to his mother: "Mom, I'm an Oriental person, therefore, I have to defeat all the whites in the film." In the context of "the United States drop[ping] eight hundred thousand tons of bombs on Cambodia, Laos and Vietnam," Prashad notes, "he had to kick Colt's ass in the Coliseum; he had to show some solidarity with the army in black pajamas."[25] In this way, Prashad's critique is multilayered in that he situates Lee historically and also credits him for negotiating the constraints placed upon him by Hollywood. "Trapped by the shackles of a racist role (in *Green Hornet* as Kato—who Frank Chin calls a glorified driver in *Slanted Screen*), Lee nonetheless broke free whenever he could, with a quiet determination."[26] In refusing to play houseboy and laundryman, according to interviews, Lee demonstrated awareness of the stereotype and declared a need to fight them.[27] Prashad situates this protest by Bruce Lee in the historical context of his emergence—such as in the Yellow Power movement, which also included the participation of Asian Americans in other civil rights organizations such as the Black Panthers.[28] Class alliances formed across racial lines. "Bruce Lee would give us the perfect allegory of both Asian American radicalism and of the Vietnam War," Prashad argues in reading Lee as one who offered young Asian Americans a way to see themselves as fighting and winning.[29]

My own work enters here, to present Bruce Lee as an embodiment of the Asian American subject beyond being simply a vessel of nationalism or Chinese cultural pride. His transnational and Asian American subjectivity gives us an opportunity to seize our definitions of gender and sexuality for Asian American men. Lee's growing up in Hong Kong during the Japanese occupation, where he became a boxing and dancing champion and lived as a child actor prior to returning to the United States as a teenager for higher education, describe what Sau-ling C. Wong and Susan Koshy discuss as new Asian American subjects.[30] Diaspora and globalization located his personhood and domestic racism characterized his experiences in the United States. Transnational popular culture—the introduction of Hong Kong martial arts to the U.S. movie industry—then signaled a triumphant return. Lee tragically died a mere month before the premiere of the film, *Enter the Dragon*, that was to signal his entrance into global stardom. Contrary to Joel Stein's assessment, Bruce Lee has achieved immortality. But what is most valuable in the legacy of Bruce Lee is the formulation of an ethical manhood that emerges from his experiences as an Asian American man.

Before I move to contextualize my own close readings of the films in order to build upon Prashad and Shu, I follow these scholars to frame Bruce Lee as a transnational phenomenon who provided an anti-imperialist critique as well as a focus on countering domestic racism. He did indeed use these justifications to explain the necessity of violence as a counter to the indignities of racism and imperialism in male experience. But what is striking in defining this manhood as not simply macho is the physical vulnerability required in his expression, specifically in terms of the emotional intimacy that counters the approach and explosion of violence as a form of ethical manhood. And then there are the peculiar workings of sex in his films that remain unaccounted for within limited definitions of patriarchy and gender hierarchy.

In this chapter, I thus provide what is missing from previous analysis: a study of intimate relations to interrupt the macho legacy of Bruce Lee. Unlike Shu's placement of Bruce Lee in the tradition of privileging the hard body, I represent Lee's success in terms of the emotions disclosed in the cinema. Lee's steely, muscled body presents an intense vulnerability even as he dominates life-and-death encounters and reveals a consciousness of the implications of sexually relating to others. In these scenes, "traditional masculine qualities" of hegemonic manhood are rendered anew in a body that almost cannot bear what the infliction of violence requires of the self. Unlike readings of Bruce Lee as an asexual person who triumphs in gender terms, I provide close readings of his sexual relations as disclosures of emotional intimacies. In these revelations of intertwined vulnerability and power, an awareness of the costs of pleasure for men in relation to others emerges. Rather than a superman of steel, we see a manhood that depends on, needs, and protects others in order to sustain the self.

Reading Sex and Emotions in Bruce Lee's Hong Kong Films

When speaking of Asian American manhoods in moving-image representations, I speak of a transnational formation. That is, industries and funds that produce the films in my study are based in both the United States and Asia and the films are seen by audiences all over the world. The movement and circulation of bodies that comprise the making of these films attest to the process of globalization itself—the transformation of filmmakers and audiences as they move across borders. Indeed, cinematic representations of Asian and Asian American men in the 1970s show us that global imperialism and U.S. domestic racism contribute to our ideas and expectations of what makes these men and how they are imbricated in each other's productions.

If not for the success of the U.S.-based television show *The Green Hornet* (1966–1967), Bruce Lee would not have made kung fu films. Recognized in the streets of Hong Kong, his star power contributed to his securing leading roles. And since his Hong Kong films made so much money, Hollywood came to him. Transnational film star Bruce Lee negotiated race, gender, class, and sex across continents, cultures, and fantasies. The documentary *Bruce Lee: The Legend* (1977) asks frequent leading lady Nora Miao how Bruce Lee's real-life experiences informed the characters in his films. She describes how in each of Bruce Lee's films he portrays a stranger in a new land. Miao attests to the life-shaping events of immigrating to the United States and the negotiations with racism there that drive his stories. In *The Big Boss* (1971), we see Bruce Lee come from China to help his cousins—migrant low-wage workers in hard-labor jobs in Thailand. In *Fist of Fury* (1971), Bruce returns home to China from abroad so as to avenge the death of his teacher, whose martial arts school is located in the nebulous space of the "international settlement" where the local police are disempowered by the Japanese colonizers. His own directorial debut, *The Way of the Dragon*, also called *Return of the Dragon* (1972), transpires in Rome, Italy, where Bruce Lee's character comes to help a Chinese restaurant owner when a local Italian man and his multiracial cast of thugs harass her. Here he comes into contact with a Korean and American nemesis. His breakthrough Hollywood film, *Enter the Dragon*, features a number of combatants from the United States (both black and white) and Australia as well as a multiracial group of women caught in the trade of sexual labor. In *Game of Death*, the film that uses 12 minutes of footage that included the real Bruce Lee, he battles against foes such as legendary NBA player and Bruce Lee student Kareem Abdul Jabbar and Dan Inosanto, a Filipino American martial arts champion. Indeed, Bruce Lee's characters exist in a world that is tied to others across and within borders. His world involves traveling bodies and multinational subjects fighting in different lands.

While we understand physical struggle among the individual representatives of nations, such as Chinese people versus Japanese people, *Fist of Fury* involves individuals representing themselves as independent fighters as well. The African American fighter Jim Williams in *Enter the Dragon* fights racism at home when the police harass him. When choosing to have sex with multiple women at once, he fulfills the stereotype of black men as hypersexual, though he also meets a death typical of African American men who cross racial lines when he is ultimately lynched—this time, for refusing to join the evil Dr. Han. While we see critiques of domestic racism as well as the transnational circulation of capital in all the films—whether through the drug trade in *The Big Boss*, the Chinese diaspora in *The Way of the Dragon*, or the moving bodies of elite athletes in *Enter The Dragon*—we also see negotiations with the ever-changing meanings of sex and desire. In close readings, I attempt to revise the romanticism of Bruce Lee's physical power to emphasize what he brings to transform our understanding of Asian American manhood. Rather than signify brute strength, Bruce Lee problematizes the costs of violence in civil society and the importance of sex in transforming gender relations.

While others claim that Bruce Lee never appeared in a sex scene, Bruce Lee engages in intimate sexual relations that comprise an expanded definition. For example, in several scenes, he engages in flirtations, nudity in bed, kissing, declaring love, investments in long term partnership, and promises of marriage—in *The Big Boss* and *Fist of Fury*. We also see him as an object of desire by Asian and white women in *The Way of the Dragon*. And while he has the option to participate in sexual relations in *Enter the Dragon*, he refuses, for reasons that are not simply the fulfillment of a straitjacketed understanding of masculine sexuality in asexuality. Close readings of the sexual and romantic encounters in Bruce Lee's films expand our understanding of sexuality beyond phallic enjoyment. An approach that insists on searching for the literal penis or the symbolic phallus cannot do justice to the rich repertoire of sexualities on display and at work in Bruce Lee's films.

The Big Boss (1971)

In *The Big Boss*, Bruce Lee's character, Cheng, goes to Thailand to join his extended family, who all work at an ice factory. Members of his family begin disappearing once they discover the boss's drug trade activities. When Cheng's closest cousin and de facto leader of the crew disappears, Cheng comes to the family's violent defense, but not without hesitation. He sacrifices love with a woman from the laboring camp as he unleashes the force of his will and body for the sake of members of his family who die at the hands of the drug lord's violent crew. The film ends with a scene where Cheng single-handedly destroys a massive gang of goons, who drastically outnumber him, in a crucial and climactic cinematic confrontation at the drug lord's compound.

For some unstated reason, at the beginning of the film, as if continuing from Bruce Lee's own life as a boxer whose mother sends him to America to get away from trouble, the character has promised his mother he will no longer fight. His vow is challenged immediately upon his arrival in Thailand. He and his uncle stop to eat at a roadside cart operated by a pretty young woman who is soon harassed by thugs demanding she "keep us company." Two of them come close to the young woman, played by Nora Miao, teasing her face with their fingers. She resists their sexual advances by attempting to maintain her dignity. But when the thugs beat up another vendor, a young boy who approaches them with rice cakes and demands payment for what they eat, Cheng almost loses his composure. His uncle stops him and instead, another young man beats up the thugs. This man, Brother Hsu, turns out to be Bruce's cousin. Early on we see that violence is a technology of control utilized by bad men over innocent women and children and used by good men such as Cheng's cousin in their defense. Cheng, his uncle, and his cousin represent a critique of a social order that privileges men who bully others.

Women also function as romantic interests, one whose love Cheng sacrifices. At the cousins' house, where all the Chinese workers sleep, Cheng meets a young girl named Chow Mei. Romantic music plays over her entry to reflect his entrancement by her. Broken out of his reverie, he stands abruptly when introduced to her. This establishes Cheng as an exceptional figure for his regal behavior among all the other men seated in the room who surround them. Cheng and Chow Mei stand eye-to-eye, he in his kung fu purple pajamas staring as she in her long braid and white shirt offers him tea. She is immediately taken with him and locks her eyes on his visage. Her thick braids frame the sides of her face as she looks at him as if they are the only ones in the room. She does not stop staring at Cheng in this alert way throughout the entire gathering of men. He pretends to pay attention to the male conversation—about a young girl exhausting an old man sexually—then deliberately turns and pauses to look at her with a giant grin. Their innocent connection seems untouched by the unsavory nature of the conversation around them. His body, directed toward the male gathering, contradicts the direction of his face, which is turned completely toward her. His eyes meet hers and his face tilts opposite hers while attentive to her mood. The film clearly establishes how they are powerfully attracted to each other.

The two-shot of the couple breaks into a complementary intercutting that suggests their compatibility. His face occupies left of screen while hers rests in the right. Both faces remain relaxed and attuned to the other. When the men's voices rise to agree that women are either a blessing or ruin to man—"they make you impotent and useless as a eunuch!"—Cheng makes a goofy face at May: his knuckles pressing on his cheek, his mouth pouting in an exaggerated manner, he turns his face to meet her gaze directly, and then stops to maintain a focus on her face. She smiles at him as he scratches his nose to sneak a peek at her face. It's a deliberate flirtation by each of them, and it occurs among men whose faces we do not see and who engage in crude banter about male fears of women's sexuality. Instead we see a sweet and tender romance unfolding between Cheng and Chow Mei, who demonstrate interest in each other's faces and characters. The romance between them is situated within a patriarchal situation that comes to transpire in a concretely dangerous reality in their next scene.

Another young man notices Chow Mei as well, but in a way that comes across differently. The son of the factory's boss and owner encounters her at the creek where she washes clothes. From the hill above her, he moves toward her aggressively, expressing his sexual desire for her. Grabbing her as her braids whips across his chest, he pulls her in for a kiss. She resists by pulling away, so that the front of her body faces the other way. Both of his hands prevent her arm from moving. She is completely pressed against him when they both see Bruce Lee's character arrive at the banks with a solidly determined, strong, and calm face. She runs to Cheng with relief. Their coupling contrasts with the contact with her assailant. While her side and shoulder fit into the nook under Cheng's arm, both her hands are free.

The hand closest to him lies on his chest while the other relaxes along her side. She rests her back on his arm and his hand supports her shoulder blades. His alert stance makes his chest face his opponent while his other hand hovers above his hip. He stares down the drug lord's son.

When the other man leaves, Chow Mei and Bruce remain holding on to each other until they realize they're still touching. First, his eyes look down toward her without moving his face. He has to contain his desire for her, so he hides his looks lest they reveal too much. She softens against his chest, then soon realizes that the threat that leads to their proximity has gone. Their faces reveal a self-consciousness of their desire for each other—which only we witness—before they immediately separate, jumping away to stand a foot apart. She looks down and he looks up to the sky as if whistling, both hands behind his back. He leaves and without his gaze upon her, she watches him go with a strong longing.

This scene's softness comes sandwiched between violence. In their meeting, we can see the emotional intimacy between Chow Mei and Cheng. Unlike Cheng's attention, which centers on his interest in her person, the other male's attention focuses on sex, as he pulls at her and demands contact. When the owner of the factory, revealed as a drug lord, commands his gang of bodyguards to attack Brother Hsu, Cheng's cousin, the violence is accompanied by the specter of sexual violence. We hear the son telling his father that he's found the perfect girl for him and then describes Chow Mei

FIGURE I   Cheng, unlike Chow Mei, realizes they are alone. And if he permits himself, his protective touch could turn potentially romantic. *The Big Boss*. Dir. Wei Lo. Golden Harvest, 1971.

in exclusively sexual terms. The drug lord and the son represent a world of violence that Bruce Lee's character opposes, not only in his disengagement with actual physical fighting or their different regard for women but in his family and co-workers' refusal to accept compensation unearned or dishonestly earned, such as the profits of the drug trade.

When Hsu disappears, Chow Mei and Cheng bond. He tenses his body in response to her shriveling in mourning and he leans toward her. She demands action and then as if this takes her strength, starts to cry, leaning her face against the balcony with both hands as support. Again the two-shot frames the faces of each character juxtaposed while they do not see each other. We see her face as Bruce Lee's Cheng comes up behind her. He wants to touch and comfort her, but his hand remains caught in the air between them. He pauses and stays behind her, aligning his body but keeping his distance—unlike the drug lord's son, who insisted on pressing his body against hers. Cheng tries to touch her again, lifting his hand to comfort her but instead he withdraws it and makes a fist. Again, his desire to touch her must be contained, so he turns the fist toward himself as a demand to rein in his emotions. He demonstrates awareness of the power of touch and withholds himself, to bow and to say words of comfort instead: "Don't cry. Brother Hsu will be okay." He steps back and reassures her with words alone, keeping his physical desire at bay. He leaves with our knowing that he does so without the touch he wants to give. When she exits the porch, we see their backs as she approaches her cottage behind the workers' house that

FIGURE 2   Cheng almost touches Chow Mei. *The Big Boss*. Dir. Wei Lo. Golden Harvest, 1971.

Cheng enters. But then they both attempt to connect face-to-face again, stopping to look at each other at the same time. He watches her leave with naked hunger on his face. Here we see desire in contrast to the violence the drug lord and his son inflict on women. Bruce Lee's character defines touch differently—as not only powerful in establishing a bond but in expressing desire, tenderness, and affection for a woman not as a right but as requiring her consent.

So far, in these scenes of love and intimacy in *The Big Boss*, we see that flirtation and tenderness between Cheng and Chow Mei contrast with the brutishness of the drug lord, his son, and his thugs. We note too that the power of touch can express desire and affection as well as threat and danger from men toward women. In the first scene, we see a culture that renders women as sexually powerful over men, women's sexuality as threatening to men's character, and a male inability to control oneself. But this discussion is rendered senseless in the face of the encounter between Cheng and Chow Mei—where recognition blossoms in a loving and respectful relationship in which the man understands his ability to display power or to wield it with consideration for others.

Women express desire for men in this film as well, which helps the audience evaluate Cheng's physical attractiveness and personal attributes. The appreciative female gazes confirm how he meets the standards of beauty for men. He returns to the cart of the woman whom his cousin protected in the opening of the film. In a close-up, the young, attractive vendor played by Nora Miao openly approves of his appearance as she gazes upon him with an inviting look and then a smile that creates a spark in the film from its wattage. Within the film's collection of many characters, the close-up of the face emanating a cherubic gaze that discloses her attraction for him stands out. She looks directly at him and her mouth slowly parts to smile. However, he does not return the flirtation, as he does with Chow Mei. He is discriminating in his allocation of desire. Neither he nor the camera returns her look, in contrast to the way the harmonious framing and intercutting of the earlier match made it seem like Cheng and Mei could kiss.

In the following scene, Cheng breaks his vow of nonviolence and beats up the drug lord's thugs at the ice factory. Dozens of men lay fallen around him like petals. He stands over them, posed in a towering lunge. The camera then focuses on his face, against the aghast and impressed countenances of his comrades, who look upon him with a new trust and support—their champion. His face shows he is uncomfortable when not looking at his enemies, despite achieving control over them and getting them to leave the factory. He soon takes over the foreman position and his happy crew dances and chants on their way home. However, Chow Mei berates him for forgetting to demand their brother Hsu's whereabouts. Penitent, Cheng promises to do better. Here, we see the woman is also the compass for doing better— she demands he do the right thing and stay focused. His physical heroism, displayed through the ability to inflict pain on dozens of men at once, is framed within his tenderness toward women, who, in Chow Mei's case, recommend men live justly and away from immorality and corruption, which women can also represent.

Next, the drug lord's agent purports to celebrate Cheng's promotion to foreman and gets him drunk in a brothel. In his alcohol-induced stupor, Cheng looks at the very elaborately made-up prostitute who seduces and distracts him so he may come to work for the drug lord. Cheng mistakes her for Chow Mei as he becomes drunk and playfully chases her around the big table in the small private room of the restaurant while the other guests laugh heartily. He ends up passed out and naked in bed with the prostitute. To emphasize that it's not Chow Mei but a more corrupt and learned woman who enjoys Bruce Lee's fit body, we see a close-up of the prostitute gazing at his nudity and placing her body on his naked chest as he sleeps. He remains innocently unaware of her desire. Sexually inspired by his physical beauty and power, she takes off her clothes as if in a ceremony and lays her naked

FIGURE 3   The prostitute relishes the feeling of Cheng's naked chest. *The Big Boss.* Dir. Wei Lo. Golden Harvest, 1971.

body on his. Her enjoyment from this bodily propinquity is palpable. She demands a response and attempts to wake him up by kissing him. The camera pans away and focuses on the curtain as the sun comes up. While we do not see them engage in sex, it presumably happens with this discrete motion of the camera. In the morning, Cheng wakes up, surprised to find the woman naked and cuddling with him. She looks at him with knowing. Disconcerted by her gaze, he quickly puts his clothes on, apologizes, and runs out of the brothel into the street, where he encounters Chow Mei. He's even more distraught at the sight of her seeing him disheveled, with the stain of sex on him. Though drunkenness liberates Cheng's repressed desire for Chow Mei, both the lead characters remain innocent, while the prostitute embodies all the sexual corruption. However, we also see Bruce Lee's character and body as an object of unbridled desire, as well as conclude that he is desirous and actional.

The power of sexuality connects Cheng with the prostitute in a new allegiance, so much so that she ends up risking her life for him in a struggle against the drug lord. When the boss kidnaps Chow Mei and kills most of his comrades, Cheng finally goes to the big boss' compound. The prostitute tries to help him, but ends up getting killed for it. The prostitute, as the one who bears and bares desire unashamedly, shows transformation through sexual experience. Her loyalty shifts to her lover and she is punished for it by the drug lord's son. Through her actions, she is redeemed in her expression of a bond with Cheng and in the process disassociates herself from the corruption of the drug lord. Thus while her work for the drug lord enables her to meet Cheng, she saves herself from the big boss and his enslavement.

At the drug lord's mansion, women provide him with intimate services such as massaging him, fanning him, bringing him an abundance of food, or flanking him in an entourage so as to verify his power. He dishonors their service when he burns the chest of a female servant with a cigar. She quietly leaves as Bruce Lee's character looks on, shocked. Such treatment of women attests to the evil of the drug lord, but also encourages us to see how other men like Cheng consider such treatment reprehensible. Thus, we see a contrast between different genders in Bruce Lee's films. Here, Cheng fights men who are brutal, immoral, and corrupt. Women stand as agents for good—either as the litmus test for measuring male characters and ensuring the safety of all others, or as those who need to be saved from corruption.

In the final fight scene, as Cheng pummels the remaining villains, Chow Mei calls the police. The film closes with Cheng surrendering to the police for unleashing his violence and for killing, even in the name of justice. His violence, however, is tempered by Chow Mei's presence, her forgiveness, and his surrender to the symbol of justice that she calls to the scene. His is an ethical manhood that accepts punishment for the costs of violence to society. Again, we see how women are the litmus test for men's ability to make the right choices, to maintain civilization without cheating the self or others. The film concludes with Chow Mei coming in with police, as a shirtless Cheng breaks the body of a man below him. The camera takes the point of view of the one being beaten. Here we see Bruce Lee's character wrestling with the ethics of violence involved in the physical and psychic costs of killing another—a prominent theme in the rest of his films. At the end of his battle, we see the connection of the emotional and the ethical in the vulnerability and regret at perpetrating violence, however necessary and honorable.

Bruce Lee's body, in flexing its sculpted form, exposes these tensions. The notion of exposure is crucial as his body often ends up unclothed in juxtaposition, mostly, to clothed opponents. Exposed in his chest and his body are the strength required of him—the flexing, the folding, the stretching, the bending, and the sweating that come from the building up and releasing of strength. The special mix of male brutality unleashed and civilized regret demonstrates an ethical struggle that is contrasted with enemies, who subscribe blindly to greed or violence. As such, Bruce Lee's character reveals the self in confrontation with the other, while his opponents do not question their violence or brutality. In the end, Chow Mei finally abandons her reserve. She rushes toward him and rests her body on his bloody chest. He embraces her and turns his face to hers. He touches her face and we see his back muscles flex from behind. His hand falls as part of his surrender; thus the film ends with his ethical submission, as well as a powerful contrast. His hurtful touch becomes a caress of tenderness.

In *The Big Boss*, Bruce Lee's character falls in love with a young woman who encourages him to fight for their community. Emotional intimacy—affection and love—from women informs Bruce Lee's character. Cheng recognizes that his actions—whether he declares his intention or affection, or not—have meaning for her and he measures his decisions around her. He finds her pleasing—and recognizes the power of touch in articulating his desire for her. Yet he won't touch her. When drunk, he imagines that he is able to reveal his desire. A lot of damage can be done within intimate relations, but here, Cheng demonstrates caution and care as important to the formation of his manhood. In order to protect her and himself from the power they hold over each other, he withholds his touch. And in the end, we see the high cost of violence when he can no longer be with her. Taken away by the police, he must give her up. In Bruce Lee's first film, we see the importance of touch—in terms of sexuality and violence—that Bruce Lee's character carefully deploys. His performance shows the strength of the male body that goes beyond the conflation of the penis and the phallus. His is not a manhood that seeks to conquer others but one that uses strength with an eye toward caring for others. Ultimately, his ethical manhood also requires him to give up his own satisfaction with his love object in order to uphold civilization.

Fist of Fury (1972)

Threaded throughout the narrative of *Fist of Fury* (also known as *The Chinese Connection*), Bruce Lee's second film, is the importance of heterosexual, long-term coupling for his character, Chen Zhen. Chen returns home to the Shanghai International Settlement and his former Chinese kung fu school to propose to his girlfriend. There, he finds his teacher has recently died a very mysterious death. A competing Japanese school now threatens the Chinese school. Like in his previous film, nations and their representatives clash, with Chen's school represented by an older teacher who restrains himself from retaliating against the bullying Japanese, who look like punk rock samurais. In *The Big Boss*, Chinese workers and Thai drug empire thugs combat each other. Here, the Japanese occupy an international area of Shanghai, and Bruce Lee's Chen defends school, people, and country.

Compared to the other students, Chen can barely stifle his rage over the arrogant Japanese, who invade their school with threats and insults. Despite his elders' warnings, Chen ends up being the one to defend and protect his school by attacking the invaders on his own. All the while, his actions are motivated and measured by his love interest, Yuan Le-erh, played by Nora Miao. Le-erh knows where to look for him when he hides to ready his attack. When she finds him in the cemetery he looks wild as he eats rabbit meat with a fierce expression on his face. He hears someone approaching and growls. She gasps and then smiles as she says, "It's me." Light, romantic music accompanies her approach. She attempts to convince him not to hide and not to take revenge on the Japanese school. She raises the issue of his trust in her, and he shakes his head with a kind of shyness—saying he's making plans to follow what he believes is the right course. He wishes to protect her from the violence entailed in his plans. She questions his refusal to involve her. "We used to trust each other before." As she turns away from him she declares, "You must know I love you." He rises to face her with his hands in air: "Yes, I love you as much as I always did." She responds with "I believe you" as he looks at her tenderly. His own response is strong: "Don't ever doubt me," as he sits back down. With tenderness and firmness in his declaration of love and devotion in this romantic exchange, Chen reveals a look of open exposure—the outpouring of emotion and the firmness of his declaration—which contrasts with his previous ferocity when preparing for his attack. While he demonstrates his vulnerability when he is around her, we do not forget his fierce ability when it comes to fighting.

While they remain fully clothed in this scene set in a cemetery and on a bench, the love smolders and sexual desire seethes between Chen Zhen and Yuan Le-erh. Chen declares his intention to propose to the fighter who embodies the adorable in her black and white ensemble with white hair clips that mimic her eyebrows and keep her hair back from her small face. They sit back to back, as if to curb the raging sexual hunger between them, as he declares his desire to marry her. When she touches him in response, he closes his eyes so as to bear the threat of his unraveling by it. She moves him excruciatingly. She sits behind him and he falls against her back with a kind of physical vulnerability he exposes to her in their intimate exchange. He smiles with a kind of longing expression as they wistfully discuss a patriarchal set-up they desired for their future long ago: where he teaches martial arts and she takes care of the house and kids. "What happened to those dreams? Do you really love me?" she asks. "You mean more to me than anyone," he says strongly, in an inter-cutting that captures them facing each other directly.

This beautiful sequence establishes their romance—as if they are about to kiss, but the actual placement of their bodies when revealed in the larger shot reminds us that they indeed face away, sitting with their backs against each other. Upon his declaration, which mixes a calm and agitated voice, she finally turns to face him. Her question "Do I?" is seductive. Excited, he slowly pulls her in after an exchange of close ups on the eyes. The first kiss, lips to lips, is tentative, but soon becomes deep. Passions are let loose and

F I G U R E 4   The kiss expresses Chen Zhen's need and desire for his fiancée. *Fist of Fury*. Dir. Wei Lo. Golden Harvest, 1972.

sexual desire set free. He holds her, cradling her torso under his as they kiss passionately. Stopping, she moves up to look at him as he holds her. As they embrace she asks him to include her in his plans—his attack on the Japanese school and his future. As in *The Big Boss*, sexuality creates a pathway for the couple to disclose their need for each other.

Chen looks down, gets up and walks away, steeling himself with his hands behind his back. His plans for her are long term. "I'm taking you away with me . . . to somewhere where they'll never find us, somewhere where we'll be safe." Here, the dialogue portends commitment to a lasting companionship where the notion of safety is not referencing them individually, but their coupling. His plans go beyond hiding at the cemetery and fighting the Japanese school; he imagines a life together elsewhere. His gauge for successful manhood is not the violence he deploys, but his more important ambition of charting a life together. He embraces her and they cuddle, until suddenly he returns to a hunting mode. His commitment to her snaps him back into focusing on avenging his teacher.

Later, we see that he must again give up the dream of coupling when he releases massive violence against the Japanese school and seeks punishment by getting shot to death. Here we see Bruce Lee's character, Chen, as a sexual being and a romantic figure. His treatment of women is indeed unlike James Bond's—with whom his characters are compared—who uses women sexually.[31] In this and his previous film, we can see that for Lee's characters, women are partners with whom he attempts to achieve recognition and mutuality, even within normative reproductive configurations. Furthermore, gender roles and scripts do not remain static, as his love interest in this film is a fighting figure who also leads him to justice, as in *The Big Boss*. In these ways, Lee presents an alternative hero in his relations with women, which don't always end with achieving sex and love in the movies. We feel their loss especially as we glimpse their powerful appearance.

While brutish men contrast with Bruce Lee's tender characters in *The Big Boss* and *Fist of Fury*, we also see a contrast in the women featured in each of these films. In *Fist of Fury*, as in *The Big Boss*, male intentions toward women are the measure of their ethical manhoods. In the Japanese characters in *Fist of Fury*, we see male consumption of women's bodies as corrupt and excessive. In a tatami room, the nemesis, Suzuki, gathers his cronies, including an effeminate Chinese traitor and a ferocious Russian fighter. A Japanese geisha entertains them with a dance that becomes a burlesque stripshow, where her traditionally coiffed hair comes to contrast with a garish costume of mere pasties and a g-string. In effect, the dance begun in geisha garb morphs into a Western woman's striptease. The geisha-turned-burlesque-performer grinds on the floor, shakes her breasts vigorously, and finally takes off her underwear and gyrates in front of the Chinese traitor, who exclaims, "Japan is great!" This scene contrasts with the previous interaction between the lovers, who negotiate with each other the most effective way to protect their love and their community. In this scene the woman speaks through her sexuality directed toward its consumption by men. Unlike the ethical manhood in relation to women offered by Bruce Lee's character, Chen, we see an exploitative community of Japanese, Russian, and Chinese men who ultimately present an unethical manhood that uses less powerful others for the sake of one's own pleasure.

Later, at the conclusion of Chen's attack, where he fights with dozens of men at the Japanese school, we see his face in pain, as in *The Big Boss*, distorting to disclose how the act of killing is one he regrets. His face expresses the dawning of a realization that his acts come at a tremendous cost to the self—including his opportunity to love. Thus his consciousness comes to peace with the release of violence that he has attempted for so long to contain. Later in the film, in battling the Russian fighter, he once again has his shirt off against a fully clothed opponent—who actually wears a tuxedo in a kind of extreme contrast. The naked body hides nothing but simply articulates raw and ready power. Here we see the blur of Bruce Lee's arms moving too fast. The camera isolates the movement like it's a dance move that needs to be taught. A new form of filmmaking anticipates the audience in awe. Unlike his having to slow down for the television cameras in *The Green Hornet*, he can unleash his fastest movements for the film camera. We also see the cutting technique of a medium close up, to a close up, and then to an extreme close up of his eyes in the fight—as well as his body shaking from the ferocity of the battle. He discloses his physical vulnerability as he displays his strength. Is it regret? Is it in the loss of physical control that consciousness finally catches up with? Upon killing the head of the Japanese school, Chen looks up—as if to repent for losing control of his body. The film concludes when he encounters his girlfriend, Le-erh, and says to the police chief, "I will pay for the lives I took." Ending the film with forgiveness from Le-erh acts as a blessing, for he acknowledges responsibility for taking lives as separate from the good he accomplishes. The last shot is the iconic scream, where he unleashes a force from within as he confronts the gunmen outside the school, leaping to a future beyond the screen. The second film thus ends like the first, where his characters lose the noble women whom they love and desire as part of the sacrifice they must make for the violence they commit. Bruce Lee's directing and writing of the next film enables special insight into his authorship of violence and sexuality beyond his performance as an actor and martial arts choreographer in his previous films.

The Way of the Dragon (1972)

Capturing the transnational movement of the film, the opening titles scroll across the screen while men in a dragon boat row across the ocean in Bruce Lee's *The Way of the Dragon*, also known as *Return of the Dragon*. Bruce Lee is a Chinese man, Tang Lung, who travels to Rome to help a beautiful restaurant owner protect herself from a "syndicate" who terrorizes her, her employees, and customers. Behind the restaurant, in a narrow alleyway, Tang Lung trains the waiters in kung fu and together they fight the multinational thugs, who seem to hail from the United States and Italy in this film, whereas *Fist of Fury* features opponents from Japan and Russia. In *The Way of the Dragon*, we see that a different notion of ethics informs the protagonist's fighting and violence. Rather than acting out of blind loyalty to a corrupt master or as a fighter-for-hire, Tang devotes himself to a non-patriarchal loyalty to community and to others beyond himself.

The opening shot of the film reveals a great deal about Bruce Lee's attention to otherness as central to his characters. The film opens to reveal a close-up of Tang Lung looking into the distance. Shadows fall on his face and the camera reveals a close-up of an older white woman who stares him down. The frame becomes a two-shot and we see them side by side, and very close with considerable space around them. As we see them within their context, the woman's audacity is astounding. Meanwhile, Tang stands very still, looking down while she looms over him. With her arms crossed upon her chest, she stares in a way that polices him into a tense humility. The shot cuts to an even wider angle and we see that she is crowding him. He clutches his bag closer to his body. When the old woman's friend arrives, she smiles broadly—in direct contrast to her open hostility toward Tang Lung. Upon her departure, he releases his breath and relaxes his posture with a great sense of relief. A kind of breathing space opens up around him.

In *The Way of the Dragon*, Bruce Lee's directorial debut, Lee chooses to focus on how his character reacts to the intense scrutiny he undergoes as a foreigner—immigrant, alien, and racialized other—in a new land and to the scrutiny of his body. This is a gaze that occurs across gender as well. Is the woman staring at his racial otherness with curiosity, resentment, fear, or desire? Her stare registers as anger, strangely. She looks mad at him even as he attempts to appease her with several smiles. Other people too stare at him as he passes by. Is it his pajama-style clothing? Or that he's hungry? His stomach growls so loudly that it draws attention, and when he finally finds food, he burps from eating too much. So Lee begins the film both seriously and comically—both threads contribute to the telling of how a Chinese tourist assumes a heroic role that also involves romance and sex at a time when Asian American men rarely controlled their appearance on screen. His body transforms under the scrutiny of various gazes.

Miss Chen, the attractive restaurateur, finds him frustrating, beginning with his lateness, which makes their meeting feel like the opening of a classic romance where misrecognition occurs before love. He irritates her with his fetishization of her car—"Is it a BMW, a Rolls?" They establish the setting of the film in inadvertently touring the city of Rome and its many recognizable tourist sites, as she drives by ruins, sculptures, and towers on her way home. As in *The Big Boss*, the woman in *The Way of the Dragon* lives separately from her comrades, the other workers in their ethnic enclave. Within this gender-segregated group, a romance brews between the sole woman and Tang Lung. Here, the romantic premise is more pronounced, with the couple's inability to communicate unless they fall within more traditional gender roles. A romance of misrecognition begins when they attempt to find a language in which to communicate, but the cross-cultural divide prevents the conversation from moving deeper. Cultural gaps stunt their connection, from his hesitation to get too comfortable around her to his dismissal of the suggestion to take a taxi when they go out or deposit his money in the bank. Bruce Lee comments on his character of Tang Lung as one who is too proud to admit he knows nothing of the new land. Miss Chen finds it frustrating.[32] Once they assume the heterosexual roles of hero-to-the-rescue and damsel-in-distress, however, we see them relate more harmoniously. Moreover, when he becomes attractive to other women and demonstrates his physical capabilities upon men who harass, Miss Chen's attraction accelerates and blooms. However, Tang Lung won't respond, for he has a higher calling as a hero whose appetite for sex must recede.

Miss Chen takes Tang Lung outside to the streets of Rome where they sit in a piazza facing each other while she lectures him on how to behave in the new country. A very attractive, slim, young white Italian woman—massive hair, fully made-up eyes—sits behind Miss Chen and tries to get Tang Lung's attention with her seductive stare. Tang Lung tries to understand the stranger's gaze as Miss Chen describes how the "foreigners" here (as she refers to Italians in Rome) are friendly, so "smile back." Miss Chen is unaware of the attention Tang Lung receives from the woman behind her. He does smile as the Italian woman smiles. "While you're here, don't be so uptight," continues Miss Chen, so he winks at the flirtatious woman. Upon receiving this gesture, the Italian woman comes over. To Miss Chen's resentment, he puts his arm around the stranger. The Italian woman caresses him and drags him away to her apartment. When she leaves him in her living room for the bathroom, he looks at himself in the mirror and practices his kicks. He evaluates his reflection. When she emerges topless, he gulps and stands up. His eyes bulge out. He hides behind a closet or goes out the door. The scene ends and cuts to his return to Miss Chen's apartment where he's met by a waiter who is supposed to take him back to the restaurant. Rather than say he was with the Italian woman, he looks down when asked where he has been. Sex is the thing to hide in his bow. While we don't quite know if he's actually had sex, we do see Tang attract attention from other women beyond Miss Chen. Others also respond to him—commenting on his size or physique—as in the scene with the wait-ers who measure Tang Lung's body by looking at him up and down, as if he were the feminine object of the male gaze. At this moment, Tang Lung emphasizes they need to watch his moves. He says "put your hip into it," in his instructions to the waiters, and we cannot but help look for that move-ment in his performance. We are made to be very aware of his magnificent body and others' measured gaze upon it.

Men of other sexualities emerge in this film to notice Lee's body as well. In various states of undress, the waiters return to the restaurant from the

FIGURE 5   Flanked by two attractive women, Bruce Lee's character negotiates his romantic and sexual possibilities. *The Way of the Dragon.* Dir. Bruce Lee. Concord Productions, 1972.

FIGURE 6   Tang Lung is admired and touched by both men and women in *The Way of the Dragon. The Way of the Dragon.* Dir. Bruce Lee. Concord Productions, 1972.

alley. One drapes his arm around the naked shoulder of another as Bruce Lee's character again heads to the restroom. A white man approaches Tang Lung as he enters the restroom stall. Tang Lung sits strangely on the toilet and the man stops to stare. Tang closes the door to prevent the white man from ogling him. Outside, when harassed by the men Miss Chen calls "thugs," this white man seems effeminate, as if he's supposed to be read as expressing male desire for Tang Lung in the restroom. Later on, at the restaurant, Mr. Ho, leader of the thugs, a flamboyant Chinese man, takes the opportunity to appreciate Tang Lung's physique as he emerges from the restroom. The gaudy and glitzy Chinese man is both brutish and soft. He threatens the restaurant by pinching and slapping the older uncle in the face, but when he sees Bruce Lee's Tang Lung, his disposition changes instantly and he flirtatiously touches him in his genital area and dares to tuck in his belt. Tang Lung looks amused yet oblivious to the thrilled response of the man upon touching him. On the left of the screen, Tang Lung fixes his pants and the other man becomes giddy with giggles. They contrast with the plainly dressed Tang Lung and, with his flamboyant costume, the queer character on the right of the screen. The other character focuses on the Tang Lung's physique and touches him several times in the area of his groin. The man is not ridiculed, however, but is simply part of a repertoire of other masculinities. In the back of the restaurant, a group of four black and white men who seem to be American and Italian threaten the large group of waiters as well as the older chef and Miss Chen. The battle is racialized—the thugs order "Chinese spare ribs," which entails hurting a waiter right on his rib cage. The gang ridicule "Chinese boxing" before Tang Lung single-handedly defeats them all, with minimal moves to flatten each opponent. He names each set of acts as "Dragon Seeks His Path" or "Dragon Whips His Tail" to impress his comrades.

During the first fighting scenes, we see Miss Chen's attitude toward Tang change. The camera zooms in toward her face as she gets a new perspective on him during his impressive performance against the multinational and multicultural thugs. After the fight, she approaches him with a giant, beaming smile on her face and invites him home. (The waiters adore him too, showing their affection by crowding around him and making him a special breakfast.) While the film is a demonstration of Bruce Lee's abilities, it also presents his magnificent body. One scene shows off his body flexing the famous "V" of his back, which stretches a significant number of inches when flexed. This is a sexualized moment. As Tang Lung flexes, he is distracted by the painting of a couple kneeling naked before each other and intertwined. This scene is followed by Miss Chen's presentation of a meal she cooks for him. Tang Lung is naked when eating with her and they share glances in what looks like a domestic scene—where he protects her and she cooks for him. As light and dreamy music wafts into the scene, we can see that she wants romance when she invites him to tour the sights of Rome, to a specific ruin of an edifice gifted by the king to his queen. She surmises that "he must have really loved her" to build such a grand edifice for her. Here, she asks Tang Lung if he's married, a question he ignores or does not hear. When they return to the restaurant, the thugs have come back and taken over. Thus while Miss Chen attempts to snag him, the romance between the two is presented as a distraction from Tang Lung's role there.

A strong magnetism emanates from Bruce Lee's character, and as a director and writer, Lee emphasizes it further in terms of how his body registers as attractive across different characters' perceptions. Each of his enemies, from the waiters who first meet him to the thugs hired to beat him up in the back of the restaurant to his ultimate competitor, the American champion, Colt, played by Chuck Norris, all pause at the sight of his physique—before they decide to move forward to attack.

Both Colt and Tang Lung are sexually objectified in this film. We are first introduced to Colt as he emerges from a plane coming from America. He walks into the camera as the shot ends on his crotch. When Colt and Tang first meet at the Coliseum, Jachinson Chan suggests that the exercises they individually conduct are a kind of homoerotic foreplay before the fight.[33] It's a comedic one that's witnessed by a cat whose perspective is privileged by the camera as it goes from one fighter to the other before and during the fight. Colt measures Tang's dancing-fighting moves in a shot that covers the length of his body before readying himself for battle. It's as if he's saying, "How can this little man beat me?" He continues to fight Tang Lung even as Colt continues to get beat, receiving several crucial kicks that injure his arm and leg to the point that he can no longer fully stand. When Tang Lung gives him the chance to stop and surrender, Colt moves in for the kill—and loses. Tang Lung covers Colt's face when he leaves him dead. Fighting garners respect from one's opponent and one's lovers.

After Tang Lung beats the famous American Colt, as well as top fighters from Korea and the famous martial arts villain Bob Wall, he says "Now that it's all finished with, I must go." He no longer engages her flirtatiously—she puts her face in her hands and then holds his hand. He responds with a very chummy goodbye instead. Here he is rendered a hero who is not sexually or romantically available to her. Although attractive and desirable, he does not desire her because sex gets in the way of his work in the world of violence. The film ends with one of the waiters reassuring Miss Chen that, "In this world of guns and knives, wherever he may go to he will always travel on his own"—as if a hero cannot afford to have sexual or romantic relations. So here we see a patriarchal definition of sexuality that still renders women threatening to male libido and strength in a way that asexuality and effeminacy does not adequately describe. It is a definition of strength that must forsake sexual relations with women. While it may render him as a macho figure who won't romance women, in a definition of male sexuality that fears women and relegates them to distraction, his is a solo manhood. While Tang Lung refuses to participate in women's sexual exploitation or return their romantic interest, to describe him as an asexual/effeminate eunuch would be imprecise for he is more like a priest or a protector with a higher calling. It is on that basis that he rejects the distracting and secular enterprise that is sex in the context of the film.

Continuing this thread of sex as separate from manhood, we see in the next film, *Enter The Dragon*, that the hero there too won't have sex with women like the other men do. The other men exploit and enjoy women sexually while Bruce Lee's character remains unavailable to participate in the trafficking of women within this world.

Enter The Dragon (1973)

To assess the sexuality of Bruce Lee's character in his Hollywood feature film debut, *Enter the Dragon*, as going even more underground is to subscribe to a sexuality that is phallic and penile. *Enter The Dragon* is a homecoming of sorts for the transnational star—truly the first Asian American lead in terms of possessing star power. That is, Lee is the choreographer of the fight sequences in the new genre of film wherein these scenes are the main attraction. The film tells the story of a noble fighter named Lee and played by Bruce Lee. He is a master of kung fu in a palatial, established, old school. At first the school seems otherworldly until we see the contemporary skyline of Hong Kong. His superior tells Lee that he must attend an international martial arts conference on the island of a suspected criminal, Dr. Han—who indeed traffics not only in drugs but in women. He operates from the island guarded by martial artists, for Dr. Han refuses to use guns in combat. Lee competes with representatives from different nations—with the other leading characters being an African American man named Williams and a white American named Roper. Each man comes to the island with differing backgrounds and concludes his visit to the island in varied ways as well. Lee fights against Han's ultimate champion in a devastating performance that guaranteed Bruce Lee's immortality in film.

The film's title, according to Bruce Lee, heralds someone of quality, thus "Enter the Dragon"—which is rather strange for its double entendre of the dragon enters and the dragon is entered. It begins with a wide shot of an immense pagoda, then pans toward a fighting arena overlooking the blue ocean. From a distance, we see a well-arranged scene of fighters in color-coordinated kung fu uniforms seated around a narrow fighting space set in a grand location—a production design to which today's contemporary battle arenas in video games are obviously linked. As the fighters—naked except for their tight, short, black trunks—confront each other, we witness a sea of black, red, blue, and yellow robes adorning the fighters. The two-shot zooms and pans in to Bruce Lee's face in profile as he looks intently at his opponent. We switch to a camera that sees from his perspective. Then we look up from the ground, tilting up slowly, and witness Bruce Lee's sinewy, muscled body as he prepares to strike out. His face conveys resolution, unflinching in its evaluation of the fighter before him. He kicks, knocking the other off his feet. In fewer than eight movements, Lee pins the other man down, dominating him and forcing him to surrender. It's an exhilarating opening for the audience: bare-hands fighting and brute strength dished out by a lithe and graceful body. Moreover, a swivel of Lee's neck reveals a beautiful face with an unwavering stare and an impact like a punch the audience can feel. At the end of the fight, we see Lee's light-hearted camaraderie with his black-clad group of fighters as he somersaults toward them in laughter. The opening thus establishes an intense charisma, an incredible handsomeness of face, and a perfectly trim body containing a mountain of strength in a scene silly and serious simultaneously.

The next scene reveals a very intense character who not only is regarded with importance but who takes his power seriously as he considers the job of taking down the notorious criminal Dr. Han. Lee listens intently to his advisors and, with an air of gravitas, delivers teachings to a young student.

This character is laudable in an era when we do not frequently see in the movies serious men of color worthy of respect as a man. We find out that Lee is driven to investigate Han's island because of an incident relating to his sister. The sister walks with her uncle as they encounter Han's martial arts crew, who immediately approach her with sex on their mind. She fights back fearlessly but to no avail—she commits suicide rather than allow herself to be raped by Han's goons. Lee visits his sister's grave before he goes to the island. As in *The Big Boss* and Bruce Lee's other previous films, his character is motivated to help out of his awareness of the vulnerability of others and his determination to defend them—unlike the other characters, such as Roper, who wishes to win only for himself (to pay his gambling debts), or Williams, who wishes to combat the racism he personally experiences at home in the United States while partaking of patriarchal sexual pleasures that contrast with Lee's noble abstention.

In *Enter the Dragon*, Bruce Lee's character contrasts with black and white manhoods—presented by the various men from the United States, Australia, and different parts of Asia who compete in the tournament on Dr. Han's island. Dr. Han is involved in sex and drug trafficking and at night, ritually offers up women for the enjoyment of the tournament fighters. The black man chooses four women, in a stereotypical representation of his sexual needs. The white man chooses one woman, the one in charge, who approves his choice of her. Bruce Lee's character, Lee, refuses to participate in the sexual traffic of women and instead assists the Asian woman, who turns out to be an undercover agent who has infiltrated Dr. Han's harem. We could read this refusal to have sex in terms of the castration of Asian men in Western film, as previous literature has done, but we can also read it in terms of protesting the exchange of women as a gift between men. Instead, Lee forms a partnership with the secret agent; he helps her free the other prisoners in Han's dungeons, while she gives him an alibi as he explores Han's island. Together, they are intent on capturing Han and freeing the women imprisoned on the island. Lee still possesses sexuality and demonstrates attraction for the agent, however, as he looks at her with desire before the need to head out to find the secret lair of the evil Dr. Han. He stops at the door and looks at her with a seductive gaze. The film ends with their mutual victory—she releases all the imprisoned women and unleashes the martial arts crew from under Han while he fights the rest. The film concludes with Lee's character overlooking a sea of injuries and a manhood successful in fulfilling his responsibilities as a

FIGURE 7   Refusing to participate in the traffic in women, Bruce Lee's character nonetheless enjoys sexual attraction as he gazes seductively at the other spy. *Enter the Dragon*. Dir. Robert Clouse. Golden Harvest, 1973.

crime fighter. Lee demonstrates rich emotions of nurturing and strength that won't dominate women but participate in the economy of protection and compassion—a caring for self and others in an ethical form of manhood.

David Bordwell says that we feel the bodily impact of Hong Kong films—they convey "filmic emotion at its most sheerly physical" through their editing, action choreography, and the talents of men like Bruce Lee.[34] But I insert the emotional power Bruce Lee brings to these scenes as that which justifies the physical and formulates the ethical manhood we can learn from today. As in his other films, Bruce Lee's character enters the scene from another country. He encounters others from other nations as well, and takes fighting them to a level where he defends justice and innocence against immorality and evil. I conclude my reading of *Enter the Dragon* when Lee comes to battle the leader of Han's ruffians, a white man with the scar on his face—evidence of his identity as the one who attempted to rape Lee's sister. At the tournament, Lee battles the would-be rapist, who charges at him with two broken bottles. Lee kills him with a kick to the groin—in other words, the site of the white man's transgressive weapon, the weapon he attempted to use against Lee's sister. Here, rather than seeing sexuality in terms of failure, we witness a noble warrior whose sexuality must be sacrificed in his dedication to community. Why, however, does he not die for the killings he commits? In this Western production, Lee no longer receives punishment for killing so many people; instead, Lee, like Roper, kills for just causes and is thus on the right side of the law. What remains is his face, tormented by the act, its muscles pulled taut and his mouth opened in an expression of pain.

In Bruce Lee's films, we see experimentation with the power of violence and sexuality—the first films influenced by censors, critics, and cultures all over Asia, and the last film influenced by the expectations of an American audience. While he has been accused of unconsciously sparking the stereotype of the asexual martial artist, Bruce Lee himself felt pigeonholed by the limited roles he could get, while at the same time he did initiate one of the few roles now available to Asian American men. In close readings of these martial arts roles, we can see that sexuality and sexual success cannot be

FIGURE 8   Tormented by the act of killing. Lee's face expresses pain. *Enter the Dragon.* Dir. Robert Clouse. Golden Harvest, 1973.

measured solely by phallic power or by a display of the power of the penis as conqueror of women. We see that a broad definition of sexuality is at work and on display, and it is significant for charting Asian and Asian American male sexuality. While this version is tender, brutish, and ferocious, most importantly, it renders sex and touch as powerful and significant for Asian and Asian American men to experience, withhold, and deploy.

Bruce Lee died just one month before the world premiere of *Enter The Dragon*. His last films, *Game of Death* and *Game of Death 2*, feature minimal footage of him, but they helped create his iconicity in the yellow and black jumpsuit, in the former, and disseminated some of the footage from the twenty films he made before turning 18 in Hong Kong in the latter. *Game of Death* features some original footage in a nostalgia project that hired a couple of look-alikes to replace Lee, resulting in strange insertions of his face on a mirror shot over someone else's body. Sammo Hung, one of Bruce Lee's successors, agreed to shoot additional shots as a form of honoring him. However, because we can no longer fully see his face, in both *Game of Death* and *Game of Death 2* we do not see his close-up interactions with women nor the bookending of violence with the pain of inflicting it on others. These last films do not have the complex intimacy of violence and vulnerability together with tenderness and strength that Bruce Lee brought to his performances. Bruce Lee demonstrates both strength and emotionality out of control, as well as nurturance and compassion—a caring for self and others in an ethical form of manhood in his own previous films. Indeed, the emotional power he brings to these scenes as that which justifies the physical, sets the scene for the thoughtful emotional encounter of both violence and sex, and formulates the ethical manhood that influenced representations of men in late-1970s film, and that we can still learn from today.

No one better exemplifies how film and television comprise transnational discourses of race, gender, and sexuality than Bruce Lee: born in the United States, raised in Hong Kong, he became a star in America, then failed, then returned to Hong Kong to become a transnational star with the support of the U.S. film industry. He achieved this global prominence through cinema's presentation of his body as one that fights within the films and outside them, against the stereotypes of Asian American men as weak, servile, and peripheral. While others blanketly declare Bruce Lee's performances to be poor, I argue that we need to situate his performances in the cinemas and heroes of the 1970s. In his performances, Clint Eastwood used small moves such as the turn of the hat or the use of a phrase to create iconic images. Similarly, Bruce Lee performed in iconic shortcuts—the movements of his head in readying for battle; the scream at inflicting violence, despite the rule of law, as he killed; his love for kung fu demonstrated in the rehearsals of exercises he performed on screen.

Bruce Lee resented the dubbing of his films in other languages. As an immigrant who struggled to learn English, he understood the difficulty of learning intonation and gesture in deciphering the meaning of language. He insisted on framing films within their cultural context and making films for those contexts. He looked forward to playing a diversity of characters and demonstrated how each of his characters possessed different qualities—defying the charge that he played himself throughout the movies. For example, he discussed the naïveté of the character in *The Big Boss* and the hardheadedness of the character in *The Way of the Dragon*. He also described the trouble with playing an Asian as an Asian American. In the only existing video interview with him, now known as "The Lost Interview," Bruce Lee is seen and heard speaking as an Asian American movie star with the jazzy intonations and contemporary slang of his time. Perhaps the critics did not detect or note these small character distinctions because his singularity as an Asian American, who uses the terms "man," "jazzy," and "in the bag" in his spoken language, is not apparent in the Mandarin-dubbed films or in his appearance. The dismissals of Bruce Lee do not account for his transnational Asian Americanness; he died imagining a life where he would live both in Hollywood and Hong Kong to best make sense of his life, work, and family. We must view him through a transnational lens of gender, race, sexuality, and industry to appreciate his legacy.

More than anything, Bruce Lee expanded our idea of sexuality beyond measuring it for phallic power or the presence of the penis. Through my close readings I have attempted to reveal his formulation of manhood beyond machismo. Bruce Lee's manhood in the movies anticipated the representation of gender and sexuality in the late 1970s, where we see emotional, nurturing, and strong, though not dominating, men—qualities we continue to demand and see today. Today, we have pretty men who star in movies as strong and more appealing partners and lovers to women. Bruce Lee's characters anticipated such a change, bridging brutish masculinities with tender manhoods—loyalty to women, commitment to community, and tenderness in the promise of family. There are also queer formations to this seemingly heteronormative ideal. Asian American men in the movies experience lack and inadequacy in terms of their roles, but Bruce Lee made a play for the heteronormal as a position available for Asian American men. However, it was not simple; it took a complex negotiation that we see in the biographic film, based on the memoirs of his white wife, Linda Lee Cadwell, played by Lauren Holly, and starring Jason Scott Lee (no relation) as Bruce Lee.

Dragon (1993): Claiming Bruce Lee

In the DVD, Bruce Lee's wife, Linda Lee Cadwell, introduces the film *Dragon*, based on her memoirs, which would focus on not just one aspect of Bruce—his ethnicity, his profession, his family, or his personality—but all the elements that compose what she calls his subjectivity as a "human being."[35] The introduction includes family photographs that humanize Lee as well as quotes and narration that drive home the magnitude of this contribution in a world where so many stereotypes about Asian American men are deeply entrenched. *Dragon* begins with Bruce Lee's travels back to the United States as a teenager and then follows the entire span of his career. The story is framed in terms of a curse—which leads not only to his death but also to his son's. More importantly, what returns in this late-twentieth-century Hollywood movie about Bruce Lee is the sex as well as the racism that he encountered in the industry that his films did not include. The young lady accosted by the Australians whom he beats up and runs after him early in the film, clutches him and says "thank you, Little Dragon [his nickname]." He shuffles her out with a kind of cute, appealing innocence that also combines seduction and eroticism, saying, "thank me later" as they bound down the stairs together. And indeed he moves energetically like he does in the original: up the stairs, through windows, still with his wet oiled chest and trim waist revealed. In this Hollywood tribute twenty-five years after his death, sex comes to describe him like never before; it is central and a natural, normal part of life for a young, virile, attractive man. People want to have sex with him, the film conveys. Unlike in the American-made films such as *Enter the Dragon*, what we see here is an insertion of a fuller picture. A virile and attractive man would of course draw potential lovers, so we see Bruce Lee almost as if he would have been in the world.

When Lee is in the United States working as a dishwasher, an attractive waitress named April attempts to get his attention by slithering against him in the kitchen. In his own room above the restaurant, he's in glasses and tight white underwear immersed in books, working on his English. As he reads in bed, a knock sounds on his James Dean-poster-adorned door. The waitress April stands there with an inviting smile. Wordlessly, he pulls her inside and lifts her against the wall to have sex with her immediately, smoothly grabbing down her underwear as she writhes and gasps. The head cook resents Lee for "getting his girl" and pulls rank to get Bruce to clean up deliberate messes on the floor. When the intimacy between the two new lovers emerges in the public space of the kitchen, the cooks gang up on Bruce Lee. The film links his autobiographical narrative with scenes from his films. Mimicking scenes from *The Way of the Dragon*, Bruce readily beats them in the back of the restaurant. The space transforms to an arena for the display of his bare-fisted fighting as the cooks wield knives and fall all over themselves. Against their gracelessness, Jason Scott Lee as Bruce Lee kicks one into a tower of boxes like in *The Way of the Dragon*, lands his feet around the foe's face, demonstrates his crying expression for inflicting pain, and licks his own blood before charging against his enemies. He also fights intelligently, taunting two guys to come at each other instead. As in *Fist of Fury*, the shot focuses on the woman's appreciation of his display of power-ful physicality; April smiles. Unlike Bruce Lee's cocky persona in interviews, Jason Scott Lee's performance possesses no such bravado. His is an innocent rendition or a romantic version of Bruce Lee as a kind of innocent.

The film describes the first meeting between Bruce and Linda Lee simi-larly. He meets his future wife, Linda, when she expresses interest in learn-ing kung fu. When he's teaching "be like water" to a group of men, she emerges into the scene with a sassy, "Is this class only for guys?" From the very beginning, she inserts her gender difference and sexually charges his class when she straddles him at the end of a demonstration. As he teaches, "it is not size or strength, but focus" that enables victory over the opponent, Linda pins Bruce on the floor and states, "I kinda like this position." Soon into their relationship, his racial difference becomes an issue not so much between but around them when others judge against their coming together. She has to lie to her mother to successfully facilitate their dating—pretend-ing to go bowling or hiding him away. Even her closest friends express shock when she dresses up for her date: "All this for a Chinese guy! I can't believe you're going out with a Chinese guy. I don't think I could kiss somebody who is not white." Linda's response is "Kiss him? At least!" Her willingness to cross racial sexual borders leads her friend to dismiss her as a "beatnik." Thus the attraction a white woman feels for a "Chinese guy" is considered adventurous and against the norm. Indeed, the restaurant on their first date won't seat them, and won't say it, so the couple waits in the bar as others get seated before them. At first, she remains innocent of these experiences, even as they transpire before her.

When Bruce and Linda watch the classic *Breakfast at Tiffany's* (1961), we see the scene excerpted of Mickey Rooney as a buck-toothed Asiatic with an exaggerated accent chastising Audrey Hepburn for her late night jaunts. The scene generates laughter in the audience, but the look of pain on Bruce Lee's face shocks Linda. Her own laughter stops—the disconnection between the image of the Asian man and the embodied Asian man next her leads to an important recognition. The theater becomes a space of racial assault, so she suggests they leave. The film is thus an opportunity to learn and display empathy as the basis for their relationship. While this is, after all, her version of events, what comes to be written here is interracial romance and love as a site of recognition across difference; through their bond, she recognizes racism and through her support, he is enabled to build an institution in a racially excluding world. Here, we see that manhood is not simply the ability to demonstrate physical domination but to develop the self within the larger field of social relations, including intimacy with others.

The couple's sex acts in the shower and in bed are also a tale of interracial and individual compatibility, aestheticized as pleasurable. They shift positions and he poses over her as she traces the contours of his chest; the camera expresses awe at the perfected torso as she rubs him. She shows off the strength of her own back muscles as she maneuvers her body to slither on top of him, his face exposing his surrender to her. Their individual and interracial compatibility is emphasized in other shots, where they conduct a kind of synchronized martial arts dance together in their apartment-cum-martial arts space. This harmony is interrupted by her difficulty in disclosing their relationship to her family. The story of Bruce Lee cannot be complete without this—the feeling of exclusion from within and because of one's intimate relations. They subsequently experience rejection by Linda's mother, who bases her response on the racial future of their children who "won't be white . . . won't be Oriental, but half-breed, they won't be accepted on either side."

The film shows Lee continually facing racism that leads to his leaving the United States. For instance when Bruce Lee played Kato on the televi-

FIGURE 9   Interracial sex as beautiful: Jason Scott Lee as Bruce Lee exposes male vulnerability in sex. *Dragon: The Bruce Lee Story*. Dir. Rob Cohen. MCA Universal, 1993.

sion series *The Green Hornet*, the studio reports, in reviewing the dailies, that "this guy Lee is awfully Oriental." The producer responds sarcastically: "He's supposed to be. He's playing Oriental. Kato is Oriental." The response: "Well, make sure he keeps the mask on." This frightening exchange establishes the setting of Lee's work as a pioneer in network television wherein he attempts to author his own contributions with his face half-covered. As Kato improves upon the direction he receives for an exciting rescue scene, the Green Hornet applauds him repeatedly with "Good work, Kato!" As the choreography continues to better the previous move, the crew is flabbergasted, and the director, impressed, neglects to signal "Cut!" Lee says, "Thought that would be a little more exciting!" From making twenty films before age 20, Lee understands the medium of moving images in relation to his body. He continues to imagine a future in the industry with a television show premised on a hero without a gun, equipped instead with Eastern kung fu. However, the television show, according to the film, becomes *Kung Fu*, starring a white man named David Carradine, as the Lee family bills mount up.

Meanwhile, in Asia the *Green Hornet* is unofficially called *The Kato Show* and Lee's visit leads to the making of *The Big Boss*, where immediately we see his screaming look of pain at inflicting force and an awesome regret at the release of violence. Their marriage teeters on the edge of breaking up—based on his disappearance into work—which the film describes as a racial mission to correct the failure of Hollywood to embrace him. "I worked in

America for ten years—it got me nothing. . . . They have a good line of B.S. It's a mountain of gold for everybody white!" Inside the interracial relation, racial injuries fester. Linda insists upon her and the family's individuality from his analysis of group racism. "I'm not America. Your kids are not America. Don't push us away! I want my kids to have a father again! This place is eating us up." Lee responds by saying he's somebody special here. He then loses control and spits out a litany of images: "just another gook in a Charlie Chan restaurant! No tickee, no shirtee. One from Column A, one from Column B, Mr. White Man? Is that who I am?" She blows up too: "I don't know who you are!" He responds by punching the closet door down. When Hollywood comes to offer *Enter the Dragon*, he accepts in order to save his American family. His Hong Kong producer, peeved that Bruce is leaving, diagnoses his decision: "You want their love so bad. Our love is not good enough for you." After his explosion of racial epithets in the earlier scene, he explains that he does not just want to put out the "beauty of our culture, a Chinese hero, but to stop breaking my wife's heart. Play with my children without looking at a clock. I need to get back to America. They are American. I will lose them." Here the film shows Bruce as an Asian American family man which is in itself Linda Lee's response to the scandals surrounding his womanizing reputation at the time of his death. In the film based on her memoirs, Bruce Lee says: "If I lose them, nothing means anything." The film concludes with Bruce Lee preparing to perform in the last shot of *Enter The Dragon*. We see Bruce and Linda's relationship mended the moment he says "I forgot to tell you I love you." This is an astounding occurrence, for Linda says that he's "never said it to me before." And to which he responds: "I meant to everyday." While his letters express love and affection in "I imagine walking with you here everyday" and other declarations of love and affection—such as his luck in having such a good wife—this conclusion aims to express that romantic characteristic. The credits inform us that three weeks before the debut of the film that made him a transnational star, Bruce Lee died in a mysterious coma, and over 25,000 people attended his funeral in Hong Kong. Linda decided to bury him in America, where he now lays next to his son, Brandon. The story of Bruce Lee's life, told by his wife, ends with family romance and a coming home to America. "While others still wonder about how he died, I prefer to remember how he lived." The conclusion of a romantic husband and father contrasts with the sexual scandal that surrounded his death, including the release of a film that supposedly dramatized his sexual days and nights. I conclude this chapter with evaluations of films that claim Bruce Lee's legacy.

Finishing the Game (2007) and *JJ Chinois: To Whom Does Bruce Lee Belong?* (2002)

Bruce Lee's iconicity belongs to many communities, including the Asian American filmmaking community and the Asian American transgender and transsexual community. In *Finishing the Game*, the celebrated filmmaker of the Sundance-hit *Better Luck Tomorrow*, which brought into the mainstream what is known as Asian American cinema, Justin Lin offers a critique of Bruceploitation movies. He creates a parody of the search "for a new" Bruce Lee in films like *Game of Death*, in order to ridicule the idea that mimicry is a tribute rather than an exploitation in the worst sense—as if Asian American men can replace each other's complex personhoods and personalities. In *Finishing the Game*, a Hollywood studio head hires his son to direct the film that would presumably be built around the ten minutes of existing footage shot before Bruce Lee's death. The film includes a number of characters including Breeze Loo, a riff on Bruce Lee, whose career is making kung fu films as an actor not a fighter. "[My acting] is all right here in the eyes" claims Breeze Loo, who has "never seen any [Bruce Lee] films" while making over fourteen that mimic them. Offering a critique of artists working in a vacuum without accounting for their context and responsibility, Breeze Loo's character is an amusing buffoon with a lot of power—so it's not so amusing after all. Others in the repertoire of Bruce Lee wannabes include Tarrick Tyler, who looks like a white guy who declares himself part Asian. In a spoken word show, he speaks of experiencing racism due to his appearance, which is clearly not Asian at all. "You call me slanty eyes, my eyes see the damage! Railroad worker emasculated half man. Pieces of me long dead on tracks railroaded everyday trapped and trapped. Never defeated, never free." Never making sense either. He is especially funny because of the lack of visible racial difference to support his claims.

While the film mainly indicts the industry and its casting system that depends on racialized roles, it also shows how specific actors negotiate the acting process. Remi Nguyen, for example, in a scene about the casting direction in the film, describes a story about leaving Saigon without his parents, showing a self-possession that the casting director responds to well, introducing us to the concept of "fuckability." The casting director reduces the process of casting to a single notion, which she defines as follows: "the question is do I need to fuck this guy." She says this specifically in reference to movies with Asian American actors' reels which in the film includes Jason Tobin from *Better Luck Tomorrow*. Justin Lin says Tobin's audition is composed of numerous roles as Chinese food delivery men.

Although the myriad manhoods presented in the film span a selection of caricatures, it is pleasurable to see Asian American actors in roles they do not usually play. For example, the character who looks most like a normative hero and likely the best contender for the Bruce Lee role based on his looks is the tall, good-looking, fit and adorned-with-a-surfer-haircut Cole Kim, who's actually sensitive, soft-spoken, earnest, and dim, and excessively adores his girlfriend/manager. Sung Kang, an actor regularly cast in Justin Lin's films, including *Better Luck Tomorrow* and *The Fast and the Furious*, usually plays cold, cool characters. But in *Finishing the Game*, he childishly pines for Saraghina Rivas, played by Monique Gabriela Curnen—even if she's in the same room. Essentially, he can't audition unless she's holding his hand.

The character Troy Poon proves to be an exception to these varied manhoods in the movie. The director Justin Lin calls the character Troy Poon the "soul" of the film; the character stars in the fictional television series *Golden Gate Guns*, a show that looks like *Miami Vice*. Played by Dustin Nguyen, formerly of the television hit *21 Jump Street*, Troy reacts to the co-lead in the old television show—a white male actor, played by James Franco—who always attempts to get Troy's character to do the grunt work of their cases, to which he responds with a line he repeats so much that it becomes famous: "Hey man, I ain't gonna do your laundry." When the show is cut (like *Green Hornet*), Troy Poon has to find a new job and goes door-to-door selling vacuum cleaners to middle-aged housewives who fawn over him and ask him to repeat that very line. When Troy Poon's agents attempt to cast him as Bruce Lee's replacement, he's offended by the idea and the very premise of the project, since he thinks Bruce Lee can never be replaced. He protests the understanding of race and Hollywood in the film: as if Asian American men are ultimately interchangeable. Justin Lin is not alone in transnational Asian cinema in imagining Bruce Lee's return. Recently for example, the *Legend of the Fist: The Return of Chen Zhen* (2010) was released in Hong Kong as a thrilling homage to Bruce Lee's *Fist of Fury*. The lead character, Chen Zhen, returns to Shanghai, after being shot at the end of the original *Fist of Fury*. Because he must hide his identity, he dons a Kato-style mask like the one from *The Green Hornet*.

Others too lay claim to the legacy of Bruce Lee, most controversially including his purported mistress. The film written by Betty Ting Pei and released by the Shaw Brothers, *I Love You Bruce Lee: His Last Days, His Last Nights* (1975), was released in the same year as the publication of Linda Lee's memoir. The film purports to present the untold story of Bruce Lee's extramarital affair and drug-consuming persona. The film supposedly represents Bruce Lee and Betty Ting Pei's last sexual encounter in her home—a seventies boudoir where she plays herself as she and her supposed lover jump on the bed, fight with pillows, kiss, have sex, and smoke pot. He complains of a headache and dies in her bedroom after she administers a powerful drug.

The artist Lynne Chan makes a parody of this work in her production *JJ Chinois* (2002), a new media work online that includes both video and a website for the lead character. The video appropriates Bruce Lee's aesthetic—his long hair, lithe body and the coolness exemplified by his pose—and transports it into a contemporary character whose sexual magnetism the video celebrates. Lynne Chan intercuts herself as a transgendered Bruce Lee with hir wild girlfriend who jumps and hula hoops on the bed, with appropriated footage from the movie *I Love You Bruce Lee*. Here Lynne Chan as Bruce Lee is a transgendered man who deploys the ingredients that compose the original's iconic recognizability—the hair, the glasses, the lean body, and strong posture—not simply as an inspiration for the forging of his/her own manhood. Indeed, manhood does not require a biological penis but can be presented in visual terms recognizable in popular culture as male. While Lynne Chan does not hide hir transgendered body—with its pierced nipples and small breasts at the opening shot or the missing bulge in hir crotch despite her brazen display of tight white bottoms and thighs opened up—we see a calculated observation of Bruce Lee's performance of masculinity in sex. Lynne Chan's Bruce Lee watches over the silly antics of Betty Ting Pei and Bruce Lee's characters. The appropriation of the representations of adulterous intimate relations is not so much a celebration, however, but a commentary on the legibility of the phallus in terms of masculine excess—in the philandering and the bodily pleasures of drug intoxication that *I Love You Bruce Lee* shamelessly asserts. How is this macho of use to the presentation of masculinity for a transgendered man in *JJ Chinois*?

The competing narrations that emerge from the sex scandal that enshrouds Bruce Lee's death becomes an opportunity to define the legacy of his manhood. In their respective works, both Betty Ting Pei and Linda Lee root out an extended terrain of the intimate—emotional, sexual, and physical—that many others wanted to know about Bruce Lee. Linda Lee reclaims him from the possession of the public in a way that hierarchizes sexual relations and privileges normative family formations so as to reposition his legacy, especially for her children. In contrast, Betty Ting Pei lauds Bruce Lee's celebrity macho and an unbridled libido. Both women ultimately posit a knowable sexuality. Thus while both open the legacy of Bruce Lee to include the husband who cares for wife and children and the lover who enjoys his own beauty as well as his sexual appeal, the assertion of identity as fixed, knowable, and certain within these polarities, follows the same thrust to conform. However, Bruce Lee's screen persona actually explodes this sort of conformity. Both the demand for the good husband and the macho philanderer valorizes normative identity and romantic virility that can never capture Bruce Lee's challenge to our very concepts of cinema and masculinity. This is what Lynne Chan's work keeps open. Ultimately, *JJ Chinois* is an example of the eternal appeal of Bruce Lee's manhood: its unknowability in its femininity and its masculinity, its excessive sexuality and its withholding of sex, its macho and its feminism, and its strength and vulnerability.

Scholarly literature evaluating Bruce Lee's impact tends to celebrate his achievement as the pinnacle of manhood in terms of patriarchy, nationalism, and violence. For Asian American men racialized as asexual and effeminate, what I call "straitjacketed" criteria for evaluating male gender and sexuality, his critical triumph over this diagnosis is an easy, feel-good conclusion that has dangerous implications: ultimately it valorizes gender hierarchy and heteronormativity.

We suffer from a definition of sexuality that centers sexual domination and prowess by men in the penis/phallus conflation. To construct sexuality in terms of its orgasmic expression and its conquering prowess in the image of the player or its patriarchal formation in the image of the good, benevolent husband at the expense of its many manifestations and parts, is to limit our understanding not only of sexuality but of race and other categories of social experience as well. Bruce Lee's legacy shapes our future image-making in his impact not only on Asian American cinema in *Finishing the Game* but in imagining manhood for transgendered men in *JJ Chinois*. Now, more than ever, to resignify Bruce Lee's sexuality means utilizing his sensibility in service of other manhoods. In the next chapter, I show the representation of Asian American men in Hollywood films in the 1980s and 1990s as a very limited terrain of situations. As Bobby Lee says in *The Slanted Screen*, a young Asian American comedian such as himself is interpellated not as a powerful martial artist but as a nerd. When a figure like Long Duck Dong arrives on screen, not only do we hear a gong, but shame dawns. In a new turn, I will argue that the shame of 1980s Asian American manhoods in the movies can actually give rise to a new frame away from racial pride to turn into a kind of joy.

TWO

On the Grounds of Shame, New Relations

Asian American Manhoods in Hollywood

As spectators, Asian American men enter into a fraught relationship with cinematic representations of straitjacket sexualities. In the documentary *The Slanted Screen* (2006), comedian Bobby Lee describes how the image of Bruce Lee permitted Asian American men a certain stature in popular culture, but soon gave way to a shameful manhood in the 1980s. Asian American men are not born into a disprized identity but may feel its beckoning in the asexuality/effeminacy/queerness assignation in movies from that era. Concerned with how falling short of normative manhood contributes shame, or humiliation, to the very being of Asian American men, I reframe the scene of the encounter between representation and the real especially in terms of racial shame and racial pride. When the particularity of individual Asian American men comes up against representations that discount one's viability in love, romance, and sex, we have a scene ripe for the emergence of new subjectivities. The instinctive response, however, is to disavow images that debase and pursue images that glorify.

In my first book, I argued that it is worth the risk of reinscribing stereotypes for Asian American women to embrace the terms of their hypersexual subjection. Rather than fear their legibility in popular culture, Asian American women can refashion their misidentification to help articulate their own sexual identities and desires. Similarly, Asian American men must somehow and in some way craft dignified manhoods on the grounds of shame, on and off screen. Doing so exposes the social process of subjectivity—the compromised character of life—in terms of coming face to face with representation as the expressions of others as projections onto the self. Confronting the force of another's definition of one's subjectivity is not solely personal but is also found in cinema. We will see that Asian American characters come to rely on others to help them counter their disparagement. This chapter revisits characters previously dismissed as shameful in the project of empowering Asian American men toward a racial pride grounded in a limited notion of manhood as elevated and lionized. Wayne Wang's *Eat a Bowl of Tea* (1989), Ang Lee's *The Wedding Banquet* (1993), and John Hughes' *Sixteen Candles* (1984) directly engage the debasement of Asian American men specifically in terms of how relations are forged to support, parley, or destroy the framework of straitjacket sexualities.

Kathryn Bond Stockton writes, "shame is a common, forceful word for disgrace."[1] Shame leading to distress and embarrassment is an intense emotion that we see represented in cinema. Each character in this chapter comes face to face with the demand to fit into straitjacket sexualities that can bestow painful experiences. I will show how the attempt to fit within limited roles points to the narrow constraints of culturally normative manhood. That is, rather than move toward pride as a response to shame, we need to critique the criteria we use for forging manhoods considered dignified. For Asian American men, the assessment of asexuality/effeminacy/queerness as lack means a failure to measure up. Beyond offering an understanding of shame that must be disavowed, I ask: What would it mean to embrace these images previously deemed humiliating or to critique the manhoods we have available? I explore if the experience of shame can potentially rewrite the terms of one's subjectivity especially in a terrain where overcompensating for macho leads to the pitfalls of gender hierarchy and heteronormativity. I will argue that shame may provide the opportunity for undoing one's position and transforming the self away from the standards that demean and degrade it into a more enriched experience of self-respect and even joy in forging one's own manhood.

I look at the iconic characters of Russell Wong as Ben Loy in *Eat a Bowl of Tea*, Winston Chao as Wai Tung in *The Wedding Banquet*, and Gedde Watanabe as Long Duk Dong in *Sixteen Candles* (1984) for the ways they embody shame as the impotent heterosexual man, the gay Asian American yuppie, and the immigrant nerd with sex on the brain, respectively. All three appear in breakthrough Hollywood films that ultimately revolve around weddings and romance—and all involve some form of humiliation.

When participating in rituals of heteronormative privilege like a wedding, these characters confront the significance of not meeting the criteria of American manhood.

Weddings in popular media, according to Chrys Ingraham, are "spectacle[s that] work ideologically, conveying to the observer/reader what they should believe about romance, weddings, marriage and heterosexuality."[2] The main concept propagated in the repetitive affirmation of weddings and heterosexual romance in popular culture is that one must marry so as to "achieve a sense of well-being, belonging, passion, morality and love. . . . Marriage is somehow linked to the natural order of the universe rather than [being conceived of as] . . . a social and cultural practice produced to serve particular interests."[3] What concerns Ingraham is the privileging of marriage and how it demarcates those outside of it as problematic and "broken," thus edifying hierarchies and limiting our imaginations in reorganizing our relations.[4] The films I study indeed support the notion that weddings signify an investment in heteronormativity vis-à-vis the family and the child, or what Lee Edelman calls reproductive futurism.[5]

In his book *No Future*, Edelman follows Leo Bersani's *Homos*, which argues that gays and lesbians experience unbelonging in a society that celebrates heterosexuality in all of its social organizations, including relations of family. Edelman instead proposes an embrace of the social rejection of gays and lesbians to formulate a kind of anti-sociality or opposition to community and the notion of a collective future. I link this move to Asian American men, rejected by heterosexuality, who need to advocate a masculinity that criticizes rather than emulates the one that deems them inadequate.

Within these films that emphasize the heterosexual imaginary in the weddings they represent, Asian American men are cast as part of a larger world of social relations—that is, their cinematic encounters provide opportunities for forging fascinating new selves. In the case of Ben Loy in *Eat a Bowl of Tea*, he stands for the reproductive future of the emergent Chinese American community. Wai Tung, a young gay businessman, chooses to enter into a heterosexual marriage while at the same time confronting his shame in *The Wedding Banquet*. Long Duk Dong transforms from a nerd to pleasure-pursuing party animal in *Sixteen Candles*. In these three characters' performances, we see a response to their interpellation by others not only through protest or overcompensation for lack, but also acquiescence and flexibility that ultimately critique the conditions and possibilities of their existence—and they do so primarily in terms of their social networks and communities located both outside and inside of the normative bounds of family and marriage. In studying the three films in this chapter, I aim to show how in the context of shame Asian American men forge communities and relations that critique gender hierarchy and heteronormativity.

In identifying shame as a force that crafts ethical manhoods for Asian American men, I first provide the discursive context of queer theory and African American studies as well as Levinasian accounts of shame that enable me to move toward recognizing the importance of community and relations with others that gender hierarchy and heteronormativity do not accommodate. Through this literature, I show how Asian American men configure new relations that support the project of ethical manhood. Moreover, I illuminate the way representations of shame can create empathetic possibilities for understanding marginalized manhoods on screen. My close readings of the films then focus on how individual desires and identities come up against community pressures and group identifications. The characters use the experience of shame to imagine and to fashion communities and relations that they need in order to refuse and reform straitjacket sexuality. In the closing moments of the chapter, I explore the significance of ethical manhoods in terms of how Asian American men wrestle with access to marriage and heterosexual practices and structures. They do so by creating supportive relations that critique the entrenchment of victimization in understanding manhood and racism. My readings privilege ways the characters formulate solutions to their limited interpellations: ethical manhoods and new intimate relations.

The Discursive Context of Shame as Possibilities for Joy

Following the work of Eve Sedgwick, Kathryn Bond Stockton, Ann Cvetkovich, and Judith Butler, I show how from the subjection of shame, ethical manhoods and communities emerge. When Asian American men fall short of normative manhood, they use the social stigma to form more supportive relations that ease the trauma of straitjacket sexualities. Shame, according to Eve Sedgwick, is an affect or a feeling that comes when one falls short of the criteria that constitute norms that organize the self. We see it in one's particular expectations of oneself—whether cultural, historical, social, or psychological. "Queer performativity," according to Sedgwick, "is the name of a strategy for the production of meaning and being, in relation to the affect of shame and to the later and related fact of stigma."[6] For her, "shame is simply the first, and remains a permanent, structuring fact of identity: one that . . . has its own, powerfully productive and powerfully social metaphoric possibilities."[7] While Sedgwick studies and understands shame as deeply embedded in the expressions of gay life, I am interested in the experiences of Asian American men who face asexuality/effeminacy/queerness as subjectivities to be feared for their power to humiliate. Moving from shame as a communal phenomenon—where a community or larger social field gazes upon, perceives, and assigns a status of failure to another—I examine how shame, as an opportunity for self-reflection, can be rejected, transformed, and redeployed to become a transgressive assessment.

Kathryn Bond Stockton describes a particular economy of manhood for black men who cannot compete within white male standards of successful masculinity, particularly in terms of economic power.[8] Due to the constraints blacks face and following black feminist theorists such as Angela Davis and Hortense Spillers, Stockton argues that black subjugation questions the male activity/female passivity dyad that organizes white hegemonic culture. She points to Toni Morrison's disagreement with the classification of the black female-led household as "a problem, a broken family."[9] Morrison instead signals the failure of the framework of the married couple and nuclear family in contemporary culture, which "isolates people into little units—people need a larger unit."[10] For Stockton, Toni Morrison's fiction expands our understanding of black life beyond debasement to sites of visionary social reorganizations whereby people nurture each in the face of painful inequalities. Here, shame is rejected to make room for the ability of the debased to take care of themselves and each other in a way that ultimately questions their social assignations as well as existing structures of relationality.

In her study of scenes of shame in lesbian life, Ann Cvetkovich shows how they generate the energies to produce an alternative culture—one that makes sense of subjection in a way that affirms and nurtures the abjected. Similarly, images of shame in Asian American life also engage the complexity of its subjects, exposing the subject's distortion and vulnerability to the image, such that, for instance, Long Duk Dong does not exemplify all Asian men, but embodies a very odd one. Representations of Asian American men in movies show ridiculous straitjacket sexualities but also isolate the marginalization of their subjects. In this way, the subjects the movies portray appear as distorted and not quite right. Thus, I use Cvetkovich's thinking to evaluate how Asian Americans deploy the social stigma associated with shamed identities in popular culture to move away from condemned subjectivities and to craft their own affirmations. I also call for a recognition of the painful implications of the abjection of Asian American men and empathy for those who are unjustly disenfranchised in and by representation.

Queer and African Americanist theorizations of shame enable me to evaluate how communities and families form in the films discussed here, to create a groundswell of support against the constricting pressures Asian American men face for supposedly falling short of the norm. For Levinas, shame can occur from "having deviated from the norm. It is the representation we form of ourselves as diminished beings with which we are pained to identify."[11] Here, we see that the encounter with an external definition of the self undergoes an intense process whereby one must make sense of an imposed identity. Yet, the image is already familiar and recognizable as the self. As such, shame is an intensely private experience. Levinas continues: "We see in shame its social aspect; we forget that its deepest manifestations are an eminently personal matter. If shame is present, it means that we cannot hide what we should like to hide. The necessity of fleeing, in order to hide oneself, is put in check by the impossibility of fleeing oneself."[12] Thus if it's true that the projection of asexuality/effeminacy/queerness as lack achieves a certain truth in popular culture, to free oneself from this position as shameful requires struggle. From here, I am interested in how shame hides not an inadequacy in meeting the norm but a marvelous originality and even plenitude that certainly includes resistance to and liberation from straitjacket sexualities.

Sexual Shame in the Face:
The Community Theater of Marriage in *Eat a Bowl of Tea*

The 1980s and 1990s witnessed Asian American men occupying secondary roles in Hollywood movies such as a triad leader and his thugs in Michael Cimino's *Year of the Dragon* (1985), which Asian American communities protested, resulting in the disclaimer that now appears in the opening credits, warning of the power of film to misidentify communities. In the same decades, the Asian American cinema movement turned to feature narrative films. The Asian American cinema movement, which emerged as part of the Civil Rights and Yellow Power movements in the 1960s, not only produced films that attempted to establish Asian Americans in history but also enrolled Asian Americans in film schools, developed nonprofit organizations focused on addressing issues of representation in public television and the film industry, and generated critical spectators in the United States either through public scholarship or intellectual production in departments of Asian American studies and programs in universities across the country. As part of this community, Wayne Wang began his career as a director with the first Asian American feature film, *Chan Is Missing* (1982), and then directed such films as *Dim Sum* (1985) and *Life Is Cheap, Toilet Paper Is Expensive* (1989). His work spans celebrated and star-studded independent films such as *Smoke* (1995) and *Blue in the Face* (1995), and Hollywood films such as *Joy Luck Club* (1993), *Maid in Manhattan* (2002), and *Snow Flower and the Secret Fan* (2011), the last based on a best-selling novel by Lisa See.

Based on the underground novel by Louis Chu, Wayne Wang's American Playhouse–sponsored *Eat a Bowl of Tea* (1989) is set in the Chinatown of New York City where a young World War II veteran, Ben Loy, played by Russell Wong, brings home a young wife from China. Unlike preceding generations, who were deprived of their wives and families, the married couple is able to establish a life together in the United States. At first, they live independently as a new couple getting to know the city until the family association intervenes. The community pressures them to procreate and raise a family to further establish Chinese Americans in the United States. The couple represents a modern Asian American generation whose reproductive responsibilities are policed by the older generation. Ben Loy experiences a form of emasculation from the pressures of his father and his community—including an interloper who seduces his sexually unsatisfied wife Mei Oi (played by Cora Miao).

Like the novel it is based on, *Eat a Bowl of Tea* addresses the painful legacy of Chinese exclusion laws. Chinese immigrants were legally deprived of heterosexuality because of exclusion laws that prevented them from participating in marriage and traditional family structures. The film shows Chinese Americans as primarily a bachelor society. Men populate Chinatown and its restaurants, gambling halls, and streets. Family associations structure Chinatown communities, helping immigrants acclimate by finding them jobs and providing social support. The Wang Family Association considers Ben Loy as one of its promising sons, especially for his military service, which "helped to prove the loyalty of Chinese Americans to their adopted country." Indeed, the 1947 War Brides Act enabled the marriage of Chinese American soldiers, heralding a new era in Chinese American communities during this time. The marriages that followed the act thus came to be public spectacles where communities were collectively invested in growing families in terms of further securing American cultural citizenship and belonging. This context shapes the marriage of Ben Loy and Mei Oi. Here, we see that the community regards the denial of marriage and heterosexuality as a public shaming or humiliation. Ben Loy's marriage to Mei Oi repairs community shame. The individual impact of that burden, however, results in Ben's impotence— which instantiates a new shame. His father, Wah Gay, describes his son's impotence and inability to father a child as a loss of face for their whole family.

The film focuses on the shame the son's impotence brings to both individuals and the Chinese American community in New York's Chinatown. The handsome Ben Loy, who has to be convinced to travel to China to find a respectable wife, participates in interracial sex prior to agreeing to his family's matchmaking efforts. In China, he falls in love with the playful and irreverent Mei Oi and brings her to the United States. When he becomes unable to sexually engage his wife, their marriage disintegrates, and she begins an affair with Ah Song, a frequent customer at Wah Gay's gambling den. When the community discovers the affair and the paternity of Mei Oi's pregnancy comes into scandalous question, the husband and wife are exiled by the family association to New Jersey. Ben Loy's father attacks Ah Song when he attempts to return to Mei Oi and cuts off his ear. In response to the mutilation and its humiliation, Ah Song calls the police, but they cannot find Wah Gay, who has fled to Mexico. The couple escapes to California in order to flee the gaze of the community. There, Ben Loy and Mei Oh return to their marriage with his virility restored, still not knowing or caring who fathered the first child and reproducing even more children. In the face of pressures by community and family, Ben Loy and Mei Oi disregard the issue of paternity in the formation of their new family. Instead, they prioritize and define their own happiness as a family.

Eat a Bowl of Tea portrays Ben Loy as a man wrestling with the infinite complexity of his individual desires, which come into conflict with the totalized definitions of marriage in the Chinese American community. That is, Ben Loy chooses a future open with possibility over a known fate in his community. In doing so, he reveals the duality that organizes our understanding of Asian American families. In *Immigrant Acts*, Lisa Lowe argues that realities and experiences exceed the frameworks of new-versus-old and tradition-versus-modernity across generations.[13] In *Eat a Bowl of Tea*, however, it's not a matter of the young promoting the modern and the old cherishing tradition. Indeed, because the Chinese American community is deprived of normative traditions of marriage and family, the older generation of men and women aspire to that which they are deprived of: companionship and the continuing of a family line. The young couple wishes for individual autonomy and modes of relationality that do not exceed these pressures. They do wish for marriage and family, to fulfill their parents' hopes as well as their own: sexual desire, emotional companionship, and children. Yet, they are part of a community that includes older members who also wish for marital love without children. Part of what they learn in America is the opportunity to construct a type of marriage and relations between husband and wife to which they had not previously had access. And in their new family formation, paternity as the ultimate emblem of patriarchy is rendered unimportant to the supportive network they form. They distill the meaning of family and community without prioritizing the needs of men. In this way, they do not necessarily represent the modern as distinct but come to include both the needs of men and women and critique the moral policing of their sexual relations across gender in their pursuit of similar goals.

Through the power of Wayne Wang's cinema we are able to see how the spatial and historical context of race organizes the characters' possibilities. A kind of sexual shame—and its recognition—shape the community and its members when disciplined by the deprivation of marriage and sexual life, both heterosexual and homosexual. This is written on the faces and bodies of the men and the single woman, Mei Oi, who are humiliated by this position. To explore new forms of sexuality is a risky path that the main characters choose in order to liberate themselves from the position of shame and harm. The risks they take ultimately critique gender and sexual roles. In the filmic representations of Asian American men in *Eat a Bowl of Tea*, we see shame as Sedgwick theorizes it: "living, as it does, on and in the muscles and capillaries of the face—[it] seems to be uniquely contagious from one person to another. And the contagiousness of shame is only facilitated by its anamorphic protean susceptibility to new expressive grammars."[14] In looking closely at scenes from the film, we witness the shame that Asian American men feel as well as their escape in the decision to participate in love, sex, desire, and romance in new ways. We see as well that they also risk the formation of a family that defies rules of patriarchy when the woman's sexual activity outside of marriage is understood as that which must be punished. Mei Oi instead finds sympathy and understanding from her husband, father, and father-in-law rather than rejection.

Eat a Bowl of Tea establishes the intensely male composition of the Chinese American community in New York City. The film opens with a two-shot of men conferring under a light in what turns out to be a gambling den, adding up what they owe each other. They seem to be in a basement, and the scene has an eerie quality, like that of Fu Manchu's Limehouse district of London. Through a voiceover that accompanies the actor Victor Wong's saunter through Chinatown, we hear about how the "Chinese came to America. They leave women behind and thought they would get rich and go back to China, become 'big shots.' The U.S. exclusion law treated them differently from the rest of immigrants." We see him go up a long set of stairs to stop at the door of a beautiful and significantly younger Chinese woman, who welcomes him inside as the voiceover emphasizes the reasons for his seeking out intimate companionship: "No Chinese woman could come to America, not even wife and not even daughter. Chinatown [is made of] dying men getting older and could not find women to marry there. There were no families!" We then see the line of men in front of the door as we realize that the woman is a prostitute. "The Second World War changed all that. China became America's ally. Congress passed new laws. Oldtimers could become citizens just like everyone else. . . . One day, they're dying off and next thing you know, they talk about arranged marriages for the kids and how many grandchildren they're going to have!" This narration establishes how the community was shamed by being deprived of the social belonging that heterosexuality bestows on citizens. And the military service of the sons brings the old men the opportunity of the family life they so long for—as grandfathers. These older men wish for grandchildren not only because they feel their mortality, but because forming a family means furthering membership in their adopted country. Children thus represent the ultimate belonging, for they offer the possibility of planting roots and securing the foundation of the Chinese American community.

Freshly discharged from military service in World War II, the tall, attractive young Chinese American Ben Loy loafs about, enjoying the company of a white woman in a dance hall who can't keep her hands off him. She sings a song about going on a slow boat to China, establishing her racialized fetish for him and rendering the sexual agency of the white woman. We see them contextualized within a roomful of Chinese American men who watch them dance. Ben Loy seems to enjoy the bachelor life, especially with his stature at the dance halls. Compared to the other Asian men in the community, the mixed race hapa actor Russell Wong indeed stands out as one who comes close to acceptable standards of male beauty. We see how Ben Loy dances with the woman as if he has many more choices, unlike the hordes of Asian men who watch them intently and upon whose faces we see expressions of intense hunger for intimate companionship.

When Ben Loy's father buys him a ticket to China to get married and bring his new wife back to the United States, Ben uses it primarily to reunite with his mother, whom his father left behind years earlier. Within an instant of his first sighting of Mei Oi, he falls in love with the way she ridicules gender norms, which reflects his own ambivalence about the institution of marriage. As she turns around to face him for the first time, she crosses her eyes. This goofy gesture makes Ben laugh and his first words include, "Want to get married?" This act thrills the community, who considers their matchmaking the main event of the town. I describe in detail the choreography of bodies and the composition of emotion in their face-to-face exchange as a way to establish the authorship of desire, love, and romance in these scenes.

Ben Loy and Mei Oi's courtship is haunted by the representations of white love in the movies. When screening a movie in the town center, Ben Loy steals a look at Mei Oi, who sits at a distance from him. In a wide shot emphasizing her distance and small stature that focuses on his position away from her, she shyly giggles. They animate each other with desire, though they do not yet know each other. What surrounds them in this public outdoor screening space, even in China, is the Hollywood production of romance. A white man and woman kiss each other on screen, saying "When I kiss you my darling the whole word belongs to us." Indeed, heterosexual romance is the privileged relation in society, for it forms the basis of a conventional family recognized by law and culture. And in this context, Mei Oi and Ben Loy keep looking at each other with silly smiles that connect them across the distance. The screen dialogue continues: "Those bells you hear are the bells of love, those doves you see are the messengers of romance."

The screening of the film is interrupted with the announcement that a fortune teller proclaims Ben Loy and Mei Oi a perfect match. While the film within the film racializes romance as white, cultural beliefs puncture the scene and tell us how customs differentiate and organize this particular ethnic romance. When alone in front of the movie screen, Mei Oi discloses to Ben Loy her desire to meet her father in America. She echoes his sentiments in ways that move him—their individual desires to see a parent brings them together. But across this cultural similarity, he insistently asks her how she feels about him as an individual. She responds by kissing him—in a passionate rush and with a curious hunger—an act that expresses her singular desire to come together with him in a proximity that foreshadows a sexual joining we do not see until the wedding night.

When we cut to the wedding scene between Mei Oi and Ben Loy, we see the bride in a traditional Chinese qipao and the groom in his U.S. military uniform. They represent different cultures within their community, but come together in a marriage that the priest proclaims as an "honoring of ancestors." It is also significant, for it is the concrete result of the 1947 War Brides Act, the reason Ben Loy could even bring a bride over from China. At this time, antimiscegenation laws ruled in most of the United States, which meant that since Chinese men could not marry outside their community, nor bring wives from China, they were essentially locked in bachelorhood. Later that night, in their bedroom, Mei Oi nervously washes her face over and over again while Ben Loy coolly waits. Their eyes meet and they smile mischievously. He approaches her from behind and gallantly carries her to bed where he poses over her as they laugh. A sheath protects them from our full view. He brings his weight on to her and she slides in place beneath him. They look upon each other, face-to-face and consume each other's bodies hungrily. To end the scenes of China with their physical coming together writes their marriage as a sexual intimacy between two that is different from what is available in the United States, where the coming together of men and women in sex is rather a group activity such as the prostitute who partners with many men outside of marriage, or the white women in dance halls who serve multiple Chinese male partners. Thus, the sex between Mei Oi and Ben Loy is a coming together significant beyond the moment of that intimate relation. The sheath that appears in China, to frame their sex scene, represents the singular couple within the privacy of that moment. In China, they do not feel the eyes of others monitoring their reproductive capacities.

FIGURE 10   A sheath shields the sex between Mei Oi and Ben Loy, indicating the privacy they enjoy in China. *Eat a Bowl of Tea.* Dir. Wayne Wang. American Playhouse, 1989.

When they arrive in New York, the couple soon realizes that their marriage actually is a public theater and does not belong to them alone. In their Chinatown ceremony, witnesses play a central role in the making of marriage as the couple publicly vows in front of their guests and families to perform their roles as husband and wife. Eve Sedgwick argues for understanding marriage as theater. "Marriage . . . like a play . . . exists in and for the eyes of others. . . . Like the most conventional definition of a play, marriage is constituted as a spectacle that denies its audience the ability either to look away from it or equally to intervene in it."[15] For the Chinese American bachelor society in New York, however, the community does intervene. The marriage presents an opportunity for them to redeem themselves from shame. When they experience the deprivation of dignity in the lack of marriage opportunities and the inability to exert their heterosexuality, this marks their lack of belonging in the United States in sexual terms. This is why Ben Loy and Mei Oi must hold a wedding banquet for the community as a kind of theater, which the couple actually seems to fear. They look scared of the well-wishers, all of whom are men.

One particular guest is Ah Song, the man Mei eventually has an affair with. While he is short and stout, he stands out because of his dapper clothes—all white and flashy in a sea of dark and no-nonsense attire—and as the only one who approaches the new couple with a confident swagger. He addresses them with: "You are so lucky, can I kiss the bride now?" This interaction expresses the way others feel about possessing not only the marriage but the bride. It is a new arrangement for a couple to exist in this space. We see it in the men's longing as expressed in their physical comportment and facial expressions when looking at the couple. It is palpable in the looks they bestow upon Mei Oi's body when they first meet her—as if men in a desert are gazing upon a life-giving oasis: a lone woman dressed as a bride. And we also see it in the emergence of Ah Song, who dares to break from the masses of unpaired men to make a bid for the bride during her wedding banquet.

The president of the Wang Family Association toasts the couple in a long speech. On stage, he speaks about the historical importance of the occasion:

> Something like this is not possible until recently. Harsh laws made family separated. Men came here and lived as outsiders who could not share with his wife, could not share with his family. Partly because of Ben Loy's service did we prove what did not need proving—the loyalty of Chinese to our adopted country. We Chinese believe in family. Friends and cousins, we now have a new generation who can enjoy what family means—many generations together! We will celebrate the birth of [our] host's first grandson. Let's not wait that long. Let's drink up!

At the conclusion of the speech, which already shows a gendered economy of value, we notice that except for the wife of the president and for Mei Oi, the hundreds of well-wishers are all men. Now that Ben Loy occupies the position of a husband, he is supported by the community and validated by the offering of a managerial position at the restaurant. He is given this position so that the community may validate and support heterosexuality and marriage for themselves, not just Ben Loy.

But Ben Loy sees marriage differently. He says, "I have plans. Save some money, go back to school." But once again, the community intervenes. He must become a father, commands his dad. "We got big face tonight, you and me. It's up to you to keep it for both of us. That means you're gonna act like a big man and become a father. Take everything seriously, twenty years from now you could be head of the whole Wang Family Association." To which

Ben Loy responds, "Dad, I think I'm gonna throw up." Here the older generation subscribes to the meaning of marriage not only in terms of kinship and community dignity but patriarchy as the epitome of masculine success. Ben Loy, however, understands it as an opportunity to reassemble the self in the face of the older generation's definition and to rebel against the teleological development of manhood assigned to him. In a particularly telling scene, we see Wah Gay visit Ben Loy at his place of work. Ben Loy sits on a stool holding papers for work and Wah Gay approaches and stands near him. The two-shot reveals contrasting figures: Ben Loy, tall, thin, and well-dressed, and Wah Gay, short, stocky, and disheveled. Wah Gay asks a rhetorical question about Ben Loy's ability to use his penis. "Do you know how to use it? It's not just for fun but for making babies!" Ben Loy cringes at his father's speaking of this problem and brushes him off while closing his eyes in shame. His father publicly confirms the source of Ben Loy's private anxieties—his inability to have sex since returning from China, which takes him to doctors and which causes a rift with his wife.

The intervention of community into their marriage prevents Ben Loy from participating in sexual relations with his increasingly sex-hungry wife. The scene of their face-to-face coming together becomes a lying down together, yet apart, looking up, as if aware of the eyes of the community policing them. Her thrill with the modern amenities of America—the faucet's running water and the convenience of fire from the stove—soon transforms into boredom and loneliness. While they make each other laugh at first, the glue of their marriage comes apart without sex. She becomes desperate for him and short-tempered too. He disappoints himself and her. When he is first unable to perform sexually, he says "I just feel like everyone is watching us." And in the next scene we do see and hear the men gossip as Mei Oi walks by, commenting on her thin frame and how she's not yet pregnant, and how Ben Loy always looks tired. And again, when Ben Loy fails in bed she looks at him patiently, declaring her love. The next day, she urges him to visit the doctor, who recommends a vacation away from the stresses of his work. What we witness at the doctor's office is Ben Loy's embarrassment when he can barely describe the situation. He says, "Once in a while now again I have this little problem . . . when I'm with my wife." When they finally flee the pressures of family and work, and live the way they want in a visit to Washington, DC, and visit the Abraham Lincoln Memorial, they are reminded of their togetherness as a couple and of their belonging as young Americans. He becomes able to have sex with his wife again, unlike at home in New York City, where he lives in shame under the pressures of the community of men.

Upon returning to New York, Ben Loy once again loses his ability to perform sexually and Mei Oi becomes more hysterical from isolation, loneliness, and desperation. She interrupts him at work, with luggage in tow as well as two tickets to Washington, DC, and a hotel reservation. He considers this a public humiliation—an acknowledgment of his inability to satisfy his wife. She bursts into tears and encounters the man who propositioned her at the wedding. We see in Ah Song's knowing gaze that crosses the distance between them that he suspects her vulnerability and identifies her as one who may consent to his predation. She retreats. At home, she expresses her fear to Ben Loy that he no longer wants her. He tries to explain his feelings of powerlessness—"I do want you. And I can't do a damn thing about it. How do you think that makes me feel?" We notice how they move apart from each other as they lay side by side but far away on their bed. Their marriage disintegrates from his sexual failure.

FIGURE 11   Despite their proximity, their distance in bed signifies Mei Oi and Ben Loy's marriage falling apart from their inability to have sex in New York. *Eat a Bowl of Tea.* Dir. Wayne Wang. American Playhouse, 1989.

In the next scene, the interloper Ah Song approaches Mei Oi on the rooftop as she hangs out the laundry. She shies away from him, with a look of fear on her face, while moving across the hallway. Then she smiles a little as he follows her all the way to her door, which he opens behind her, then touches her face and slinks in. We see them post-coital. She lies in bed and he fixes his suit coat, smiling. "Can I see you tomorrow? If you agree, put out the fishbowl." She is definitely an agent who chooses to act on her desire. The next day, she puts out the sign for him to return. When she does see Ben Loy, they fight and she declares her loneliness and wish to go home to China. She becomes more intimate with her lover, whom she kisses on the mouth as she nestles in his arms and on his chest in bed. The gossip about her husband's impotence continues. We hear that the Chinese community is indeed in a hurry to get a baby and in this respect, Ben Loy disappoints. When Mei Oi does become pregnant, he is of course surprised and needs the reassurance of the date of their trip to Washington, DC. The baby's pending arrival begins to change things for her. She's happy the grandfathers will be pleased even if the baby's a girl. Here we see the importance of any reproductive future over the gendered specificity of continuing their lineage. She now refuses the attentions of her lover Ah Song and his invitation to go away to Miami, but not before the neighbor sees them kiss and suspects they are lovers. The gossip spreads. "He goes up to her apartment while the poor bastard's at work. When a woman's horny, she'll take anyone." Here we see in this film the persistence of the organization of relations between Asian American women and men: her hypersexuality and his castration—as the source of their shame.

Losing face, or the infliction of shame by the community upon him and his family, leads Ben Loy's father to explode: "Ben Loy, are you possessed by demons? I'm going to beat the hell out of you! What do you think you're doing, you son of a bitch!" He wields a knife over his son. They both do lose face. The Wang Family Association demotes Ben Loy from his job, and he becomes a line worker in a fortune cookie company in New Jersey. Ben Loy then declares himself officially a loser, humiliated and shamed by his own family. Despite Ben Loy's physical attractiveness, it is actually the more homely character who ends up fulfilling masculine standards of virility. The world must indeed seem topsy-turvy when the one possessing more hegemonic traits of these two Asian Americans loses his wife to the other.

When Ben Loy and Mei Oi fight, however, we see their spunk return. Ben Loy says, "Frankly, I'm disappointed in your taste. To be taken in by a heel like that is beyond me." She retorts, "At least he paid attention to me. You married me to please your father!" And he responds, "Maybe you wanted a ticket to the USA!" And she blurts out, "You could have any woman for price of ticket!" Sexual shame drives them into this place where they are physically punished and hungry not only for sex but affection. In this way, sexual shame permeates the scenes of this film in terms of the experiences and realities of the characters. They are haunted by ideas about their sexuality, aggravating their concrete everyday life to the point where Ben Loy and Mei Oi don't know what they want.

Ah Song returns from Miami and is ousted by the community. When he attempts to return to Mei Oi's apartment, Mei's father Wah Gay cuts off Ah Song's ear—essentially castrating the interloper's body. Rather than keep the problem within the family association, the interloper calls the police, so now both grandfathers flee New York City—one to escape punishment and the other in support of friendship and family. Their departure becomes an opportunity for Ben Loy and Mei Oi to make up and reunite on new terms. Similarly, Ah Song protests the community's laws on keeping their problems in-house. Ah Song is a crucial figure—for while he fails the gendered description of manly beauty, he achieves virility. He defies his role as unattractive and demonstrates that failure to meet hegemonic standards of beauty does not preclude sexual prowess.

Similarly, Ben Loy won't adhere to the importance of paternity when he declares his love for Mei Oi. He further demonstrates no interest in the true paternity of her child though it may be Ah Song. He is more concerned that the problem of their marriage is his and Mei Oi's rather than the community's. Ben Loy wants to place at the center his own needs and his own family rather than the wishes of the larger community. He no longer feels guilty in prioritizing his own desires. He will be with her and the baby, depart from the pressures of his ethnic group in New York City, and move to San Francisco to explore a new industry, radio, in Chinatown. The film ends with the reunion of their fathers—Wah Gay who butchered Ah Song and eventually escaped to Havana and Mr. Lee, who left for Chicago. Wah Gay speaks Spanish to his grandson, and Mei Oi is pregnant again. They then move away from New York's Chinatown, fleeing the conventional mores of Chinese America and sever the tradition of working in restaurants. They instead live away from the ethnic enclave, behind a white picket fence and with a backyard, making the norm accommodate their difference.

Levinas's notions of totality (absolute and infallible knowledge) and infinity (promising possibility) can help us to understand the significance of not making paternity an issue. By reformulating family as an institution in which the members support each other rather than one that privileges male subjectivity, we come to see the importance of flight and risk in the exploration of new relations. Ben Loy moves away from the shame inflicted by community, rejecting its terms when he expresses no concern for the paternity of Mei Oi's baby, and insists on continuing in the marriage despite the couple's mutual disappointments. A search for desire, love, romance, and sex—an exploration of the unknown—is what they choose to embark upon in marriage. Not knowing what they want and how they feel, such unknowing animates them into the enthusiastic action of intimacy that leads to adventure. Intimacy—sexual and emotional entanglement—binds them together in this new exploration across the United States. Their companionship produces enjoyment, and they do things for each other to create more pleasure, such as purchasing an expensive television and planning a trip to enjoy sex with each other. Recreation characterizes the journey to a new place for Mei Oi and the movement from bachelor to husband for Ben Loy—this movement transforms them and their spaces beyond their ethnic enclave and marriage as solely for reproduction.

What we see at work here fulfills what José Esteban Muñoz identifies as "queer futurity."[16] While Muñoz's work is grounded in queer theory and queerness as homosexual, in this specific scenario of New York City's bachelor society of Chinese American men, the characters are constructed as outside heteronormativity. They are structurally represented as antisocial or outside of heterosexual community. Ben Loy's abjection is based on his inability to perform sexually. The result is that he experiences a terrorized heterosexuality—he is rendered inadequate in ways that are punitive so that his existing community becomes unbearable. Muñoz describes a moment in LeRoi Jones' *The Toilet* where two boys—one white, named Karolis, one black, named Foots—who carry on an affair are discovered. The group that is usually led by Foots drags him to the bathroom and beats Karolis, waiting for Foots to finish the job. When Foots sees Karolis, he has to hide his concern and his affection. Only later, when the group leaves does Foots return to cradle Karolis in his arms. Muñoz describes a queer time in this place where the gesture of affection expresses a "not-yet-here"—that is, the boys cannot openly express their love lest they both become victims of violence. A "queer temporality of the gestural, a temporality that sidesteps straight time's heteronormative bent . . . [can be seen in] queer futurity['s] . . . opening or horizon."[17] Muñoz sees this moment as a critique of Lee Edelman's recommendation of no future and no children for queers, which is to "give up hope and embrace a certain negation endemic to our abjection within the symbolic. What we get, in exchange for giving up on futurity, abandoning politics and hope, is a certain jouissance that at once defines and negates us."[18]

Muñoz is concerned about the lack of racial analysis in Edelman—who disavows children as the future. Children of color, queer children, and queer children of color, according to Muñoz, are not the "sovereign princes of futurity."[19] He asks, how is Edelman's monolithic understanding of the child always already white, without accounting for the nearness to death that children of color and queer children experience? Similarly, death haunts the bachelor communities in *Eat a Bowl of Tea* in ways that fuel the pressures Ben Loy feels. These pressures force him to bend the usual arrangements of family—he forgives the affair and negates the question of his child's paternity and his wife's fidelity. Doing so brings rewards when he gets a suburban paradise and the opportunity to explore new financial paths. The rearrangement of the confines of heterosexuality for the couple then allows for the trappings of heterosexual life that becomes linked to economic mobility and national belonging.

Deprived of heterosexuality in the sense of their exclusion from the institution of marriage, and even deprived of privacy, Ben Loy and Mei Oi's marriage relates to queer studies of negativity and the reproductive future. Muñoz enables me to identify the way this new family formation refuses gender hierarchy and heteronormativity, accomplished through an ethical manhood that refuses the logic of failed heterosexuality and accepts the disintegration of marriage as a mutual responsibility, rather than perpetually punishing the wife for her sexual indiscretion. Both the new manhood and family formation destabilize patriarchy and transcend the failures of heterosexual macho expectations assigned to Ben Loy. The couple shifts the terms of acceptable marriage in order to redefine gender in their family. And in so doing, they show the transgressive fissures even in the most idyllic picture of heterosexual marriage, economic mobility, and national belonging for racialized subjects.

The Wedding Banquet

Ang Lee's *The Wedding Banquet* shows how an Asian American immigrant gay male character named Wai Tung attempts to resolve the shame that defines his homosexuality within and outside his family. He poses in a fake marriage with an Asian American woman concocted by his white, live-in boyfriend. While the ruse at first seems to address some of the concerns and expectations of the parental generation, the performance has other, deleterious and unplanned results. The faux marriage results in a real pregnancy, the bond between the gay couple gradually disintegrates, and the inauthentic marriage predominates in the presence of the parents, who nurture it. Here I show how an ethical Asian American manhood emerges in relation to confronting one's queer sexuality and in the process redefines kinship, much in the way José Muñoz celebrates the rearrangement of community relations and structures in his queer utopia. I extend Muñoz's argument to say that not only an ethical manhood but community forms in the attempt to accommodate those who fail to meet the normative expectations of men and women in traditional family formations such as marriage. Like Ben Loy and Wah Gay in *Eat a Bowl of Tea*, Wai Tung expresses a need for others to help support his new self formation. In *The Wedding Banquet* the characters forge new socialities that ultimately bring them out of their old situations and into joyful new scenes where they take care of self and others.

My reading also extends the work of David Eng and Mark Chiang in redefining an ethical manhood that emerges from the representation of transnational marriage. Within the context of his career as one of the most successful Hollywood directors of our time, Ang Lee has told stories not only about Asian American men but contemporary gay cowboys, in *Brokeback Mountain* (2005); English women without rights to inherit property, in *Sense and Sensibility* (1995); and even fantastic superheroes like *The Hulk* (2003). In each of his films, he attends to the dramas of difference and inequality in everyday life. His films reveal the details that construct manhood and womanhood in the cultures that contextualize his stories.

In *The Wedding Banquet*, Wai Tung is a young, gay, urban, professional Chinese American immigrant businessman who owns property in Brooklyn. He rents to a young Chinese illegal immigrant painter and restaurant worker named Wei Wei, who fosters a romantic interest in him despite her knowledge of his gay sexuality and of his boyfriend Simon, a physical therapist, great cook, AIDS activist, and live-in lover who is also white, handsome, fit, ever nurturing, and Wai Tung's idealized dream of a partner. His parents' only son, Wai Tung faces the unremitting pressure of his family to marry. Even from a distant Taiwan, their force is tangible in New York City. The pressure bears down powerfully; he hears that his father has escaped from the clutches of death, supposedly motivated by his one last wish: the possibility of holding his first grandchild. Wai Tung's mother persistently asks him to describe his perfect woman so she may enter him into an international marriage service. Complaining of physical ailments that prevent his mother from writing, she records cassette tapes for him to listen to while working out. At the gym, he listens absent-mindedly to her complaints of various illnesses. He drops his weights on the ground when he realizes she's sent an actual woman who possesses a Ph.D., sings opera, and speaks five languages to meet him as a potential mate. His lover, Simon, concocts a plan for Wai Tung and Wei Wei to marry so she may get a green card and he may finally be relieved of the pressures to marry. Little do they know that the plan—which puts them within the grasp of heteronormativity's power—will put them at risk and change them in unanticipated ways. The faux marriage challenges their love and friendship, as well as Wei Wei's independence.

The literary scholar Mark Chiang argues that Wai Tung's coming out as a gay man represents not only a sexual emergence but a racial one too. However, it is an emergence that, according to Chiang, complies with Asian patriarchy when the gay man is subsumed in the father's agenda of reproductive futurity.[20] Indeed, in an effort to ensure the reproductive continuity of his family line, the father will not publicly acknowledge his son's sexual identity even though he knows he's gay. At the end of the film, the father recruits his son's lover, Simon, in this ruse to further humiliate their gay sexuality into silence. Queer Asian American studies anthologies such as David Eng and Alice Hom's *Q & A* and Russell Leong's *Asian American Sexualities* chronicle the different ways coming out registers as important or not in gay Asian American life.[21] Coming out could mean the relinquishing of family, which is usually a haven in a racist world. Thus Wai Tung may not come out to his family for reasons that include his unwillingness to lose them and find himself entirely without a racial community. The shame assigned to gay men then is especially aggravated in the case of Wai

Tung. David Eng describes how in the "traumatic displacement from a lost heterosexual 'origin,' questions of political membership and the impossibilities of full social recognition dog the queer subject in a mainstream society impelled by the presumptions of compulsory heterosexuality."[22] Here he describes the perpetual deprivation of home and national belonging that gay Asian Americans experience as a kind of "impossible arrival," which we can use to rethink the creative making of home within this abjection.[23] In my reading of this film, I show how queer rearrangements expand new kin relations that serve the needs not only of the patriarch but of the feminist women and queer men who are usually shamed and punished by heterosexual normativity, as well as racial and gendered hierarchy. José Esteban Muñoz's argument about queer futurity is relevant here as well—when both Simon and Wai Tung embrace their roles as fathers as a positive dimension of their lives and an affirmation of their family formation as gay men.

Overjoyed at the news of Wai Tung's engagement, his family decides to visit for their son's wedding. Alarmed, the gay couple needs to "straighten" their home, which also entails "Asianizing" it for the visit. We see them attempt to delete the traces of their gay life by filling their space with Asian cultural objects and signs. Several pictures of erotic entanglements must come down. Earrings come off of Simon. Simon must educate Wei Wei on the map of their everyday life: locating for her where Wai Tung lounges after work and where he keeps his underwear. Modern paintings are replaced by scrolls of Chinese calligraphy.

When Wai Tung and Wei Wei marry in City Hall, his parents are extremely disappointed by the simplicity of the ceremony and the lack of a celebration. At the restaurant later that night, Wai Tung's father's former driver-turned-restaurant-owner offers to host a grand wedding banquet for his master. This arrangement is a trap—not because the gift comes from the hierarchies of the old country that constitute their ethnic heritage, but because it becomes the gateway for rituals of heterosexuality to enter their relations. Trapped by the social rituals of marriage and their sentimental significance in society as breeders for the ethnic community, Wai Tung and Wei Wei are both seduced out of their subjectivities as gay male and independent female artist into the romance of community heterosexuality that culminates in drunken sex on their wedding night—as enabled by the "invasion" of the honeymoon suite by Wai Tung's friends. Here we see the function of community as normalizing the gay men and female artist into acceptable roles within heterosexual romance: Simon becomes best friend and Wai Tung and Wei Wei become husband and wife.

Wai Tung's friends are composed of young and old—parents and children—though mostly of his peers: working young adults. They play mahjong, drink alcohol, and supervise the games that sexually titillate the couple, such as kissing various places on the body while lying down on the bed blindfolded. This affectionate and loving welcome to heterosexuality is contrasted with the hateful regard they usually receive as a gay man and the undervalued consideration of the single woman artist who barely makes ends meet. While Wai Tung adores his lover and loves his life as a gay man in New York, he is not out to his old school friends, some of whom he sees on the streets. His lover and gay friend receive disparaging glares from their white conservative neighbors. Wei Wei also feels the pressure as an illegal immigrant and poor artist who lives in squatter conditions: broken sink, broken air conditioning, and broken heater. She fears deportation and INS raids, which already took away her best friend.

Wai Tung and Wei Wei attempt to negotiate their gender roles as subjects struggling to cope with their socially disprized identities. From the very beginning, she flirts with Wai Tung: "I always fall for handsome gay men" intercuts with "when will you fix the sink?" When she describes losing her job and her deported best friend, she hugs Wai Tung as they both sweat profusely. Her caressing hand makes him visibly uncomfortable and he pushes her away, agreeing to accept her painting in lieu of three months' rent. She may be using feminine wiles to get what she wants while also expressing desire for him. To be sure, Wei Wei uses her art practice to secure some freedom. It pays her rent and acts as the primary reason for her living in a New York tenement: to live as an artist and forge a fulfilling life as a painter, rather than a conventional role as wife and mother. The primary wound of the film, however, is the silence Wai Tung abides regarding his sexuality. We learn this when Wai Tung confesses to Simon the pain he experiences in having to lie.

When Wai Tung's parents meet Wei Wei, they are pleased: "She'll make lots of babies." Wai Tung's father confirms the importance of heterosexual manhood when he says that Wai Tung now bears the responsibility of continuing the Gao family line. The deception deepens when they lie about Wei Wei's cooking abilities. She lounges as Simon cooks, and then they switch places when the mother walks in the kitchen. While Simon acts as their son's best friend, we can see that he actually enjoys and performs his real-life role as Wai Tung's domestic partner, a role he must hide. The heteronormative masquerade generates tremendous affirmation from Wai Tung's family—a distinct contrast to their previous disappointments. The father compliments Wei Wei's (actually Simon's) cooking—as better than that of their revered cook in Taiwan. Wei Wei is so moved by Wai Tung's parents that she comes to miss her own family. A kind of homecoming occurs in her relationship with his parents. She compliments in a very detailed way the perfection of Wai Tung's father's calligraphy. The father is moved to tears. His daughter-in-law validates his patriarchal role. Wei Wei becomes "speechless" at her in-law's presentation of jewelry and clothing from Japan, Malaysia, and mainland China. The accoutrements of heterosexual sexuality provide emotional pleasure to its participants. It seduces them into the confines of gender roles that constrict their actual desires.

Wai Tung is overwhelmed by his parents' love as expressed in very physical and even lovingly violent terms: the mother pretends to eat his arm and the father playfully beats his chest. The parents put great weight on the heterosexuality of their son and the significance of marriage in describing a spiritual bond that passes across generations and on how fate brings the coupling of their son and his wife. Throughout, Wai Tung's actual partner, Simon, is deemed inappropriate, giving presents to the parents that point out their ailments and age—a blood pressure monitor and skin cream that targets wrinkles. This is in addition to his humiliation as the "landlord" who must witness his lover's charade and endure his lies about their relationship. Wai Tung tells him, "we should have moved you out." While he says this gently and Simon does not respond with shock, we slowly see the gradual disintegration of their romance. Like Ben Loy and Mei Oi, they no longer have sex or sleep together. Simon goes out, Wai Tung waits for him. They cannot have sex in the house and tension arises. Here, sex lubricates their bond much like it did with Ben Loy and Mei Oi. Without sex and other pleasures, their connection as lovers dissipates while the silence required by the conventional family deepens.

On the day of the wedding banquet, Wai Tung gazes at Wei Wei in her white wedding dress. The father's speech describes a romantic scenario where Wei Wei and Wai Tung take care of each other and help each other succeed as a married couple. They have their photographs taken as a married couple—elaborate glamour shots in romantic marriage sets. A baby boy jumps on their honeymoon bed to invite the hurried arrival of sons. The guests make noise with their wine glasses, demanding a kiss, then a more passionate one. The toasts at each table get more raucous as each guest demands his own dedicated speech and drink. In response to a white couple who express surprise at the boisterousness of the Chinese, Ang Lee, in a cameo appearance as a wedding banquet guest chimes in, "It's 5,000 years of sexual repression" unleashed in the wedding banquet. After Simon takes Wai Tung's parents home, we see various drunken men vomiting in the bathroom. Then a large crowd enacts an invasion of the newlyweds' hotel room. They force them to play games that Wai Tung and especially Wei Wei seem to enjoy. While blindfolded, he eats fruit from her clothed body, which is lying beneath him on the elaborately decorated bed. Before the guests leave, they demand that the couple get under the sheets and take off all their clothes. When the party finally leaves, the couple cuddles in bed, naked and exhausted. When she realizes he has an erection, she accuses him: "Liar, you told me women don't excite you." He doesn't intend to have sex with her—and he's surprised she's intent on having have sex with him. She's crossing a boundary—which generates a curious response in him. Rather than adamantly insisting on stopping her, he asks, "Wei Wei, what's your hand doing?" as if it is disembodied from her. She considers his ambivalence a form of willingness to her

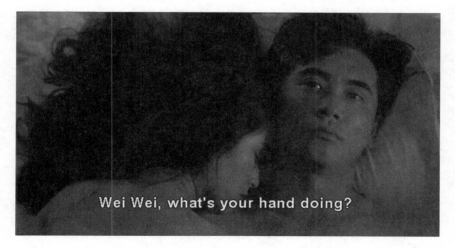

FIGURE 12   In *The Wedding Banquet*, Wei Wei attempts again to reach Wai Tung sexually. *The Wedding Banquet*. Dir. Ang Lee. Ang Lee Productions, Central Motion Pictures Corporation, and Good Machine, 1993.

mounting him with a forceful declaration: "I'm liberating you." We can interpret this statement as her granting him freedom from the confines of one sexual identity or his fixed conception of self but also a kind of extraction from their desire to defy traditional roles. Heterosexual sex either expands their identities or constrains them into normative identities. The next day, Wai Tung picks Simon up from a volunteer shift at an Act Up booth, which displays placards stating, Silence Equals Death. He does not disclose what he did with Wei Wei the night before. When they get home, the two men make out, taking off each other's clothes as they climb up the stairs, only to find that Wai Tung's father is there. Again, the lovers cannot have the sex that they so want. The movie depicts a deprivation of both gay sex and gay sexuality because of the heteronormative push by the family.

When Simon discovers Wei Wei is pregnant, he freaks out, yelling that in his description of how "things got out of hand," Wai Tung did not admit to actual sex. When his father has a minor stroke soon after this incident, Wai Tung can no longer bear his secret and comes out to his mother. "The marriage is a fraud. Simon is my real friend and lover. I'm gay and Simon is my lover. We've been living together for five years. It's hard for a gay man to find compatibility so I treasure Simon so much. If not for father's need for a grandchild and your nagging, I was happy with the way it was." Despite his confession of love for Simon, the hardship of queer life in a heterosexual world that includes the displaced pressures from her and his father and the painful silence he must bear, the mother recruits him into continuing to hide himself. She makes him promise to protect his father from the truth. She says the father cannot know for "it will kill him." In a sense, she threatens him with the death of his father so that Wai Tung will keep silent.

In a form of gender role negotiation that prioritizes the patriarchal power of her husband while accommodating the needs of her son, the mother then surprisingly attempts to get to know Simon. She accepts the opportunity to change her own attitude because, as Wei Wei explains, Wai Tung and Simon truly are gay and his mother can't expect them to change. The mother actually accepts the need for her to expand her traditional ideas of family. In this vein, small transformations occur that nonetheless indicate the power of patriarchy in preventing fundamental transformation. The father shows small changes as well. When Simon cooks, the father offers to do the dishes.

But the breakup of the gay couple looms—when the parents go, Simon proposes to leave too. The nurturing and love they demonstrated at the beginning of the film disappears as Wai Tung becomes a father and a good son. The marriage also faces a breakup. Wei Wei attempts to reclaim her freedom as a single woman, and to flee motherhood and conventional gender roles. She returns the gifts to the mother, who asks if Wei Wei can return the love as well. Wei Wei explains that she intends to have an abortion: "I can't do it [become a mother], I also have a future." Her future prioritizes her own needs and desires as an artist rather than as a mother or wife. She disagrees with Wai Tung's mother, who places more importance on the patriarchal order—the protection of husbands from having to change, procreation, and perpetuation of the family line—than on the needs and desires of the self. She tells Wai Tung she gave up too much for a green card. She renders herself as more than a womb, the identity by which she is recognized by the family, especially the older generation.

Wai Tung's parents insist on pushing Wai Tung, Simon, and Wei Wei into heteronormativity and gender hierarchy even if they remain aware of the falsity of these roles. In the next scene, we realize the father knows about Simon and his son's relationship. He gives Simon a present to acknowledge his relation to Wai Tung. He actually says Simon is also his son—because of his loving and caring relationship with Wai Tung. The father shares his knowledge of the forming of a new kinship, for he watches, hears, and learns. Yet he insists on keeping his knowledge a secret from everyone else. "If I didn't tell a lie, I'd never get [a] grandchild." He refuses a social recognition of that change—and instead maintains his identity as one who cannot change. While Mark Chiang argues this exchange is a cooptation of the gay man to bolster the patriarchy of the father, I argue that a different recognition actually transpires, in exceeding this formulation. "I don't understand," says Simon. And the father responds exactly, "I don't understand [either]." Here we see that across their differences lies an agreement to accept and respect, even without understanding. The film ultimately envisions a new family formation where the child conceived that night pleases Wai Tung's father, whose family line continues, and reunites Simon and Wai Tung as two fathers. Wei Wei gains a rent-free apartment that will enable her to pursue both a partial motherhood and a full career. The gay men and the feminist woman, representatives of groups traditionally shamed and deprived of kin relations, come to form a new family where the child will have two devoted fathers and a mother who is financially able to pursue a full life with a career as well as motherhood. The child also fulfills the grandparents' wishes and the grandparents implicitly have to accept the new family formation when they entrust the care of their grandchild to Wai Tung, Wei Wei, and Simon—thus supporting gay and feminist subjectivities.

In *The Wedding Banquet*, we see the shame that the gay Asian American man has to bear under the perpetual pressure his parents deploy in roping him into heterosexual marriage and the intense deception it requires. He must lie about what gives him pleasure and fulfillment: sex and love with Simon, who understands, knows, and recognizes him in his cultural difference and in his individual personality. In the process of getting married, however, the rituals of gift-giving and the words of reassurance, affirmation, and confirmation create a deep shame and self-disappointment that is violent. The film climaxes with the emergence of the pain the characters bear for betraying heteronormativity and gender hierarchy. When Simon nurtures Wai Tung, when Wei Wei prioritizes her career, and when Wai Tung enjoys sex and love with Simon, we see them energized to embrace their shame and refuse to accept their lives within a framework of debasement. They can and do form a supportive family that recognizes their differences.

The marriage starts as an attempt to resolve the shame of homosexuality. Their acknowledgment of the lie and its correction regenerates pleasure for Wai Tung in reclaiming Simon's love and for Wei Wei in launching her career. Here, an ethical Asian American manhood emerges in relation to the confrontation of one's queer sexuality and the efforts to redefine kinship to include both its traditional and nontraditional members: two parents, husband, and gay boyfriend as fathers, friends, and mothers. New kinships form and in the process, a new manhood is redefined. What we see in the close of *The Wedding Banquet* is a kind of heterosexual queerness in its offering, in Muñoz's terms, a new collectivity. Moreover, we see the formation of a new family and home—arenas that traditionally exclude gay Asian Americans and punish feminist Asian American women.

Sixteen Candles

The hit teen movie *Sixteen Candles* skyrocketed John Hughes' directorial career. *Sixteen Candles* is the first of his wildly and widely successful teen movies from the 1980s including *The Breakfast Club* (1985), *Weird Science* (1985) and *Ferris Bueller's Day Off* (1986). These films are part of and are in con-

versation with the genre of the teen film in the 1980s that expressed anxieties about the changing demographics of the United States and the identity
politics of race, sex, gender, and class, particularly in terms of shame. While
Sixteen Candles features a white heterosexual wedding, it includes an iconic
role in the Asian nerd whose subjectivity is not central to the romance, but
nonetheless comments on it. The character Long Duk Dong is so prominent that it his picture that appears on the DVD cover and represents the
film visually in prominent ways.

Like Wayne Wang and Ang Lee, the filmmaker John Hughes tells stories
that reveal anxieties about difference—including those of class, race, ability, and sexuality. Each of them has made films, highly profitable in terms
of box office draw, focused on differences. I study *Sixteen Candles*, a film
about high school aged youth and their angst about belonging (popularity),
recognition (style), and pleasure (sex and love)—a "white" Hollywood film,
alongside Asian American cinema for its racial representation of a shamed
Asian American manhood and its engagement with that shame. I explore
what it means to embrace pleasure-seeking instantiated by the controversial
character of Long Duk Dong as a remedy to his assignation into an undesirable position as one deprived of belonging, recognition, and pleasure in
sociality.

Within the mainly white cast, I focus my reading on the disparaging representation of Long Duk Dong—the exchange student with the bad bowl
haircut and accent who, enslaved by his host family (the elderly grandparents of the protagonist), is also the butt of savage jokes from across all generations from the sassy preteen Mike, Sam's brother, to her grandparents. A
gong bangs every time we hear Long Duk Dong's name. The film concludes
with violence inflicted upon Dong by the white male romantic lead, Jake,
and even his host mother, the lead's grandmother. He lies down on the
ground with a black eye after getting kicked in the stomach by his host
mother for screaming: "No more yanky my wanky . . . the Donger needs
food!" The film begins with equal outrageousness when Dong attempts
to flirt with the young female lead with another inane yet quotable line:
"What's happenin', hot stuff?" I revisit the "Donger" in order to more fully
contextualize him and how he travels from ridicule and shame to empowerment by rejecting his assignation. He instead embraces the bacchanalia of
U.S. high school culture exemplified by his outrageous actions, which include "bag[ging] a babe" while riding a stationary bicycle. Long Duk Dong

transforms within and beyond the film in ways that make it politically viable to embrace his legacy for forging ethical Asian American manhoods.

Primarily discussed as the quintessential stereotype and referenced widely by Asian American comics and bloggers to this very day, more than twenty-five years after his appearance on screen, Long Duk Dong is a caricature of a nerdy immigrant Asian man in America who does, as NPR says, "have the time of his life."[24] Armed as we are with the notion of negotiating one's lot in Hollywood and the recognition that audiences today are more politically sophisticated and racially sensitive, I suggest we might be at a point where we can recognize the ambivalences in Long Duk Dong's representation. Thus, beyond his negative image, we can recognize the radical disjuncture he represents for many Asian American men.

Sixteen Candles explores teen life in an era of intense social conservatism. Its treatment of the character of Long Duk Dong as a caricature or an exaggerated fantasy of difference reflects the fact that it was produced in the Reagan era.[25] In the late 1980s and early 1990s, Asia emerged as an economic yellow peril with the rise of the tiger economies.[26] Rapid economic development in Asia led to fears that America was at a competitive disadvantage and its industries might be taken over by Asian enterprises. In this context, we see anxieties not only about racial difference but fears of economic disadvantage. It was this kind of yellow peril paranoia that led to brutal crimes, such as the murder in Detroit of Vincent Chin, a Chinese American engineer mistaken for a Japanese, in the 1980s. Yet, this reading—which links representation in such a direct way to history—does not allow for us to address the more exceptional and ambivalent representation that is Long Duk Dong.

In *Sixteen Candles*, Samantha Baker, played by Molly Ringwald, is an anxious sixteen-year-old white girl with spunky fashion tastes whose family forgets her birthday on the eve of her more traditionally beautiful sister's wedding. She also nurses a desperate crush on a seemingly unattainable senior classmate named Jake Ryan, the handsome brown-haired white male jock, played by Michael Schoeffling, who also has a girlfriend who's more traditionally desirable as a voluptuous and womanly long-haired blond versus a short-haired, redhead, and boy-figured Sam. Samantha's pursued, however, by the king of the geeks, a skinny and scrawny freshman called Farmer Ted, played by Anthony Michael Hall. Racial difference is prominent here; the population is all white except for one black boy among the geeky white boys, and Long Duk Dong, who is the only non-white character with any speaking lines. Within the sea of anxiety from different camps of the school, Long Duk Dong is unleashed as a party animal who dons a kimono to drop from a tree as he yells "Banzai!" and delivers now classic, quotable lines such as "Oh, sexy girlfriend!"

Long Duk Dong is hosted by Samantha's grandparents as a foreign exchange student. From the beginning, Samantha's family regards him with contempt. Her little brother snidely remarks, "His name is Long Duk Dong," as an extra-diegetic gong rings out. "He's totally bizarre. Let's burn the sheets and mattresses after he leaves." Or from the lead character herself, "There's a very weird Chinese guy in Mike's room." At another point, as an example of her brother Mike's horrible lot in life, he complains: "I sleep under a Chinaman named after a duck's dork." In these lines, we can assess that he's not just a Chinese guy, but a very weird one, indicating that he may be exceptionally strange, and maybe so aside from his racial background. The comments at the same time reflect a debasement of racial difference. The barrage of name-calling from many directions puts Dong in a humiliated position as the butt of jokes. The audience is not aware of his feelings about occupying this position until the dinner scene, where we see the family staring at him as he eats.

A shot from the head of the table shows his perspective of several non-Asian people gawking at him and interrogating him about the quiche he eats. We then see how Long Duk Dong looks afraid as these very weird white people stare him down. The father nods his head vigorously and the grandparents look at him like he's an alien from another planet. Yet, even in this frame, Long Duk Dong is ridiculed by the film, which has him eating quiche with chopsticks while some kind of Oriental music plays. The dinner conversation reveals the monstrosity of his situation: how his host parents treat him as cheap labor, making him mow the lawn to save grandpa from his hernia (or "hyena" in Dong-speak), wash the dishes, and do the laundry—fulfilling the role, "you betcha," of the good Chinaman. So while the film bullies Long Duk Dong by its debasement of his character as laughable, we see from Long Duck Dong's perspective the disparaging and mocking regard of the white family within the film as well.

Despite Samantha's protests, Long Duk Dong goes to her high school dance. There, he meets Marlene, a very tall, large, strong, and buxom athlete whose breasts serve as a pillow for his head while they slow dance. The dialogue when they meet uses his name as fodder for laughter yet again. Their comedic interchange follows, showing off Gedde Watanabe's comic timing as he sniffles between his lines. She asks, "What's your name?" He replies, "Long." "What's your last name?" "Dong." "What's your middle name?" "Duk." She welcomes him into her chest. Their relation blossoms, so that Marlene ends up thanking Samantha for "loaning me the Donger, he's really bitchin'." And while fondling Marlene, Long Duk Dong coos "I've never been so happy my whole life. . . . Now I have a place to put my hand." Long Duk Dong transforms from petrified specimen on a petri dish—ridiculed as contagious, diseased—to a teen who achieves the joy of sexual and romantic fulfillment, which actually organizes the pursuits of all the teens in the film. The girl who provides this for him, however, is far being an exemplar of the traditionally desirable woman—she is large, manly, and aggressive—though rather attractive as well. Long Duk Dong transforms—from the slick, oily-haired bowl-hair style and tucked-in-shirts teen who hugs on Marlene on the dance floor crying to a full-fledged stud who drives his host parents' car wildly, hair tousled and smoking a cigarette with arms around his beautiful girlfriend whose face beams with adoration.

Unlike the geeks led by Farmer Ted, whom Long Duk Dong welcomes to a party at Jake's while riding the front door like a horse, Dong actually participates in sex. He does not have to pretend to get it, nor does his ridiculed stature or the lack of conventional beauty of his partner get in the way of his enjoyment. He also does not get beaten by jocks like Farmer Ted and his friends do. When he does come into violent confrontation with a white

FIGURE 13   Long Duk Dong thrills his girlfriend when he finds a place to put his hand. *Sixteen Candles*. Dir. John Hughes. Universal Pictures, 1984.

man, it is in the form of an equal beating and a mutual recognition. After the party, Jake surveys the damage to his house and after releasing Farmer Ted from his prison inside a glass coffee table, finds Long Duk Dong in a tree. Dong shocks him by jumping on him while yelling "Banzai!" Later, when Long Duk Dong opens the door to Jake looking for Samantha, he accuses him of "beat[ing] up my face." Jake explains: "You grabbed my nuts." We discover that Dong actually defends himself in the physical confrontation and explains, "Oh, I thought you were my new American-style girlfriend." He not only fights for himself, refusing to live silently under the name-calling, but even stuns and feminizes the hero by mistaking him for his own girlfriend. So while the Donger remains on the periphery, he comes into his own as a subject who won't accept being pigeonholed, but pursues enjoyment on his own terms. He certainly speaks to Jake not from a position of inferiority, as does Farmer Ted, but from a position that is not disparaged or undervalued compared to the white male lead.

Twenty-five years after Long Duk Dong's big screen debut, National Public Radio's *In Character* program revisited the character as the "last of the stereotypes."[27] Presuming an audience that no longer tolerates caricature and cultural critics who appreciate what Gedde Watanabe did in the context of limited roles for Asian American actors, the news item explores the power and resonance of the stereotype—as funny and as somehow long-lasting. Indeed, Gedde Watanabe's performance as an Asian American playing an Asian caricature is part of what makes possible the character's redeemability, unlike Mickey Rooney's performance in *Breakfast at Tiffany's* of another Asian caricature.

Indeed, there is much to love about Long Duk Dong. John Hughes' film aligns with Wayne Wang's and Ang Lee's in commenting on the shaming of Asian American men by American popular culture and advises them to recognize they do not have to partake in their naming into straitjacket sexualities. Unlike Wang and Lee, however, Hughes as director ridicules the character through extra-diegetic means as well as within the character's relations with others in the film. Thus, consciously or not, Hughes uses the comedic form to provide a recommendation for Asian American men to enjoy themselves outside of their naming and to refuse to accept that humiliation. Moreover, we learn about the fantasy-production of the white male lead character as well. Both are characters who represent not the typical white and Asian American men but exceptions. Long Duk Dong's and

Farmer Ted's presence at the margins indeed makes us more aware of Jake, the center—even here when played by Michael Schoeffling with such loneliness and isolation. In recognizing the exaggeration of Long Duk Dong, we can also find Jake Ryan impossible, unattainable, and hopelessly fantastic as well. Both characters seek to transform: away from insensitivity in the case of Jake and away from humiliation in the case of Long Duk Dong. While in Long Duk Dong we find a commingling of the endearing and pleasurable and the humiliating and embarrassing, he does move from an abject position to one where he can seek and find enjoyment. And Jake does find someone to love him as he wishes. Both are fantasies of the sensitive jock and the bacchanalian geek.

Yet we look upon these two characters differently within a hierarchy of racialized gender. We gaze upon Jake with longing as we look upon Long Duk Dong with anxiety. This anxiety is politically productive, however. Kent Ono, in a study of Japanese American internment films, recommends spectators remain anxious in their viewing of movies in the context of U.S. industry films' tradition of misrepresenting racial others.[28] What good can come from a bad image like that of Long Duk Dong? Earlier I noted Leo Bersani. His recommendation in "Is the Rectum a Grave?" is to embrace homophobic images of homosexuality. Similarly, here I conclude to embrace racially unflattering images.[29] Bersani posits the importance of stopping the "the denial of the value of powerlessness in both men and women . . . a more radical disintegration and humiliation of the self," for it celebrates how sexuality can transform the self.[30]

Twenty-five-plus years later, it's true that within *Sixteen Candles* we see many aspects of the complexity of Long Duk Dong's character. The first is his performance as the good foreign exchange student, with mannerisms of docility as he raises his head timidly to the crowd of the white family watching him eat quiche. Then there's the crying boy nestling against the big-breasted female at the dance. There's the party animal who drops Samantha off at home before driving into a parked car with kids making out in it. He opens the door, while riding it, for the geeks who fear their death at the party. Long Duk Dong shows no fear. He has sex on a bike. He jumps on Jake from a tree. He passes out on the lawn, yelling irreverent sexual innuendo to his host mom. And finally, he mistakes Jake for his girlfriend. We can tell through the gradual dishevelment of his pomaded hair how wild he gets, and at the end of the film he's loose.

Long Duk Dong's transformation is not simply from repression to liberation. He resonates across these decades for other reasons, which lie in the
power of interpretation. The impact of Long Duk Dong's character can be
seen in the way prominent Asian American cultural producers discuss how
his image shaped their youth—for instance, as cited in the NPR story, the
founders of the magazine and empire *Giant Robot*, Eric Nakamura and Martin Wong, describe a turn from the reputation of Bruce Lee kicking ass to the
imposition of the ridiculed Long Duk Dong. Without question, the straitjacket characterization inflicts pain. Yet, we also need to tread carefully in
positing the opposite: to declare a successful manhood for Lung Duk Dong
while ignoring insensitive conquering of women that Jake Ryan protests or
the refusal to acknowledge the privileging of a sexual conquest narrative.

Gedde Watanabe did not realize the impact of his role as Long Duk
Dong—he was trying to make people laugh, he says. He also has had to
live with the disparaging power of the character to shame Asian American
men, as his public encounters remind him. In 2008 Watanabe said, "People
still come up to me to this day and quote my lines." He admits he was "a
bit naïve" about "making people laugh. . . . I didn't realize how it was going
to affect people. . . . Yet, it's funny too . . . at the same time, I laugh at the
character. It's an odd animal." Indeed, Watanabe, as Martin Wong describes
to NPR, has to carry the baggage of the image, as do the Asian American
men who are mistaken for and misnamed by him. He is, as the NPR story
argues, an indication of the continuing dearth of roles for Asian American men in Hollywood movies. Watanabe says, "We really need an Asian
American star, and it hasn't happened."

Beyond the lack of heroes, what would prevent Long Duk Dong's rec-
lamation from ridicule is the framework of straitjacket sexuality—that
asexuality/effeminacy/queerness as lack—which victimizes Asian American
men into positions that are undesirable within the context of heteronormativity and gender hierarchy. A straitjacketed perception would romanticize
the position of Jake Ryan, the ideal white male, as more desirable. Long
Duk Dong would not be seen as one with true and genuine responses to
the denigration and disparagement of his difference—he is not supposed
to laugh it off, for he must be serious in fighting his shame and humiliation. But he seeks pleasure instead. For that, NPR calls his image a "stain"
that cannot be removed. The image is indeed a record of his humiliation
as an Asian American character in a white movie, which continues to be

distributed, re-released and celebrated to this day, and for which the actor had to hide his American heritage. But we must remember he drunkenly disavowed his hailing within a raucous celebration that earns him a place of rapport with the lead, to participate in a male homosociality.

In reframing Long Duk Dong, I confront two approaches to his image. First, we can approach him with ambivalence and laugh at the excellent exaggerations of this exceptional image—a really, really weird guy who enjoys his new country and actively tries to figure out its slang, saying "What's happenin', hot stuff" as he endures his enslavement as a houseboy by his host grandparents. We can say that despite the forces of shame, which Long Duck Dong may not be aware of as a character from Asia rather than an Asian American, he enjoys his surroundings and his opportunities. He deploys laughter in the face of his abjection.

The second approach is to take him very seriously especially in terms of the lack of desirability, for this is a powerful position. If so, the question I would ask is: Would I want my sons to watch this movie? A straitjacketed perspective would say his letting go of inhibition is a small a victory in the face of his unfair representation—especially with that extra-diegetic gong. The pleasure-seeking in small and individual terms is inconsequential in the face of this force. And this is why we would want what Gedde Watanabe wants: a star, or two or three or more, to fight off the shame that his performance of inanity does not quite fend off. Indeed, Long Duck Dong's wildness in the face of brutality indexes the limited choices Asian American men possess on the movie screen and off. More choices must be made available in the face of racializations and attributions that come from beyond one's purview. We need to remember the existence of these images as hailing of Asian American men and informing others. They indicate for Asian American men a history, one they are not born into but one they learn and confront.

To fight them off can be a truly enriching and creative part of life. It can transcend everyday images through humor, as in the case of Wong Fu Productions; through incisive, intelligent anger, as in the case of the Angry Asian Man; and even through the Geeky Asian Guy—all enterprises produced by Asian American men who contribute massively to our knowledge and culture through online media. Their contribution takes us far beyond the characterization of the Asian American man as an extremely weird guy à la Long Duk Dong. The significance of Long Duk Dong arises in an entry of the

Geeky Asian Guy Blog. In April 2010, the blog reflects on Long Duk Dong in terms of the anti-immigration legislation recently passed in Arizona:

> Here's the thing—when you grow up as an Asian American male, you convince yourself that there's no way anyone would ever confuse you with Long Duk Dong. You speak perfect English. You have better clothes and better hair (at least some of the time). You take pains to avoid acting in a childlike or giggly manner. . . .
>
> Yep, there's no way anyone would think you were FOB.
>
> Yet, deep down, I know that an awful lot of people in America just don't see that much of a difference between me and Long Duk Dong.
>
> And if I were living in Arizona, that would scare the crap out of me.[31]

Here we see the power of stereotypes in freezing images of individuals to stand in for groups in a widely circulated manner. The images compose our shared vocabularies and perceptions of each other in such a way that Asian American men persist as the undervalued other. As Gedde Watanabe diagnoses, we can counter these images with heroic ones—central ones, where Asian Americans do not merely provide peripheral amusement but can become a heroic Jake Ryan, with kind studliness, giving up his insensitive girlfriend for one he can truly love and who can love him back and expressing his disgust for the debauchery of white jock life. To compare Jake Ryan to Long Duck Dong is to see the inequalities in representation as well as two fantasy productions. The film ends, undeniably, with a respectful regard for Long Duk Dong by the white male lead and a relationship with a girlfriend who feels lucky in lining up with him. In the face of hostility, the Donger makes a community and even a home among his adoptive family when he finally releases his particular personality.

This chapter critiques the coexistence of: 1) the harm inflicted by his image, and 2) the harmlessness of the ridiculous image of Long Duk Dong, whom Gedde Watanabe plays so well. When the film was re-released in 2011 for special Valentine's Day weekend screenings across the country and in Canada, Long Duk Dong in the previews is no longer an extremely weird guy but just one of Samantha's friends, an excessive party animal.[32] He is presented not as alien but as belonging. To study closely the events in the film is to recognize this transformation. To confront feelings of ambivalence regarding this image is to see the power of caricature, even to those caricatured. As I write about Long Duk Dong now, I realize my own ambivalence, both loving and resenting him. Long Duk Dong is simultaneously horrible and silly, but most of all, deserving of a multidimensional response. His image is so of his era—when anxieties about racial difference manifested in such extreme caricature. But it is because of this extreme image of Asian American manhood that we can imagine many more possibilities that are similarly strange, disgusting, fun, and cool in ways that exceed racial essentialization. Long Duk Dong makes room for Asian American male characters that are not simply boring Jake Ryan heroes but villains, lovers, and even more complex characters.

I embrace the ambivalences of Long Duk Dong's image for representation does not directly shape reality nor reality directly shape representation. We can imagine many more manifestations of Asian American manhood in the movies because of Long Duk Dong, who remains popular and continues to appear for he is a bizarre character that can be read in a myriad of ways: funny, powerful, studly, and geeky. And Gedde Watanabe delivers a knock-out performance of an exceptionally bizarre guy. A straitjacketed spectatorial response would deny that over-the-top performance and remain anxiously hopeless in assessing his image. The lesson for Asian American men is to look closely at this image and to realize it does not mirror them. It is laughable—yes; endearing—yes; horrible—yes; and fantasy production—yes. It shapes subjectivities, but in ways that do not disallow Asian American men from speaking back or speaking out about the richness of their own lives—as men truly distant from Long Duk Dong. The power of anxiety remains and must inform the power of interpretation to critique and recast these images.

In Closing: The Power of Shame

The films *Eat a Bowl of Tea*, *The Wedding Banquet*, and *Sixteen Candles* articulate worlds of racial inequality, heteronormativity, and gender hierarchy. In evaluating how they work against and with the images of Asian American men as shamed and debased in their race, sexuality, and gender, we need to account for the context of the performances as well as the performances themselves. In these films, the performances of sex occur in the setting of heterosexual marriage and the romantic comedy form, which ultimately serves as a commentary on the diverse ways we can forge family and kinship when we acknowledge the failures of heteronormativity and gender scripts for racialized men.

I close with a formulation of a public mourning of the straitjacket assignation of sexuality for Asian American men so as to call attention to the manhood that must be constructed in its face. As Judith Butler points out, we cannot overcome our vulnerability. If we accept the precarious finitude of life—or the ongoing struggle men must take on to shape their manhoods—we can craft a new politics that will not fear the otherness assigned to us or succumb to a finitude of self in the singular model of the hero. To aspire to one role would constitute the death of imagination. And it would be to deny the fascinating drama of relating individual particularity to the epistemic violence of representation. To attend to the transformations possible in the face of challenges is to address the pain and harm inflicted by existing representations as well as the possibilities of forging new manhoods and new relations to accommodate a self-respecting subjectivity.

In *Eat a Bowl of Tea*, heterosexual marriage is redefined and recast in such a way that it becomes unlike heteronormativity and gender hierarchy. We see in Russell Wong's character in *Eat a Bowl of Tea* a tolerant and feminized man who celebrates the configuration of his new masculinity away from tradition and the heteronormative community of the New York Chinatown ethnic enclave. In *The Wedding Banquet*, marriage is remade in the context of a queer and feminist family. The film recommends tolerance and respect even when the characters do not understand difference. *Sixteen Candles* captures the debasing of Long Duk Dong's Asian American male difference by the elderly and the young—which does not preclude him from making friends and finding a girlfriend who appreciates his difference. He refuses to accept his humiliation and counters the insanity of those who regard him, with more insanity. He out-crazies racist regard by becoming inane. In the film's conclusion, we recognize that he cannot simply be relegated to moronic status. He competes, carves out his own space, derives pleasure, and achieves recognition where there was no space, just pain and misrecognition.

We learn about available manhoods in film production and can measure their qualities in terms of how they account for their own power as they recognize their hailing by and into positions of shame. Indeed, we as spectators engage viewing as a political practice, keeping sharp our critique as we approach representations. As filmmakers and critics, we must recognize how Asian American manhoods are dramas that are full of potential for the telling of stories located at the crossroads of pride and shame—where joy is located in multiple sites beyond the hero.

I conclude with the lesson that manhood is that which is learned. Cinema gives us an opportunity to teach about manhood, which must be ascertained from others, such as in the shared communal and perhaps even ethical networks of cinema viewing and making. This chapter accounts for ethical manhoods, communities, and filmmaking forms in terms of cinema's accountability to Asian American men on and off screen. The next chapter studies the contemporary articulations of Asian American manhood in hit movies by young Asian American men, which includes *The Debut,* an attempt to move away from an enthrallment with whiteness to assert a love for one's heritage. It also shows how the film *Charlotte Sometimes* maps a world for Asian American men and women where sexual repression and sexual liberation are their assigned roles. In these movies, the scenes of rivalry regarding the circuits of desire, love, sex, and romance illustrate how the characters' actions as Asian American men and women become engagements of power and privilege—in feeling and inflicting pain. We will see in that chapter the significance of romance and intimate relations for Asian American representations as a site fraught with possibility—for reinscribing power relations and for crafting ethical selves and relations. I then conclude the chapter with an analysis of the work of Justin Lin and *Better Luck Tomorrow*'s unlikely refusal of responsibility. Instead, it privileges subjects of infinity as the solution to the problem of Asian American men's sexual problems in the movies. Through his work, I discuss cinema as a technology that can formulate ethical manhoods.

THREE

The Marvelous Plenty
of Asian American Men

Independent Film as a Technology of Ethics

Historically, as we have seen in my study so far, social formations such as marriage are contested terrains for Asian Americans. Asian American men endured "a kind of public shaming ritual performed by state and local officials" when negotiating laws and exclusions that declared miscegenation illegal.[1] Indeed, heterosexuality itself has a tainted history for Asian American men—who were prevented from marriage and family unification—as evident in the fostering of bachelor societies.[2] The haphazard deployment of scientific discourses of racial classification and the inconsistent use of popular culture to determine the visibility of racial difference in the many court cases that challenged anti-miscegenation laws revealed the frustrating inconsistencies in the definition of race.[3] Today, independent films by and about Asian American men explore issues of romance, sex, and love, and trace the subject formation of Asian American men as they come to terms with their own genders and sexualities as constricted by laws and popular culture in history. The critically noted films *The Debut* (2000), *Charlotte Sometimes* (2002), and *Better Luck Tomorrow* (2003) chart Asian American male subjectivities in between the poles of lack and macho. These independent films threaten to center phallic power in telling stories that hinge on male rivalry over women and in using women as property and possessions in the organization of heterosexual relations. Since heterosexuality and manhood historically have been denied Asian American men, they have become the terrain of struggle in which men claim the right to define and control their masculinity.

While gender remains a problem, Asian American filmmakers seek to improve romantic and intimate relations with others. Independent films about Asian American men capture subjects wrestling with the importance of acknowledging male power and the risks of expressing vulnerability, especially when relating to subjects they desire. By using the medium of film to engage the marvelous particularity of stories about race, sexuality, and gender that Asian American men face, we witness an ethical dilemma regarding such questions as whether to extol the regulation of desire and whether to condone or condemn interracial dating—which is considered a traitorous kind of race suicide or, conversely, a salve and step forward in racial progress. Independent Asian American male filmmakers try to escape the binary frame of manhood as weak or strong by revealing how the social forces of race, gender, class, and sexuality inform choices and desires but in ways that do not preclude the particularities of individual attractions, preferences, and histories.

This chapter adopts an ethical approach in studying the racial politics of intimate relations. To get out of straitjacket sexuality requires recognizing that Asian American manhoods contain group identification as well as individual particularity. This recognition allows me to make a recommendation regarding how to approach images of shame imposed by others but accepted as part of the self: strive for a remarkable originality that comes only from within. Film is a mesmerizing medium for capturing the process of subject formation where men wrestle with self and group identity in owning both their lack and their macho.

One way to make apparent the coexistence of lack and macho is to locate how straitjacket sexuality assigns Asian American men to a position of lack, which when understood as inadequacy leads to overcompensation in the form of macho. If we acknowledge the possession of both lack and power, we can shift our understanding of Asian American male sexuality and gender toward a position of need—or the recognition that subjects depend on others while also holding the ability to hurt others. For the philosopher Emmanuel Levinas, "need . . . turns us toward something other than ourselves. Therefore it appears upon initial analysis like an insufficiency. . . . Habitually interpreted as a lack, it would indicate some weakness of our human constitution."[4] I will show how the focus on themes of sexuality by Asian American male filmmakers accomplishes an ethical task. They acknowledge vulnerability not as a weakness but as a position of transformation and change toward the possibility of ethical manhoods, to culminate in a kind of "peace-with-self"[5] or what I call a calm manhood that transcends the male malaise of lack and macho.

What we discover in Gene Cajayon's *The Debut*, Eric Byler's *Charlotte Sometimes*, and Justin Lin's *Better Luck Tomorrow* is the plenitude of Asian American male actualities and desires—the best counter to the assignation of lack precisely is the acknowledgment of the self that needs others. To recognize one's need for others is an act of "vulnerable strength"—à la Bruce Lee—but also an act that counters straitjacket sexuality by forming communities like those discussed in Chapter Two. In such communities new manhoods are supported not by macho or castration but by the unique ways men survive straitjacket sexuality.

Released early in the twenty-first century, the Asian American male films discussed in this chapter helped to establish a viable voice in U.S. industry cinema precisely because they use the medium as a technology of ethics—in unabashedly showing subjects undone by their interpellation and embarking on a process of unraveling themselves toward new ethical manhoods. To approach film as a technology of ethics is to use Levinas's philosophy of relating to the other. He describes the highest form of ethics as a responsibility to care for the other, but this does not necessarily always require mutuality; when caring for a young child, for example, the parent does not and cannot expect reciprocal treatment. Ethical Asian American manhood rests in the awareness of one's position of power so as to decenter oneself in questioning how one impacts others. If facing the other makes one aware of the ability to affect the other, I look to film as a technology for figuring ethical manhoods. Through 1) the power of touch, which Levinas defines as "not as palpation but as caress"; 2) the work of speech, "not as the traffic of information but as contact"; and 3) the face-to-face encounter, the self–other encounter in representation, I show how we need to account for the particularities of desire across difference in formulating new ethical selves.[6]

First, I describe the importance of using Levinas in studying the romance and rivalry Asian American men experience in independent films. In formulating an ethical Asian American manhood and film as a technology of ethics, I situate the filmmakers' work within cinematic history. I then read the films *The Debut*, *Charlotte Sometimes*, and *Better Luck Tomorrow* to ask how characters proceed in making demands upon self and other so as to know more about how Asian American men and women recognize themselves and others as social beings, especially in sexual acts and other intimacies. I evaluate how these scenes become places where they engage power and privilege, particularly in feeling and inflicting power, and how they reveal an understanding of the ethical significance of behaviors and choices.

Asian American Romance On and Off Screen: Bringing in Levinas

Like other racialized communities, Asian Americans experience pressures regarding coupling in terms of gendered hierarchies of sex. In September 2010, the online magazine *Madame Noir* published "8 Reasons to Date a White Man," which prompted much response and a panel discussion at Columbia University entitled "8 Reasons to Discuss Romance in the Black Community." One panelist shared how the long history of racism at the site of sexuality informs African American romantic practices and futures. A recent article on *Love Jones* (1997), an independent film about African Americans in love, critiques the lack of conceptualization of "romance in our own terms." The article calls attention to the importance of independent films in articulating visions of racialized love beyond stereotypes while also acknowledging the sexual subjection of racialized subjects.[7] In recent years, Columbia and Cornell universities have produced disturbing findings in their research on male desirability according to race. Among all racial groups, excluding Asian American women, Asian American men ranked at the bottom, under white, black, and Latino men. African American women also ranked at the bottom among all racial groups in the hierarchy of desirability according to race.[8]

Asian American men's lowly place in the hierarchy of desirability is a loaded issue. For example, the filmmaker Eric Byler explicates the politics of sex in contemporary Asian American gender relations to include sexual relations between white men and Asian American women, which he relates to the lack of desire for Asian American men. In an interview with Oliver Wang, Eric Byler rhetorically asked "What's the truth?"

> The truth is that those Asian girls who you see walking down the street with white guys that bugs you so much, they go home and they have sex. It's not just that they have coffee and it's not just that they go to bars or whatever, they go home and have sex. And if you really want to deal with

how you feel about it—and I want you to deal with it in the most personal way—then watch this movie and decide where you stand.[9]

Here, Byler indicates the problematic way Asian American men can perceive relations between white men and Asian American women. Undergirding their irritation at glimpsing public intimacy are private sexual activities. Such intimacy is perceived as threatening to Asian American male subjectivity—as if women betray Asian American men through sex acts with men other than Asian Americans. What we see here are links to Yen Le Espiritu's argument that the sexuality of Filipina American women is made to stand for the larger community, and thus these women are subject to moral judgment for their choice of partners.[10] Byler places Asian American men at a crossroads in determining their identity and their sexuality as men when they see Asian American women with white men.

And Byler goes further when, on a panel with the film critic Roger Ebert, he speaks about the relationships between Asian American men and women:

> I saw a lot of couplings between Asian men and women that are platonic where he would pretend not to love her and she would pretend not to know. It's not necessarily an Asian American thing . . . but there is suspicion among Asian American men somehow that the choice as to whether the new person in your life is going to be a lover or friend is somehow contingent upon race. . . . As you come of age, you ask what kind of sexual being am I going to be—in the media, usually an Asian man's a technician and he's never a lover and if he expresses sexual desire it's ugly or unwanted. Where do I fit as a sexual being?—[as a man,] the more you repress your sex desire the more you will fit in. Asian girls grow up as if sex is all we want from them—the more sexy, the more beautiful . . . where exotification equals acceptance. . . . These creatures don't know how to interact very well—they slide into friendship and there's a fundamental lie at the core, which leads to very difficult situations.[11]

In Eric Byler's assertion that Asian American men do not want to "slide into a friendship" with Asian American women where there is a "fundamental lie at the core" is a deep question about what kind of sexual being an Asian American is going to be in a society where perhaps for other categories of people it is a given. If there are questions about the sexuality of Asian Americans as a group and as individuals, Byler is right to work in film, a medium that structures and forms our ideas about masculinity and sexuality. But it is necessary to interrogate the structure of Byler's assertion that male and female friendship represents a form of castration. In a sense, within the logic of straitjacket sexuality the platonic relation turns the Asian American man female.

To move beyond this frame, we may extend the platonic friendship so that the function of the women Asian American men desire goes beyond feminizing them into a castrating friendship. The women in the films I discuss here cannot simply be friends, for if they are, then men have to move beyond articulating female subjectivities as property and possessions. Friendship can transform social relations for Asian American men and women, especially if it requires an Asian American masculinity that is not about aggression toward women or traditional gender relations of female ownership by men. In other words, friendship can expand acceptable relations between Asian American men and women—if one rejects the unchanging male self that depends on conquering women to bolster male subjectivity. That Asian American men experience disadvantages in the heterosexual marketplace and structural inequality—whether in institutions of government or family—may be framed as a weakness that leads to anxiety and an inability to recognize the importance of redefining relations between men and women.[12]

In this chapter we will see how independent filmmakers work through issues of ethical manhood—some successfully, some not. Since manhood must always be understood within a larger field of social relations, it is crucial to acknowledge the implications of seeing oneself as victimized by other desires and relations and equally crucial to imagine new subjectivities and relations. Indeed, the films I study in this chapter reveal how romance introduces difficult challenges for Asian American manhood in terms of rivalry between men and competing visions of mutuality and accountability among Asian American men and women. The challenge is not only to account for the wielding of privilege and power within romance, but to care for the self and other/s. Focusing on formulations of power and freedom within relations of sex, love, and desire for Asian American men in the most current independent filmic representations of romance allows us to see how Asian American men use film to provide opportunities for fashioning ethical selves that account for how they hurt. They don't always do this successfully, though it is important that they try.

In the current proliferation of bromances, hangovers, and other unabashed reclamations of lost manhood that include homosociality and embracing their feminine within, Asian American men participate in reassertions of traditional masculinity.[13] I consider films as attempts to author manhoods within differing situations and structures, including racial, sexual, gendered, and classed personalities—or each character's specific desires and ways of coping with and acting out norms. When Asian American men fall into the trap of centralizing their victimized subjectivity as men, the result is the definition of male subjectivity as a totality rather than an infinity.

I turn to Emmanuel Levinas, whose discussions of the face-to-face, touch, and the work of speech inform my method, which arrests the specific way film operates as a technology of ethics. In cinematic representations of romance there is always mystery and unpredictability in the narrative. This is part of what pleases us as viewers—to see a relationship blossom despite obstacles and misunderstandings. I study these scenes of intimate relations closely—expanding too our understanding beyond genital sex—so as to attend to how the act of relating to one another becomes an undoing of the self. Cinema exploits the fact that we cannot fully know the other as subjects apart from us despite our wish to know and be close to the other. The possibility of the unexpected always arises, and if we anticipate the other, to use Levinas's terms, he or she becomes a totality rather than an infinity. Totality I define as a subjectivity that is known, while infinity is a subjectivity that is not yet, and can never be, fully known. Within the cinematic frame, relationships are the scenes where an ever-changing subject transpires before us and with us. Thus, love and sex are vital in cinema, offering to an audience the experience of fascination with the unfolding of one's love object. When no longer beguiling or if seemingly possessed in total, love can die because the object of desire no longer has mystery. When the unknown becomes known, it can be thrown away. Thus I interrogate these films by and about Asian American male filmmakers for their definition of their characters in terms of fixity (totality) and ever-changing complexity (infinity) as they wrestle with what it means to be men within relations of love, romance, and sex.

Informed by Levinas's idea of totality and infinity, I examine descriptions in both the directors' and actors' words in the process of representing love, romance, and sex. When they describe the script as a living object, although it is ink on paper, or the film as not coming to life until spoken in the movie, I note that it is the same for feelings and touching. That is, films come to find meaning in both the "saying" of the script (in its actual speech), and in the "said" (in its performances of touching and other bodily acts as expressions of feeling). This is the source of the power of cinema—the moment when the actors' work and interpretation come together with the filmmakers' for the sake of the audience. Hence, the unpredictability that charges intimate relations—how will this person respond to my touch?—thrives in the cinematic form as its filmmakers and actors come together, committed to representing a dynamic encounter.

No matter the number of takes or the extent of editing and its cutting and juxtaposing scenes, it is the actors and director who form the meaning of the film. Touch, speech, and look, especially on faces, significantly help to articulate the meaning of a film. While the director has intentions, they do not come to life until the actor enacts and interprets the role. Through the skill of the director and the actor, we recognize falling in love, the power of sex in achieving intimacy, and the ability of speech and the look to create feelings of attachment that fulfill romance. Cinema not only uses this phenomenon in depicting love, but makes it recognizable in our understanding of cinema as an ethical event. Using Levinas, I assert the importance of the power of touch, the work of speech, and the face-to-face encounter as attempts to connect across the vast distance between self and other in love so as to show the power of cinema as a technology of ethics. Filmmakers use this technology to offer social critique by creating subjects whom we may evaluate for their ethics—the ability to go beyond themselves and to use their power to care for others as well.

The Material Context of Asian American Filmmaking by and about Men

In Russell Leong's *Moving the Image*, we see a chronicle of Asian American filmmaking for social change that emerged in the 1960s and 1970s as a result of the Civil Rights movement. The UCLA-based ethnocommunications program shattered the lily-white demographics of one of the nation's top film schools with the enrollment of filmmakers who changed the media landscape of the United States.[14] Since then Asian Americans have been moving through the hallways of the most prominent film schools. These filmmakers often feel pigeonholed by the classifications and categories of race, yet they devote themselves to telling Asian American stories creatively while simultaneously developing their craft. Their coming into filmmaking is contextual-ized by a bombardment of stereotypes—or limited representations, usually derogatory—which they undo with works that present richer characters and situations. Films by Asian American men intervene in what can be described as the torturous experience of enduring images of asexuality and abnormal-ity, suffering as the butt of jokes, and being relegated to peripheral status in a world of white men and women as central and heroic figures. While film-makers may set out these goals in their filmmaking, we as spectators can also recognize the ambivalences in the production of meaning and in the risk of reinscribing the limits Asian American actors face in the cinema.

Michael Kimmel describes how "George Stade, writing in the *New York Times Book Review* in 1984 . . . bemoaned the current wimpiness of fictional male characters." Stade asserts that "protagonists no longer venture forth, they retreat, admit defeat, take the heat, all with a sheepish grin. . . . [They are] preadolescent mama's boys, alternately bratty and eager to please."[15] If white men resent movements that take away their privileges without an as-sessment of those privileges, Asian American manhoods relate to this devel-opment. Indeed, they similarly experience "male malaise" or "yearning for a deeper, more authentic version of masculinity than the one on offer from consumer society."[16] U.S. cinema produces what Michael Kimmel character-izes as anxiety, which has led to a crisis of masculinity during the post–Civil Rights, post–John Wayne era. In this larger context, attitudes of entitlement lead to perceptions of victimization as a de rigueur understanding of mascu-linity that needs to assert itself in a world still dominated by men.

While others have discussed the institutional matrix in filmmaking and race, such as how the need and desire for certain images are created by the industry, how the distribution of funds precludes a diversity of authors, and how filmmakers must struggle for institutional and governmental sup-port,[17] I am primarily concerned with how men have come to make Asian American narrative feature films in recent years. Do Asian American male filmmakers seem to get the lion's share of narrative filmmaking funding while Asian American women mainly work in the realm of documentaries? Is there a gender-genre assignation in Asian American filmmaking, where women act as housekeepers of the community in reporting and archiving stories while men take charge of myth-making and fantasy production? The lack of Asian American female participation, moreover, illustrates the larger problem of a lack of women directors in U.S. industry cinema.

Asian American cinema from the 1990s to the present has moved from an imagery-for-action framework to one where social change occurs through dramatic narrative. By enabling audiences to experience the struggles, missteps, and resolutions of Asian American characters, thereby encouraging the viewer to sympathize with and root for them, these films invite us to identify with someone who could possibly be a friend, a lover, an ally. In this way, these cinemas accord worth and power to those who would otherwise be deemed different. Asian American men occupy the lead roles in teen blockbuster stoner films such as *Harold and Kumar Go to White Castle* (2004) and its sequel, *Harold and Kumar Escape from Guantanamo Bay* (2008). These films veer away from the white guys who usually make fun of the Asian geeks and instead follow the latter as they navigate the fascinating terrors and strange comedies of racism on a road trip across the Northeast in the former title and on a flight where they are misrecognized as terrorists in the latter. Imagine an American Long Duk Dong as a normal person, not the butt of jokes but someone we follow to see how he goes beyond being simply the hero or the butt of jokes. *Better Luck Tomorrow* director Justin Lin has directed several big-budget Hollywood films in recent decades, including the popular franchise *The Fast and the Furious*. These Hollywood films authored by filmmakers who right the wrongs of stereotypical, two-dimensional images of Asian Americans have captured the industry's attention to the extent that most screens in the United States now carry such works with big box office opening weekends. Filmmakers are doing more by creating myths about what is possible for Asian American lives than can be achieved by the modest goal of securing cinematic presence or simply presenting racial difference on screen.

One hundred years after the birth of cinematic mass culture, we are at a significant moment in the history of American movies. The output of Hollywood representations authored by Asian American filmmakers today puts Asian American men and women, usually cast in peripheral roles, in actual speaking parts and as substantial characters. These filmmakers often risk their own financial security to make these products that alter the status of Asian Americans in the cinematic imaginary. Movies teach men and women how to move, look, and love; thus I see these movies as significant to the everyday in their assertion of a very different presence for Asian Americans. They help inform our choices of how to construct our genders and sexualities in the ethical network of cinema going and making. Primarily authored by Asian American men, these films, however, have not settled the question of narrative filmmaking as a man's trade in terms of the lack of women directors of any racial and ethnic background.

As for the issue of gender in the stories Asian American men tell in the movies, if the stories are constrained within straitjacket conceptions of manhood, sexuality, and racial identity in the asexuality/effeminacy-versus-macho divide, then these men address their deprivation without fully using the power of cinema to forge truly different realities—such as a wider range of sexual and gender practices for Asian American men and women. Thus this chapter focuses on the romantic entanglements of Asian American men to account not only for structural inequalities but to index the complexity of individual desire and lived practices. To do so helps us to imagine the marvelous plentitude of Asian American manhoods.

Mutual Desire for Conventional Coupling in *The Debut* (2000)

The Debut by Gene Cajayon is the first narrative feature film about contemporary Filipino Americans to have screened widely in the United States. It focuses on the struggles of Ben Mercado, a Filipino American high schooler who's received a full scholarship to UCLA but has his heart set on professional art school. He clashes with his father about his career choice, and on the night of his sister's "debut," a confrontation of competing definitions of family, community, and romance occurs. Through Ben's drawings, we understand his world is white and see he is not—and this becomes a site of confusion. Played by handsome Dante Basco, who also appeared in the Hollywood movie *Hook* (1993), Ben Mercado is attracted and attractive to Jennifer, a young white woman who shows him her artwork. As they melt into each other, nearness and conversational insights exciting them, her friend glares with disapproval from a nearby car. Ben's friend, on the other hand, approves. He observes, "Whew—she's on your nuts like a squirrel." In this scene, the film establishes Ben within a white America where his viability as a romantic prospect is debated in racial and gendered terms.

Though Ben's friends—who appear white—accept him, he avoids inviting them to his house for its explosion of ethnic difference. They engineer their way into his home nonetheless—demonstrating amused appreciation of decorations like the man in the barrel with the penis-surprise and the giant fork and spoon on the wall (a staple decoration in Filipino house-holds). They especially welcome Ben's generous mother, who offers them food. Ben fears the ethnic cornucopia will corrupt their perception of him and damage what he deems is his almost perfect acceptance among whites.

Ben's sister, Rose, rebukes him for hanging out with white male friends—characterizing him as resentful of his brownness and thus using his friends as a conferral of his desired-for whiteness. The film posits a binary between his friends, representing America, and the ethnic homogeneity of Asia, represented by the household. The bind that marks Ben's understanding of culture centers on his father, who is intent on Ben following the tradi-tional path to success—becoming a doctor—while Ben prefers pursuing his passion for art. The sister's debut party, however, exceeds this binary of old-versus-new and tradition-versus-modernity when it brings Ben to a Fili-pino American culture that's hybrid in its music, dance, fashion, and other expressive arts. Within the party, however, he comes to represent white-ness and his rival blackness, while his sister and her friends (both men and women) embody Filipino brownness, which here mixes hip hop urbanity with cultural history from the homeland, embodied in performances of tra-ditional music and dance.

At the debut, Ben's object of desire is a woman named Annabelle, played by Joy Bisco, a slim, small, and brown-skinned Filipina American beauty. Their coupling is constructed within a rivalry for the woman between two men who represent different aspects of Filipino American masculinity. In the hallway of the auditorium where the debut is held, Ben walks toward his former childhood friend Augusto, who in his gangster swagger, heroic demeanor, and fashion is racialized as black to Ben's whiteness. Augusto, Annabelle's ex-boyfriend, corners her and gets in her face, demanding she accept his expensive pager. She refuses. Augusto threatens her with a men-acing posture—and Ben rescues her by putting his face between theirs—allowing her escape. Augusto and Ben stand face-to-face—and then Ben leaves the confrontation to run after Annabelle, who won't look at him, but instead calls him and all men dogs. He calmly says "nice to meet you too," disarming her, so she stops to look at him. They face each other. From this moment when they lock their physical alignments together, they enter a flir-tation of gazes up and down to search each other's faces for an indication of feelings for the other. A rivalry frames Annabelle's choices—white and black versions of brown maleness. No matter whom she chooses, the result will lead to violence. Augusto functions as the rival, he who flaunts an aggressive masculinity that's street and volatile. Annabelle becomes for Ben a vessel for redeeming the culture from which he flees and he becomes for her a romantic, masculine hero to her feminine heroine. In this way, the film fulfills a wish for white heteronormativity for a brown leading man and woman.

While the older folks dance the electric slide inside the auditorium, Annabelle brings Ben to the heart of a Filipino American low-rider, balling and hanging out on the basketball court culture outside. There they rehearse the courtship ritual of smooth lines and moves in a metacinematic commentary on teen romance. He discloses in an important way his philosophy of manhood—I don't beat people up because they look at me funny—in a critique of Augusto's "barkada," or gang of friends. She shares her ability to speak Tagalog, which compels him and further secures how she represents a homecoming for him. Then he's touching her, face-to-face, as they move toward erotic relations. He'll try a "classic backrub"—a corny device that results in a palm-to-palm touching of hands that makes her face change to an expression of desire as they sit together against a car. Augusto notices this—as do his friends.

This tender physical connection between man and woman, in a writing of conventional heterosexuality especially for the feminine as soft and mas-

FIGURE 14   Ben and Annabelle touch and change the dynamics of the space between them. *The Debut.* Dir. Gene Cajayon. Sony Pictures, 2000.

culine as hard, leads to male-on-male violence and aggression. Soon, Ben's playing basketball against Augusto, who fouls him, requiring Ben and his team to walk away so as to avoid a brawl. Here, we see that Augusto's hyper-macho version of Filipino American masculinity is hardly admirable for he bullies others and aggressively approaches women—unlike Ben, who avoids conflict and rescues women. In this world, Ben achieves heroic masculinity against a perverse one by Augusto. He represents a protective yet not frightening manhood.

Outside the community, however, Ben finds himself an inadequate man. At the party, to which he flees, he encounters a white girl who calls him "chink" and classifies him in racially disparaging terms. He responds passively with "I'm not Chinese" and retreats outside, cutting across the frenzy of white head-banging bodies to sit in front of a parked car, a position that emphasizes his weakness and vulnerability. He asks his white friends to return to the sanctuary of his family's party. The world of white male grunge is represented as unreceptive to Ben, especially in the form of hostile women and unreliable white men. His friends barely defend him and he must leave rather than negotiate his presence there or present a calm, assured, and confident manhood that won't let others define him. In this way, Ben fails as a romantic figure in the world outside the Filipino American community—he cannot speak for himself nor can he compel others to defend him in a community of support. Within the Filipino American community, he speaks and offers a different masculinity—one that walks away from violence with calm, cool confidence. But instead, here he cries and runs away, infantilized. The force of racism is so strong that it defeats him, making the ethnic home an enclave of safety. Against whiteness, he fails.

Within his own community, a different story about violence and male subjectivity transpires. That is, among his own people, he succeeds. Later, Augusto sees Ben and Annabelle almost kiss, which enrages him, releasing a force so strong that both young men lose themselves in a brawl—hitting each other in the hallway with bewildered faces of not knowing what will transpire next. The physical fight is a struggle between two manhoods—one hypermasculine (macho) and the other eunuchoid (castrated)—which won't survive outside the community. But violence brings the family together. Augusto never speaks of his father's death while smoldering with resentment about his mother's new, white husband. He defends his mother when his stepfather belittles her after the fight. The mother slaps her son instead—over and over again for disrespecting her husband—and Augusto is left crying and ashamed at the public announcement of his secondary place within his family. Ben's father, Roland, receives the wrath of his own father, who places responsibility for the party's failure and inadequacy on his son's failings. Ben's father is a postal worker rather than a doctor. The bad feelings with his own father lead Ben's father to reconcile with his son over his choice to pursue art. Ben and his father attain a new manhood on their own terms with this act of self-definition—a moment of recognition where the father realizes he can release his own hopes from his son's future.

Ben, damaged and formerly seduced by communities outside, ultimately comes to belong to his Filipino American community by way of the woman. The physicality of the fight with Augusto is subdued by the next scene, in which Ben walks Annabelle to her car, where they kiss. She is contrasted with the white girl, Jennifer, who expresses excitement over Ben, making plans to meet him at the party but then won't come to his defense when he's racially slighted. It is Annabelle who, in order to defend and protect Ben, calls for the community to stop the fight. In this film, the white world is rendered unmovable, while everyone is welcomed to the Filipino American community. Romance with the young woman, whom the directors deliberately cast as a dark-skinned *morena* beauty, represents a return to the fold of family and community.

Women continue the logic of the film, which places Asia and America in a binary formation. Ben chooses Annabelle as he does his Filipino community while pursuing his passion for art—framed as an American action, unlike his father's Filipino-good-son sacrifice of his passion for music. This kind of convergence shows this as an Asian American film with concrete recommendations for living a life where culture is binary, so that both sides are included in its conclusion. The film consciously sees itself as representing the Filipino American community: it romanticizes that community and tells to a wide audience what is, essentially, a Filipino American story in gendered and sexual terms of securing a viable manhood that ultimately is a totalized masculinity.

For Ben the achievement of a dignified manhood is through the pursuit of his passion for art and coupling with the woman who represents community belonging. Yet, his manhood fails to work outside of the community, part of the film's argument to stay within one's ethnic group, rendering it the proper place for brown men to achieve viable manhoods. It is a manhood that cares for the self—in the pursuit of a man's passions—yet the man settles for the woman as a connection to community. He accepts her partnership for he must occupy a world of same-race love as the privileged option for his manhood. As a man terrorized by white racism in a way he does not confront, his is a partially successful manhood.

Both the Filipina American woman and Filipino American man want to belong together in a mutual love. They regard each other's totality with mutual desire—she wishes for him to be heroic and he wishes for her to be his country. They remain on an island together, in the Filipina/o American community, where they occupy conventional roles of coupled man and woman. The film attempts to access what is not previously within grasp—a Filipino American manhood that loves its brownness and forsakes its adoration of whiteness. This small pleasure accompanies the thrill of seeing male romantic leads from the Philippines like Tirso Cruz III and the legendary actor Eddie Garcia alongside Filipino American child star Dante Basco. However, the role of traditional hero and heroine is not problematized but wished for, indicating the pain of deprivation from these visibilities. I now move to a film that refuses to aspire to whiteness and instead explores the way in which Asian American men and women critique traditional coupling and create new identities in the face of their differing racial sexualizations by gender.

Psychosexual Entanglements in *Charlotte Sometimes* (2002)

Eric Byler's *Charlotte Sometimes* privileges the romantic relationships and psychosexual dynamics of four racialized subjects. I attend to the bodies and read the choreography of the two Asian American women, one Asian American man, and a biracial Asian American man so as to show that touch functions as speech. The lead character, Michael, a mechanic, manages responsibilities for chauffeuring his aunt while owning a family repair shop specializing in German cars, and serving as a landlord to Lori and her hapa (biracial Asian and white) boyfriend Justin. Lori and Justin enjoy a vigorous sex life that she ritually finishes off by leaving to cuddle with Michael upstairs. Together, Lori and Michael watch movies, share physically intertwined company, and enjoy familiarity and emotional intimacy. A mysterious stranger who becomes close to Michael breaks this habitual pattern and the four embark on a sexually volatile relationship that reveals much about the power of social assignation and relations with others in terms of the self.

The film was nominated for the Independent Spirit Awards—often described as the Oscars of independent cinema—in two categories: Best Picture (the Cassavetes Award) and Best Supporting Actress (for Jacqueline Kim).[18] The gorgeous *Charlotte Sometimes* also enjoys high regard as the first film shot on DV to be converted to 35 mm—an innovation that has benefited the industry as a whole. The film toured universities and has enjoyed wide educational and home distribution as well as journalistic coverage.[19] As I quote above, Eric Byler presents the premise of the film to be the coming together of Asian American women (who grow up encouraged to act hypersexually) and Asian American men (who are told to act asexually). These men and women meet in a particular exploration of how race, sexuality, and desire converge in erotic romance where Asian American men and women occupy roles that represent the binary poles of their sexualities. The Asian American man relates to characters who are actually sisters, Lori and Darcy/Charlotte (the mysterious newcomer), and enters a rivalry with Justin, who represents the threat of another masculinity in the commingling of white and Asian sexualities in one hapa body.

I map the intimate relations as entanglements that identify the vision of ethical relationality this film advocates. While it frames Asian American race and sex as gendered experiences, the film concludes with the aggression of men and the madness of women in the formulation of character and the definition of the self in relation to others—especially as they engage in sex and other intimate acts on screen. In *Time and the Other*, Levinas poses that "to say the sexual duality presupposes a whole is to posit in advance love as fusion. The pathos of love consists to the contrary, in an insurmountable duality of beings; it is a relationship with what forever slips away."[20] That is, we cannot have certainty of the other, but we may acknowledge the other's betrayal and loyalty when we experience existence side by side or when we experience life's events, whether painful or joyous.

What I find useful in evaluating the gendered experiences of race and racism is Levinas's conception of intimate relations not as fusion and convergence but as of the face-to-face. At the moment of intimate encounter, we recognize each other as apart from the self. In *Charlotte Sometimes*, Michael attempts to formulate an ethical manhood in the face of lies. When learning the facts of others' actions, he does not abandon them but attempts to reach out to them so as to register his feelings and perhaps forge a coexistence. In his encounters with others, secrets are revealed. And though his secrets are not fully revealed, we do see a concern for others that is of importance to his self. However, this is rendered problematically, as weak and asexual in Michael and strong and hypersexual in Justin.

Despite the binary formulation of male and female characters within the repressed/liberated sexuality divide, the film commits to these characters by taking the time and space to tell their stories vis-à-vis their attachments to others and their own relationship to aloneness. In deft movements that utilize production design, camera movement, and performance, the first act of the film establishes a strange love triangle between the two men and one woman—an Asian American man, an Asian American woman, and a biracial hapa man. Their racial identities matter because the social context of their lives shapes their relationships.

The first sex scene unfolds in a way that shows the architecture and space where these relationships transpire. A duplex sits on a hill along a narrow and curved street. The double garage doors open together, although the stalls are separate. Parking his beat-up car, Michael goes upstairs to a space full of books to sit and read after a long day of work. He sits on a towel so his mechanic's uniform won't stain his couch. Already we see his meticulousness and neatness in a set design that captures the mid-20s age of haphazard arrangement of space in the small apartment with fabrics and screens delineating rooms. His care of space allows for a welcoming of others despite his predilection for solitude. Soon, coming into the same garage, Justin enters the downstairs door and takes off his suit, while Lori lies flat under the covers. Justin acknowledges her only at the very last moment when he pulls off the sheets to reveal her naked; he gets on top of her as she squeals with thrill. As Michael's quiet time is interrupted by their pleasure-making, we come to understand their proximity within the house, now split into two: one for Lori and her boyfriend and the other for Michael. To avoid hearing Lori and her boyfriend breathe, pant, and moan with intensity, Michael leaves for the neighborhood bar, which welcomes him warmly. First the waitress flirts with him and then the bartender approaches with a hearty hand-slapping greeting. He settles into his urban, contemporary American club crowded with other young people, while a notable African American singer performs. It is this club that situates Michael in a cosmopolitan Los Angeles where he—attractive, brooding, quiet—makes a home, both alone and among others with whom he shares feelings of attraction, familiarity, or neighborly kindness. It is also the place where he meets a stranger who transforms his relationships and threatens the comforts of his everyday rituals.

Evaluating intimate relations in terms of the face-to-face, the work of speech and the power of touch enhances understanding of the couplings in the film. The face, for actors, is an expressive tool. Levinas discusses it as "straightaway ethical," for it is the face that prevents us from killing the other, or at least makes it difficult.[21] He says "the skin of the face is that which stays most naked, most destitute. . . . There is an essential poverty in the face. The proof of this is that one tries to mask this poverty by putting on poses, by taking on a countenance."[22] For an actor to use the face is to lay bare, "without defense" the character's emotions and responses to others. The face "exposes" the self in certain moments in its small expressions. The work of speech in the film can be understood by distinguishing between the saying (actual speech) and the said (bodily and facial performances). The saying are the words spoken. The said is the "excess"[23] or everything else that speaks, including intonation, the tilt of the head, or fingers touching the other's skin as words are spoken or not. In Levinas, the said is preceded by saying, wherein "saying opens me to the other . . . before saying what is said, before the said uttered . . . forms a screen between me and the other. A saying without words, but not with empty hands. . . . If silence speaks . . . saying bears witness to the other of the Infinite . . . which in the Saying awakens me."[24] Thus here, I describe instances where face-to-face encounters epitomize a declaration of responsibility for the other, which touch attempts to bridge, and speech may rip and rend. This is how I approach *Charlotte Sometimes* and the representation of Asian American men and women in romantic love as a technology of ethical life.

On the night we meet them, Lori and Justin lie awake after energetic sex that nevertheless does not end with the lovers coming together face-to-face. She gets up and goes to the nearby bathroom, then wordlessly goes upstairs. However, she does give Justin a judgmental look. Justin, though awake, remains silent. He looks at her, waiting. But she goes elsewhere for companionship—which must hurt him. She walks upstairs—an assertion of desire and need, walking up the red stairs between the apartments and knocks on the door. In the time Michael takes to open the door there is a pregnancy of possibility; just by virtue of his lingering for unnecessary seconds in his kitchen, we realize he understands the difficulty of opening the door and the implications of letting her in.

When Lori does come in, she glides her body across Michael's unmoving stance. She's palpably thrilled to come inside, with a beaming smile directed at him. But they also never achieve the face-to-face encounter, despite the heat they generate in each other's presence. They avoid looking directly at each other at the same time; yet their shoulders rub in a form of bodily speech that articulates desire. They settle on the couch to watch anime long into the night; she drapes her legs over him as her face finds a home in his chest. Her body's movements comprise the said. Yet no saying occurs. They avoid each other's gazes, never achieving the face-to-face encounter where emotions spill out and confess with the nakedness of their expressions. Instead, they continue not to comment—on his desire for her, and her pretense of not noticing it, especially as the one who enters this relation as already recently, and loudly, sexually sated. With Justin, she does not enjoy a full-force face-to-face acknowledgment of the self in their romance though he tries. After sex, he grips at her shoulders and arms as she looks at then looks away from him. She flees from him as if repulsed by his inability to express in speech what sex does not.

I focus on the face-to-face encounter, the work of speech, and the power of touch so as to home in on what comprises their relation. Downstairs, in the morning, Justin wears only pants, revealing a muscular and athletic body. As he brushes his teeth, he realizes Lori did not come home. Strangely, he changes first to his suit, and then goes upstairs with an impatience that shows in his gait and tone. Apologetic in her murmurs, Lori chases him down like a puppy, hopping behind him with questions as he rushes off to work. Justin obviously disapproves of her emotional infidelity while Michael resents his physical deprivation. Michael finds his own bed when he gets up from the sofa where she slept on him. We then see Lori in her own bed. Each alone, with naked face of doubt, desire, and confusion, trapped in this vexed triangle.

In the next scene, we see Lori rehearsing her lines for "a lesbian movie"— she practices her inflections and tone by saying something in different ways. She then goes to see Michael at work, where we see them interact with an enormous expression of emotions left unsaid in speech but spoken loudly through their bodies and faces. Here, Lori and Michael enjoy coming together. Dressed in light-colored jeans and a pink top, she waves her long hair about her body as she walks to the car shop. He is on his break, sitting in a beat-up car. She joins him in the car and plays with her hair, which frames her carefully made-up face as she gazes at him coyly. Michael, on the verge of confronting his feelings for her, immediately asks about Justin, "Was he mad?" He continues to face away from her. She can't stand his questioning, so she looks ahead—away from his face—then glances at him, then looks down. Her little utterance of "He knows we're just friends" is accompanied by a wary look back, which Michael does not notice though he winces. In this meeting, we discover they do not acknowledge their feelings for each other—they avoid an intimate confrontation. Yet, the expression of discomfort on their faces—which only we see since they are turned away from each other—expresses their acknowledgment of the odd dynamics of their strange and awkward relationship of postcoital, emotional intimacy without sex. She asks if he would agree to getting fixed up with a date—an idea he resists by saying "I'm not afraid to be alone." She responds by saying she knows it, as if telling him that indeed, she recognizes him.

Alone means not touching others. In togetherness, touch attempts to reach out of aloneness. In *Charlotte Sometimes*, sex functions as what Michael will call "a short cut" in which he does not want to participate. He and the new love interest Darcy/Charlotte decide they will avoid short cuts and instead find other ways of getting to know each other. Lori and Justin, however, achieve validation of existence via intense penetration. Justin's vigorous assertions that make use of his entire body weight over her during intercourse confirm his physicality and hers. Confirmed in physical terms also is the emotional distance between two subjects even during sex. That is, despite penetration as an intimate coming together of two bodies that may lead to orgasm—or a physical undoing of the body's coherence—a long distance may persist. Psyches and emotions may not meet, despite physical meeting, as in the case of Lori and Justin.

In a combination of aloneness and togetherness, when we see Justin and Lori in sex, we see Michael alone in a harsh isolation. The next time we see the strong sexual coming together of Justin's smothering Lori with his entire body weight, Michael must leave his house again. He returns, however, so as to confront the force that compels his flight. Alone in his apartment, he approaches the wall on the other side of which Justin and Lori have sex. He touches the wall with his palms as if to touch her—or be part of them or attempt to see them. However, we are the ones who see the couple engage and plunge through touch into each other in the intercutting. The entrenchment of her repeated sex with Justin—followed by a hunger for fully clothed intimacy with Michael—disturbs him, but he can't stop letting her into his home and heart. In this scene, no words are spoken but the power of touch on the wall comes through in the overwhelming emotions that rush into him. In Michael's performance, we are told by the director, the actor punched a hole in the wall. As part of directing his character, or to drive home the shame of his character's castration, Byler directs Michael to fix the hole and films him doing so.

Later that night, Lori knocks on Michael's door. Unlike the first time she knocks, he waits much longer than a few seconds. It seems as if he really won't answer. He's already in bed and has turned off the light. She gives up, walks all the way down the red stairs, but then when she hits the bottom, his door opens. She turns to face him across the distance, to run up. Their ritual of bodies close and faces not facing each other resumes. During Lori and Michael's cuddling, we see his pent-up rage as he barely keeps himself contained. The phallic structure of the story is revealed here—he is a eunuch-in-waiting for her. As one who is desired, she castrates Michael with her friendship, which here is the extraction of emotional companionship after her sexual needs are satiated by another. She feels his discomfort. Unlike Michael, she reveals it in her eyes but she won't address it either. She is constructed here as the one with the power to subjugate Michael by refusing to fulfill his desire. It is the framework of speech that helps us comprehend what is happening, for he will never speak of his desire and she will not acknowledge her knowing. Between Lori and Justin, however, a bodily expression of desire takes stage as does a judgment against her for wielding her power over Michael, which he suffers in silence.

The next morning, while Michael is doing his usual chores around the house, Justin decides to use his electric toothbrush to sexually arouse the sleeping Lori under the sheets. Both the hapa man and the Asian American woman embody sexual vigor in contrast to the Asian American man's sexual stupor. She awakens to a mutual bodily hunger for consumption that ignites upon sight of Justin. From the window where Michael passes earlier, we see Justin swivel his hips as he kneels before her face against the bedroom wall. A telephone call from Lori's mother, who is insistent on talking about someone named Charlotte, interrupts the scene. As Lori speaks with her mother, Justin calls his mother. Talking to both their mothers on the phone, they also face away from each other. What is said is a simultaneous dismissal of their mothers—they don't seem to understand them. Despite the intensity of their sexual encounters, here we see two who do not connect with each other.

In this scene we also see that what binds both men is the wound of strait-jacket sexuality, which Lori heals with her body in the form of sexual touch. While Lori opens physically to Justin, she closes emotionally. We see Lori engage with Justin wholly in physical, sexual terms. And Justin meanwhile cares for her outside of sex in the power of his looks to her, and his physical positioning of hugging her as she turns away. It is an action that begs for her to face him—as if he's pulling her from the back—but she won't do it. Before the blow job she initiates, Justin expresses care for her, though brusquely, telling her to get up and get dressed so he can take her out. Through fellatio, Lori invites him to consume her—expressing the enjoyment of flirtation and sex. But she won't meet his needs emotionally—she teases him with it and withholds the face-to-face.

In the next sex scene, Lori's acts petulantly, demanding Justin's loyalty despite her refusal to meet his emotional needs. She teases him and again initiates a sexual encounter. As they move from one position to the other, she insists over and over again that he tell her he loves her; finally, succumbs in his "Yes." Moving on to another position where she's lying down and he looms over different parts of her, he asks, as her sexual ecstasy escalates, for her to say instead that she hates him—for this is what she speaks when she leaves him after sex. The saying of the body is not enough for her—she demands he say he loves her in order to humiliate him. In this struggle of the saying and the said, the couple becomes completely exhausted. Side by side, they face up and away from each other. Her face expresses distress as he repeatedly asks if she's okay, his concern earnest. At first she shakes her head no, then turns away to say yes, she's okay. He looks to her face, wanting clarification, but won't ask for it. She gets up to close herself in the bathroom, looking at herself in the mirror. We don't know why she's at an impasse; something about the sexual experience and the exchange moves her. The reasons are plentiful: she cannot achieve emotional connection with him. She experiences emptiness from the physicality of sex with a man she won't open up to emotionally, though she punishes herself for it. She cannot confess the content of her psychic trauma to Justin, although it is their physical experience together that leads her there. In this way, she won't disclose herself to him in the sex act and instead flees to Michael, the repository of her intimacy. But this time, he's with someone else and won't let her in. This film unabashedly confronts the language of sex and what it can achieve for the forging of Asian American manhoods.

Earlier that night, Michael notices someone at the bar—whether it's her pose, dressed all in black and legs crossed in a strong diagonal, her super-chiseled chin and her high cheekbones—whatever it may be, she stuns him. A different saying and said occurs here in how the face, speech, and the body are utilized in ways unlike Justin and Lori's dynamics. She catches his gaze, he turns away. Then he looks at her, which she returns in an invit-ing way, expressing curiosity. At this concentrated and forceful moment, he suddenly leaves. He goes home to stare at Lori's window, then closes the ga-rage to return to the bar. Upon his return, he finds the compelling woman at the door, and is taken aback by her strong and deep look at him—and again he retreats. But then, he turns around, finally admitting that she's why he returned. He stands upright, with discomfort, his face indicating how very hard he is working to reach out for her. He asks her out to eat, but she, in a calm voice and with a look of awareness—acknowledging his discom-fort with himself—suggests a walk, to which he responds with a nodding silence. She gives him the okay to come along with a movement of her head. Here, in his passivity and her aggressiveness, we see the characters confront social ideas about their race and sexuality in their everyday lives. That is, Michael will not speak out and assert his desires, while the woman in his life copes with the desires projected upon her. This personal and intimate en-gagement of these social roles shows us a main character who learns to care for himself in a way that disciplines the woman to follow his lead.

The face-to-face Darcy, the woman Michael meets in the bar, compels him to action—to go outside of himself and his usual self-containment. Judith Butler describes the other's power to undo one's self: "It may be . . . that despite one's efforts, one is undone, in the face of the other, by the touch, by the scent, by the feel, by the prospect of the touch, by the memory of the feel."[25] At the bar, across a crowded and loud room, Michael notices Darcy and she him to the extent that they begin to openly stare at each other. The intensity of the look increases so that he or she must rise up, but he looks away. Michael, as Darcy looks to him in an acknowledgment of a mu-tual stare that declares desire for the other, instead not only looks away but leaves. In the opportunity to rise to the other's openness, he fails, as Justin fails Lori. In how we respond to the presence of the other before us, our histories and desires are revealed. In this case, both Asian American men are unable to express what they need. Butler continues, "And so when we speak about my sexuality, or my gender, as we do (as we must) we mean something complicated by it."[26] The other compels one's histories and in the encounter presents an opportunity to undo one's past and remake the future in the present. Asian American men must, indeed, take the risk of expressing their vulnerability, as these men yet do not.

Later on, Michael reveals himself to Darcy—discloses his past in describing where he grew up and his everyday rituals around the house he owns. They peel at each other's histories—who are you and what leads you here to me. She reveals herself, even if she (Charlotte) uses a fake name (Darcy) to meet Michael. As she says, "I'd like to stay with you tonight but if I do . . ." her words are interrupted by Lori's knocking. Finally, it seems, Darcy's presence enables Michael to close the door on Lori. His coupling enables him to abandon the damaging ritual with her. Instead, he joins with Darcy, with whom he can connect emotionally and with whom he won't engage in bodily intimacy.

In the morning, as if sensing his loosening from her, Lori goes to Michael and drapes her body, breasts, breath, and hair all over him as an assertion of the possibilities of the said and what could still transpire between them. She playfully interrogates him about the woman in his house the night before, but does so by deploying sexually arousing tricks. What begins as a friendly conversation on his bed changes when she blows on his back with her mouth—which he must feel, not only the air but the puckering of her mouth and its movement toward his skin. He keeps putting his face down and off camera—trying to achieve some distance as if he's going to burst, confounded by her proximity. It seems as if his perceived success with another woman thrills her, yet compels her to remind him of intimacy with her—but which he cannot have despite her flirtations. They do not look at each other face-to-face. She looks at him, from the back, but he remains intent on reading the book he holds, looking away. He won't face her in case turning to do so will make him come undone. Lori, as Michael's original other, moves him so powerfully that he threatens to explode out of himself, but still he won't face her. Nor will he speak words, even if his body craves hers and takes pleasure in her nearness.

Individual meetings and encounters such as these between others occur within a sociality where racial misrecognition transpires everyday. At the bar, a white man sends Darcy a rose, ignoring Michael as her companion. Michael takes this as an affront to his manhood, but keeps quiet. Darcy senses his discomfort and initiates the action for them to leave together. He remains passive, she asserts and protects. On their walk home, Darcy bluntly speaks about her temporary status—she's here, then gone. When Darcy says she's not his type anyway since guys like her to be "cute, small and with a pretty little voice," Jacqueline Kim's performance reveals remarkable complexity—for the lines can be read as petulant and pouting, but she is matter of fact. The social assignations for Asian American women's hypersexuality find a place in their discussion. Michael poses a question: "Don't you notice how men always stare at you?" To this question about confronting her hypersexualization in everyday life as an Asian American woman, she replies: "The truth is, men don't want to be with me at all. They only think they do." If we recall Eric Byler's premise for the movie, then Darcy points to the fantasy of the hypersexual Asian woman who organizes others' perceptions of her. I appreciate this production of an Asian American woman who is not constructed as one who benefits from this sexual racialization, a misrecognition she has to confront everyday. Eric Byler says that Michael and Darcy share the fear of never being worth loving, so that really "when you think about it" they are the perfect pair. But what's imperfect and radically incompatible is the different ways they respond to their racial sexualization; she confronts it aggressively, while it weakens him.

In the apartment, as if fulfilling this script, Darcy initiates sexual intimacy by attempting to kiss Michael, while simultaneously warning him of her unavailability by saying, "I don't have any boyfriends in this city." They stand in the kitchen, measuring each other's responses. "Other cities?" he asks. She teases him with her response: "Those cities are very far away." In this scene, we have a truly straightforward face-to-face choreography unlike other moments in the film. And Michael and Darcy almost have sex, the kind she classifies as "simply fun [and for] tonight." Within their physical coming together in this scene, Darcy advances and Michael retreats, insisting "there are other ways to get to know someone." Darcy comes hither with "sex is faster." But Michael won't participate, asking instead for what she cannot give: time. They come to an agreement that sex simply provides a shortcut to getting to know each other and the pact is for them to disallow that sort of shortchanging. Instead, he hopes for intimacy and not simply sex. He would rather explore where they could end up rather than letting sex decide now. In this way, as Eric Byler says, Michael emerges as the hero for his high principles. Here sex becomes the privileged way of generating principles, particularly by not participating in it. Here, it is an ethical formation of manhood that's important in a world where sex is a litmus test. For Michael and Darcy in this scene, sex and the language of bodily intimacy and touch (the said) are not as desirable as the intimacy achieved through speaking (the saying)—what I consider a more ethical relationship.

What happens when the four characters come together, each with his or her own relationship to saying (in the sense of verbal speech that attempts to achieve intimacy) and the said (non-verbal speech that conveys desire for intimacy)? The next day, Darcy meets Justin, and we see a woman vying for the possibilities of two men. As the one who acts as the aggressor with Michael, she is intrigued by what could happen between herself and Justin, she being the one who tries to move away from the said of the body and Justin the one who dominates speaking through sex. Michael makes space for this to occur—as if he's confident in his intimacy with Darcy, or resigned to asexuality in the face of Justin's hybridity. In a shot that's a triptych of Darcy through the window on the left, with Justin, his back toward us, in the center, on the landing, and Michael at the open door on the right, the men gaze upon Darcy, who arranges to take them all out to lunch. The two couples come together at a restaurant where Darcy is as charismatic, charming, and aggressive as Lori is cute, cautious, and passive in her quiet self-embracing containment. Byler says he created binary characters for the women and the men. Here, Darcy taunts Justin and Lori—asking Justin about what part of him is Asian and daring Lori to reveal they are sisters. Lori is frustrated. Here we don't see her deploy her usual beaming smile but instead she glares at Darcy, demanding she come to the restroom, where she confronts her and reveals her identity as the one she was going to fix up with Michael. The actress Eugenia Yuan, who played Lori, describes how Lori did not bow down to Charlotte/Darcy in each of their interactions. In their face-to-face encounters, she exudes power in her violent stare at Darcy. Each woman is familiar with the other but ultimately they do not know each other, even as sisters who see the other in themselves. At a barbeque on the rooftop, Lori warns Darcy, "Stay away from Justin, he might be the one for me. I might marry him." And, "He's like a brother to me, Michael. Please just keep it real." Darcy's response is that Lori must regard her as totally monstrous. In these speeches, Lori expresses distrust of Darcy. And Darcy later explains that while she did not accept Lori's invitation to the barbeque, she came to see how she lived anyway, out of interest and curiosity about her sister.

Critics celebrate Jacqueline Kim's performance as the "sparkplug" of the movie. The filmmaker Greg Pak characterizes her as "sexually destructive."[27] Others describe the cast as comprising "extremely familiar types: you've got the introverted Asian dude, the cutesy Asian girl, the acerbic sexually aggressive dragon lady, and the corporate tool."[28] Eric Byler describes his directing as "the Byler technique," where actors don't know each other's motivations. He aspires for them to listen and to respond, as if they are not being photographed. As a director, Byler hopes to capture an actor realizing the meaning of the line for the first time as the take is shot. The scene he uses as an example is Darcy's taunting of Justin regarding his biracial background—"Did your mother teach you to use chopsticks?" Matt Westmore, as Justin, responds well: "Actually, I don't remember learning," which to Byler, himself hapa, means "all of me is Asian."[29] In the next scene, Darcy offers herself to Michael, inviting him to travel with her. But he's distracted by Lori's giggling; he won't go with Darcy not because he's a good nephew, mechanic, or landlord. He won't leave the one he loves, despite her lack of availability. Darcy recognizes this and departs, which humiliates Michael in the face of the others, according to Byler. But here, humiliating Michael is actually Darcy's way of defending herself—to hold her subjectivity intact in the face of his distance.

In the next scene we see Lori and Justin in bed, and once again we witness the failure of the relationship in their lack of face-to-face togetherness. When Justin refuses to go with Lori on vacation, she screams at him, exploding with her repressed emotions. We are forewarned as we see her weeping in the bathroom after their last sex act. She's devastated and screaming at him: "Do you know what you are, you're a user!" This scene indicates that she does not tell him everything. Yet soon enough, they revert to entanglement in their sexual rituals as he returns to bed, touching her. She's gleeful when they do in fact go to Monterey together. Their absence then enables Michael to discover Lori and Darcy's secret.

Now it's Michael knocking on Lori's door, oddly suspicious. He opens it in search of something and finds childhood photographs of Lori with a sister. We begin to understand Darcy and Lori's relationship. The double love triangles—Lori-Michael-Justin and Darcy-Michael-Justin—collapse when Michael discovers the sisterly relationship. Two results: the first, violence between Darcy and Michael, and the second, shattering of the self in the sex act, with us, the audience, unsure of what assembly and reassembly of self might be possible for Darcy and Justin—what I consider the more promising action in the film.

The threat of violent sex comes between Michael and Darcy. Upon discovering Darcy's identity as Lori's sister, Michael welcomes Darcy to his home and cooks her dinner. He moves toward her aggressively, grabbing at her neck to kiss her as if thirsty. She's stunned by his force. He declares that he's changed his mind about disavowing sex. He breaks the no "short cuts" bargain and after a long hug that indicates their intimate knowledge, he attempts to kiss her. Her complaints of "Michael, Michael, stop" continues with a looking for clarification of his changed behavior. She says "Michael, it's not the right time." With frustration, he retorts, "last week it was." The violent potential behind his quiet demeanor of his actually causing her psychic harm and material pain is frightening. Still attempting to make sense of what's transpiring between them outside of their understanding, she asks: "You want to make love to me?" His angry rejoinder confounds deeply: "I want to fuck you. Fuck you so hard you scream." What's frightening about him here is that he never speaks out, and when he finally does, he says this—unleashing all this male aggression as a form of punishment for her deception. She says "Stop"—a rightful demand. If ethics are the ability to make decisions that are good for oneself and others, his declaration to "fuck" her are bad ethics. He wants to discipline her for castrating him through deception. Upon his failed attempt at sex with Darcy, Michael discloses his knowledge of her: "I know you," a brutal declaration considering his intent to fuck her so as to punish her. She begins to apologize for her performance: "It does not mean . . . please know that I . . ." but he cuts her off, hatefully.

In the next scene, it is dawn and Darcy is at the neighborhood bakery, where she runs into Justin. He blocks her from leaving and tells her to let her cab go so he can take her instead. A change in her stance occurs; at this moment, she seems to accept his perception of her, following her previously "unwise" choices. Is it that she agrees to his recognition of her as sexually available? They drive on desolate roads. At a motel, their sexual encounter is a full revelation, as much as possible, of the self—and for both. Eric Byler describes the sex scene as an event he built with the characters for a long time.

> I never rehearsed Matt and Jacqueline beyond seeing them together at auditions. I knew right away I had the chemistry I was looking for—and because so much of it depended on strangers discovering one another, I tried

to separate them and even instructed Matt not to socialize with Jacqueline during production. Jacqueline later said she had the impression that Matt didn't like her, which served her well in scenes with him, because she was all the more guarded, all the more insecure, and all the more aggressive.[30]

"Insecure" as a word choice is revealing—with Michael she is aggressive, but with Justin she becomes less certain.

Why does the character choose to have sex with Justin—to disclose herself in sex—but not with Michael? Unlike Lori, whom we know enjoys sex, here Darcy weeps as Justin fucks her with the vigor he demonstrates in earlier scenes of sex. He is moved by her, however, grasping for her as she faces away. He behaves this way with Lori as well—sex opens up the space between him and a woman, but he does not know how to act at that moment. Here he attempts to connect with Darcy—for she's actually speaking verbally about what it means as they are having sex—unlike Lori, who simply vanishes upstairs to find intimacy with another after he gives himself to her. Justin shows vulnerability and strength in sex—he speaks through a powerful sexual penetration that attempts to overwhelm the woman with his body, but the sex act opens him to her as well. It's as if this is how he knows to speak—through the racialization of the sexualized hapa. Darcy

FIGURE 15   Charlotte speaks to Justin of the devastating and painful power of sex. *Charlotte Sometimes.* Dir. Eric Byler. Arts Alliance America, 2002.

whispers as we see her face beneath his: "It does not wait anymore, it does not wait till afterwards. I feel it as I am coming. Loneliness, disgust. I wish I did not have to do this." She talks about the attempt to achieve intimacy through sex that always fails the promise of the power of touch. That is, the attribution of hypersexuality leads to sex and it never satisfies—and in its nakedness the attempt to connect out of aloneness becomes ugly. This explains why she has to do it; but why with this man?

While whom we partner with may be expected or surprising and could go in a different direction despite our tastes, Jacqueline Kim makes the observation that sometimes people have sex with those they believe are not the one. Is it because at least Justin speaks, even in flat, monotonous physical terms? Or is it that he's not a potential rapist/stalker but just a brooding, silent guy who aggressively touched her? Unlike Michael, Justin is not full of pent-up, displaced, frightening rage. He actually expresses desire and lets it speak out of his body. If sex is a way to reach others, to move oneself out of the body into ecstasy so that one nears death and evacuates the self through orgasm—exposing the past, present, and future—what transpires between Darcy and Justin is meaningful.

After Lori finds out about Darcy and Justin, she packs up Justin's things and he leaves. The force of sexuality binds her to Justin but does not connect them. On the contrary, when Michael and Lori finally discuss their relationship, it's as if they've survived a war. Lori pathologizes Darcy as a liar, which Michael won't agree with. What is it about the other that makes us unravel? Lori asks for Michael's forgiveness, which leads them to finally achieve a face-to-face encounter. Michael looms over her, and she expresses surprise at his decisiveness, finally looking upon and touching his face. They begin to kiss in a new face-to-face encounter that they've never experienced before. Their mouths and bodies move toward a kiss that we don't actually see but likely happens as the last frame shows her with mouth open and his lips almost covering hers. The Asian American man, patriarchal, and psychotically silent and passive, finally gets the cute and coy girl. While Lori participates in duping Michael, he understands her as victimized by her sister. Meanwhile, the hapa man and the woman made deranged and schizophrenic are gone.

In making films like this, Asian American filmmakers venture to formulate viable manhoods for Asian Americans. But rather than the main character, Michael, and the lead, Lori, following a more ethical path, it is the characters Darcy and Justin who instead embark on the road of unknown questions opened by sex and intimacy. I'd rather go with them than continue with the formation of this heteronormative coupling between a repressed man and manipulative woman. Within the romance of missteps that keep heroes apart, figures like Darcy and Justin are usually distractions—she seduces the hero with her body and wiles, and he is nothing but an aggressor toward the heroine—both are totalized identities that try to achieve a fixed destination of happily ever after. In *Charlotte Sometimes*, the central roles are the weaker yet more conventionally gendered man and woman. The hero of Justin and heroine of Darcy are stronger characters when they confront their socializations and their desires with the risk of going toward the unknown—so that they remain more actively engaged in the process and search for betterment.

To use Levinas's terms, Darcy and Justin pursue infinity while Lori and Michael struggle to maintain the self and their coupling as a totality. The former two seek love as a continual shifting while the latter move toward love as assigned roles. What I mean is that Darcy and Justin are both moved by each other in terms of "an awakening to proximity [and] responsibility to the neighbor"[31] in each other's presence. Levinas describes proximity as "irreducible to consciousness . . . a relationship with what cannot be resolved into 'images' and exposed. It is a relationship not with what is inordinate . . . but . . . commensurable with it . . . frustrating any schematism."[32] Proximity in the film is the capacity to become undone in the presence of the other; something about the other captures the self so that one feels responsible to and for the other. This occurs in the scene of romantic love. Romance indeed opens up possibilities for social transformation and also functions as an opportunity for keeping us entrenched in further edifying inequality, especially between Asian American men and women. The two films studied in this chapter so far star the Asian American couple who strives for normalcy in their coupling where the man is strong and the woman needs him to be.

Eric Byler declares his commitment to the complexity of Asian American cinemas in his statement that "neither race nor gender is the key to understanding" *Charlotte Sometimes*. He intends to make the film "as complex and ambiguous as life itself."[33] While Byler argues that race, gender, and sex are complex and ambiguous and part of what makes cinema great, here he privileges what he calls the "personal and artistic" versus "cultural or diversity training." Hence, he privileges film and performance, which fall away when the focus is on platforms of proper political representation—that is, when the performance is judged on whether it meets the standards of proper political representation. In the commentary accompanying the film, Byler describes how in his directing he forgot about ethnicity and instead focused on the human. He defines politics against art—as if the ethnic and racial experience is not always political and as if the political is not complex beyond diatribe. Rather than continue with this binary between race and politics, we must recognize that film has the capacity to show the drama of the political in ways that even the director cannot control.

An online controversy erupted around the racial authorship of *Charlotte Sometimes*—specifically surrounding the sexuality of the Asian American man and the biracial Asian American man. Byler's interlocutors refused to acknowledge his biracialness, classifying his perspective as inauthentic and, moreover, white, and thus reestablishing for the new generation the asexuality of Asian American men.[34] Byler calls this a problematic judgment by patriarchal Asian American men who prefer to solve Asian American male sexual problems in representation with counter-images such as an "Asian super man having sex with eight girls at a time."[35] Thus, Byler understands this problem and in the making of the film successfully addresses sex in its gendered and racial complexity—as differing for men and women.

In the *Film Journal*, Byler speaks about leaving the room for all the sex scenes except one—allowing for the actors, armed with their motivations, to perform. He also describes putting the actors in charge of their rehearsals and allowing them to keep secrets from the director.[36] He did this so as to place himself at the level of the viewer, who knows little about the characters except what transpires on the screen. The faith Byler has in the power of actors to make sense of their roles and the events they need to experience produces revelatory acting. The sex scenes in particular, which I describe as precoital and postcoital, as well as the actual engulfing of bodies, are unlike the "short cut" the film describes in getting to know people. Sexual encounters are engagements with the other that have the potential to move you to ecstasy, kill you with pain, free you with joy—and explode your self out of the body.

Better Luck Tomorrow (2003)

Better Luck Tomorrow launched the Hollywood directing career of Justin Lin, who has since made a big-budget action film, and directed three films in the big-budget, high-grossing and global hit series *The Fast and the Furious* (2006,

2009, and 2011), as well as independent Asian American films, including *Finishing the Game: The Search for a New Bruce Lee* (2007). In each of his films, masculinity and manhood persist as themes and *Better Luck Tomorrow* in particular offers a critique of form as well as content. It's for "Asian reasons" that Justin Lin counters the Hollywood film depiction of Asian Americans and instead in *Better Luck Tomorrow* develops a multiplicity of characters that show a range of possibilities for Asian American men.[37] In terms of love, sex, and desire, *Better Luck Tomorrow* depicts a rivalry between men for a woman who is not only beautiful but also complex: Stephanie, the cheerleader and adoptee in a white family who wants to be a cop, does her own homework, and may or may not be a porn star. While the structure of the male rivalry persists, she is a partner whose desirability is rich and unconventional. The chance that she may be a porn star points to the projection of hypersexual fantasy upon Asian American women. But the film does not condemn her, for she may also be an empowered sexual woman when we combine that identity with her other qualities. Unlike *The Debut* and *Charlotte Sometimes*, *Better Luck Tomorrow* does not celebrate the heteronormative couple but instead presents two subjects who are unreliable and untrustworthy even as they seek each other's proximity such as in the kiss where they do not see each other's faces.

Individual and group identity for men is at the fore of the story in *Better Luck Tomorrow*. In suburban Orange County, a multiethnic group of high school age Asian American boys manage to get excellent grades while pursuing a range of financially lucrative criminal activities. Their activities culminate in the murder of Steve, the lead character Ben's competition for the female love interest, Stephanie. While the young men look individually unraveled in the yearbook pictures closing the movie, Ben and Stephanie drive away in her convertible.

The young men in this movie seek a viable manhood for themselves beyond their Ivy League–bound futures and the daily experience with racism and gendered racism. In the hallways of their school, particularly in sports, Asian Americans don't compete. The lead character, Ben, works to join the basketball team but spends the season on the bench. His new friend Daric, the class president and school paper editor as well an Asian American man, writes a front-page article for the school paper protesting the tokenization of Ben as the only Asian on the team—and doesn't get to play. Ben resents the attention for he lives quietly and intensely—working on building his SAT vocabulary words and diligently feeding his fish. Daric entices him to

FIGURE 16   After killing Steve, Ben kisses Stephanie at the party. *Better Luck Tomorrow*. Dir. Justin Lin. MTV Films, 2003.

a life of hustling cheat-sheets at first, then consuming prostitutes while on an Academic Decathlon trip to Las Vegas and finally, descending into drugs, guns, and murder.

Ben's quiet way is exemplified in his silent pining away for his lab partner Stephanie, whose slave he wishes to be—offering to do all the work and helping her make signs for her student body election campaign. She's tough—wants to do the work herself and finds in Ben a safe friendship, which irritates him considering his competition with her boyfriend, the more handsome, richer, and much cooler BMW-driving Steve, also Asian American and also competitive in college admissions terms. Worse, however, Ben thinks he discovers Steve cheating on Stephanie with an Academic Decathlon teammate, a white girl. Steve asks Ben to take Stephanie to a dance, where they slow dance, but when he is about to profess his love, Steve awaits in the parking lot, standing coolly by his BMW. In effect, Steve castrates Ben and rewards himself with Stephanie without entertaining her or courting her in the dance. In the competition for the woman, the clash between two forms of masculinity, one passive and the other aggressive, is resolved through violence when Ben kills Steve. Ben's achieving the prize of the woman in driving away with Stephanie results from his deliberate act of masculine aggression.

So it is through unrequited desire and competition for love that once again male rivalry for a woman structures the narrative. Racial problems emerge as masculine—Ben fights the role of the castrated man. In the scenes discussed above, we see Ben, who's short and a distance away from hegemonic masculine beauty, competing with a wealthier, taller, and better looking fellow Asian American man. Ben warms up to Stephanie, but Steve reaps the rewards. When helping her with the poster by working side by side, Ben is substituted when Steve picks Stephanie up on his scooter and they drive away with their fit bodies tightly entwined. They leave Ben on the sidewalk looking at their beautiful physical convergence with yearning.

Privileging the phallus and the penis in this story leads to Ben's body functioning as a loaded gun that explodes in the act of killing the other who reaped the rewards of his romantic work. Desire undoes him: he uses his explosive rage to justify his killing of Steve, whom he considers slighted him in the worst sense—by denying him his pleasure. This leads to such psychic pain and injury that in Ben's eyes murder becomes the only way to achieve relief and access literal and symbolic power in social life where women are the prize. Here, the heroic Asian American man is unethical in his acts of murder and cheating but it is not a subjectivity without consequences. The film ends with a series of yearbook photographs where the men look damaged. Their lives are in complete upheaval.

In the final scene, Stephanie is driving her new Audi convertible to pick up Ben on the street. They are mysteries to each other still. They look to each other, but neither is entirely forthcoming. Ben feels guilty for lying to Stephanie—in not disclosing his knowledge of Steve's whereabouts. But she's going her own way. She's determined to get out of her situation, and men don't matter—whether Steve or Ben, she will leave this place and become a cop. The film may continue so she catches him, later in life. She kisses Ben, the model minority gone awry, the eunuch turned hyper-phallus who emerges damaged. And we don't know if she knows or ultimately cares about him.

Justin Lin's myth-making in this film includes Asian American men who claim aggression and rage—in the face of their violation as men. This is not a refusal of ethics but the dramatization of the real consequences of aggression. To reach for phallic power to remedy the wound of asexuality and effeminacy will kill you as a consequence of hurting others.

FIGURE 17   Still mysteries to each other, the two protagonists ready to drive off screen. *Better Luck Tomorrow*. Dir. Justin Lin. MTV Films, 2003.

Ben claims a narcissism that Asian American men presumably deserve to possess—a renegade manhood that poses a menace to society as he drives off with an unknowing and unknowable woman whose dead boyfriend she keeps calling on his cell phone. Within the context of Asian American male castration in the cinema, we have an artful rage in this film. It's a manhood that claims subjectivity outside available ones, commenting on the violence of the limited choices available to Asian American men with a device that's open-ended and promising.

Better Luck Tomorrow ultimately presents a Long Duk Dong strategy of outdoing the craziness of the interpellation of Asian American men. *Better Luck Tomorrow* thus presents the infinity of Asian American manhood. I consider this move an important strategy to keep the subjectivities of Asian American men at the forefront of cinema-making. We don't know if Ben will turn on Stephanie, or she him. Unlike *The Debut*'s privileging of totality in the certainty of its desire to occupy heroic roles of heteronormative man and woman, or *Charlotte Sometimes*' privileging of the totalized couple, we have *Better Luck Tomorrow*'s suspicious leads driving into the distance with futures uncertain, like the uncoupled and critical subjectivities of Darcy and Justin. Meanwhile, the characters leave behind the wreckage of their hailing as hypersexual Asian American woman and eunuchoid Asian American man in a marvelous use of cinematic form.

In these films, men compete over women in a binary struggle and within this structure, they are engulfed in violent relations that ultimately dislodge the primacy of the phallus as the basis for gender hierarchy and sexual heteronormativity. They do so with the dynamic ways gender is imagined and sex presented. Cajayon, Byler, and Lin describe the contexts for the formations of their manhoods differently. Cajayon presents a competition for women in terms of Asian American masculinities racialized as either black or white, with women the terrain for establishing community and home. In *The Debut*, the love interest also demands a particular form of masculinity for her man and the sister polices him into returning to the community. Lin points to the castration of Asian American men by others and the female love interest remains a prize, despite her own suspicious subjectivity, for the demonstration of aggression. The woman indeed presents a complex identity herself—she may be the one to turn on him as she maintains toughness in her performance, a withholding of herself from the hero as well. Byler presents Justin, the mixed race Asian American, struggling with sexuality—he uses the language of fucking to speak intimately but cannot come up with the words to connect beyond sex. The hypersexual Asian American woman in Darcy/Charlotte attempts to find belonging outside of sex in the face of her hailing. For Michael, silence is a virtue but it is a pent-up rage that erupts in the form of sexual aggression as punishment of women. Lori, coy and manipulative, looks for a boss man to dominate her—as part of her desire.

The characters in the films discussed above represent positions that are part of a binary—the cute girl versus the threatening woman, the asexual Asian man and the sexually powerful hapa in *Charlotte Sometimes*; the thug versus the prep in *The Debut*; and the eunuch versus the womanizer in *Better Luck Tomorrow*. These characters allow us to identify the crises the filmmakers confront and how they resolve those crises with films that function as wishes for better realities that honor the complex and rich lived experiences of Asian American men. They want the Asian American guy to get the Asian American girl, they attempt to render women's sexuality with complexity, and they have their characters kill their rivals with their privileged and idealized manhoods—whether they are ethical or flagrantly not. What we see are the plentiful complexities of Asian American life and the fascinating ways men confront their sexual racializations. Both lack and macho are at the disposal of the Asian American male characters. And the Asian American women similarly confront these in their own expectations and perceptions. Both attempt to free Asian American men from the binary of competition for women as property and emblem of patriarchy so as to break out of the constraints of straitjacket sexuality. These characters provide us with a wealth of manhoods in between lack and macho.[38]

All of these filmmakers demonstrate a love for Asian American culture in taking seriously the complexity and bottomless wealth of a racialized experience as that which their films address. It is this, the ultimate description of filmmaking as a technology of ethics, that these filmmakers attempt. These filmmakers forge characters who, despite their flaws, sometimes succeed in caring for others. To achieve responsibility for the other becomes an ethical ideal. Levinas presents "responsibility as the essential, primary and fundamental structure of subjectivity. . . . I understand responsibility as responsibility for the Other. . . . To do something for the Other. To give. To be human spirit, that's it. . . . [The face of the Other] ordains me to serve him."[39] Here, the other puts into question one's own being and in romance, responsibility for the other becomes the basis of one's being. To be awakened by the other to care, beyond one's self, is to live a truly rich life.[40] In these filmmakers' focus on the larger community as that minefield of complexity and the risking of financial well-being in order to tell stories, they make a declaration of love, to awaken others, in their devotion to their cinematic work as technology of ethics.

In Conclusion: Cinema as a Technology of Ethics

Emmanuel Levinas argues that love is not the convergence of two but the face-to-face encounter of radical alterity. His theory of alterity posits the other as incomprehensible. In our encounter with the other, we attempt to cross the chasm that separates our non-consumptive relation. The focus on the individual in the present moment of facing the other includes our attempts through touch—whether physical, verbal, or psychic—to engage their difference and distance as that which we will never fully understand.[41] I study cinematic representations of the encounter between others as a moment where self and other relate and engage in their particular concreteness, knowing that in that present moment when the other stands before us, we can never fully comprehend one's separation, secrets, and histories. The best thing in the face of such seeming futility is to care, to arrive at a position of responsibility in our recognition of the other—it is precisely there to which we owe the possibility of our own self-understanding as well as a larger understanding of the world and the best way to live in it. In this way, we have a responsibility to the other. Rather than emphasizing a totalizing background, Levinas points to the importance of the situation in shaping how the subject arises. The situation is the moment when one meets the other who has the special potential, in his totality (the known) and infinity (the unknown), to put the whole self into question.

Cinema attends to such situations as scenes or actions that occur in set locations. In the writing of a film, a scene begins every time the actors enter a new location. In these spaces, encounters transpire in order to produce opportunities for identities to arise in response to the conditions and the actions the actors choose to perform within the situation.[42] For Levinas, "radical attention [is] given to the urgent preoccupations of the moment."[43] When filmmakers plan scenes or shoot them, they do not film ideas but attend to the concrete moment of bodies in spaces—adorned decisively and moving in ways that need measuring for focus and light—and made believable only with the actor's presence, so that representation and reality combine. Moreover, the actor's speech and the screenwriter's words matter. In this way, speech is a privileged mode of knowing another—it is, according to Levinas "the condition of any conscious grasp" of the other's being, making interlocution an attempt to bridge the distance between two subjectivities.[44] I pay attention, then, not only to the power of touch and the face-to-face interacting in the space between people as a crucial part of what is said between people, but also speech itself—what people say to each other in order to understand the other before them. In this way, we can see how the other reveals one's subjectivity and witness its transformation.

If characters remain the same, we cannot fully understand the other's power to discombobulate the self. In the encounter of romance that involves sex, love, desire, and erotics, cinema arrests a particular intensity of self-questioning brought on by the facticity of the other's distance and proximity. To accept how the other has power in unsettling the unity of the self is to bind oneself to the other—a choice that Levinas calls altruistic.[45] In that, when one chooses to fall for another, it becomes an investment not only in oneself but in a larger sociality as "a supporter of the Universe." This for Levinas is "happy" in the sense that when one invests in the other for the self, one gives up totality and absolute self-knowledge as a goal; however, in the infinity of the other lies the endless possibilities for one's own future as ever-changing and ever-growing. To embrace the confusion that the other compels in us is to understand the world in terms of the "idea of the infinite," where one's being is not unmoving but mutable.[46] This is where the power of film, not simply as an aesthetic enterprise but a teaching tool for ethical life, lies: its ability to prompt audiences to change their perceptions. And if political ecstasy happens, to use Kaja Silverman's term that describes the ability of cinema to move people, then this power is even more significant if it results in an ethical outcome: how to care for others and a larger society beyond one's own.

In studying the encounters between others in love, romance, and desire, we see the utility of social categories of gender, sex, and race. Films by Asian American men are stories about Asian American manhoods—told through courtship in terms of what it feels like to be an object looked upon as a source of love and desire for and by another. For a man or woman to take responsibility for another is to compose an ethics of personhood of the highest order because, ultimately, it is a feeling of responsibility for another whom one may not know at all or for whom one has preconceived notions supported by popular culture.[47] For Asian American men deprived of the romantic hero role in representation, the forming of subjectivity that does more than keep in thrall to self becomes an important goal in terms of what kind of manhood they can form. Rather than a hyper and brutish masculinity traditionally allocated to the white male hero in the romance, new objectives may form in the romantic relationship where Asian American men need affirmation and Asian American women share power.

In my analysis of these Asian American independent films, I am interested in the ethics of romance—or the process that makes way for love beyond mutuality between two others. In this context of mutuality, or making equally important each other's subjectivity, what emerges is the importance of accountability within a relation where various inequalities are at play.

Cinematic romance focuses on encounters between others who come together in recognition of dramatic alterity that invites, compels, or even requires them to analyze the situation of the other. Transformation occurs in the political power of interpretation when the viewer makes sense of the film's language: its speech, set design, and performances. For Levinas, as in the narrative cinema, the other is not an "empirical fact."[48] The other does not come with his or her meaning plainly written but comes to be an adventure, exploration, and mystery to dissect, navigate, and negotiate as one character learns about him or herself through the other. In this sense, my method of looking to the event and the subjectivities involved in the unraveling and possibilities of that relationship is to honor the complexity of the experience of inequality, social hierarchy, and resistance. Unlike filmmakers who say "I make films that forget ethnicity or gender or sex and simply tell the story," I point to the hierarchies of the world that inform our selves and acknowledge how actors and subjects relate in dynamic and dialectic relations to and with others.

A technology of ethics, then, is to create a worthwhile cinema through the power of the image and the power to imagine moving people to want to do the right thing for oneself and others. This is a good litmus test by which to evaluate the achievement of these films—especially in terms of forging an ethical manhood. We see the achievement in how we learn about manhood, race, and romance from the movies as a technology of ethics. Like Gedde Watanabe as Long Duk Dong, the characters and roles presented in these films are men dissatisfied with the imposition of Asian American male lack. Rather than simply escape their assignation of straitjacket sexuality, the characters portrayed acknowledge the impossibility of getting out of it entirely. What becomes important to their characters is the shifting of one's perspective in order to get out of the mode of suffering from straitjacket sexuality. They transcend the male malaise that droops like a bag to make Asian American men unsexy; they instead map out concrete new directions in establishing a calm and peace with oneself. I now move to the fraught sexualities expressed by Asian American men working in pornography and related genres so that I may confront the ways in which sex acts figure in the forging of ethical Asian American manhoods.

FOUR

Assembling Asian American Men in Pornography

Shattering the Self toward Ethical Manhoods

A malaise shackles recent cultural production about Asian American male sexuality, indicating its continuing status as fraught and unhinged. Unlike in the independent films discussed in the preceding chapter, lack rears its head to once again frame racialized sexuality for Asian American men in recent popular culture. Darrell Hamamoto's pornography projects *Skin on Skin* (2004) and *Yellowcaust* (2003) and its companion documentary, James Hou's *Masters of the Pillow* (2003), present an Asian American anxiety regarding castrated heterosexual manhood, which they propose to solve by paving access to phallic and penile power in pornography. While I believe pornography can be a viable site for the exploration and expression of sexuality, I am concerned with identifying problems of racialized sexuality in terms of the need to access heteronormative, heterosexist, and patriarchal masculinity. Darrell Hamamoto's figuration that fantasies about whiteness are indications of colonialism in the deepest parts of the racial self reflects a problematic view of sexuality as a tool for racial conquest and phallic power that needs to be usurped. Such an approach captures the qualitatively different position of Asian American men in terms of their power. In my first book, I argued for the necessity of politically productive perverse Asian American women or what Eve Oishi calls "bad Asians," who subvert the constraints of various forms of normativity.[1] The ethical dilemma Asian American men confront is that, in order to form male badness, they would

Parts of this chapter first appeared as an article in *Journal of Asian American Studies*, Volume 13, Issue 3, June 2010, pages 163–189. Copyright 2010 The Johns Hopkins University Press.

need to reject responsibility and ethics. Asian American men need to account for their differently gendered position in terms of their definitions and understandings of sexuality. Thankfully, other works of pornography by Asian American men define the scene of the racialized heterosexual sex act as sites for the engagement of fantasy that includes phallic power as a force to be wrangled with and undone rather than pursued and recovered.

As a genre doggedly focused on arousing physical pleasure, pornography provides an explicitness that differs from other depictions of sexuality, as it captures anxieties about the literal absence of the Asian American penis and its attendant lack of symbolic power in the phallus. Richard Fung's famous essay, "Looking for My Penis," argues that when we do see Asian American men in pornography, their frequent appearance as the "bottom" verifies an undesirable position indicative of their marginality. As I have shown in this book, heterosexual Asian American men attempt to redress their absence on screen as part of a larger problem of straitjacket sexuality. This ultimately undervalues asexuality/effeminacy/queerness in the effort to instead recover the penis and to privilege manhood in terms that Michele Wallace plainly calls "macho" in reference to heteronormative phallic power.[2] In this chapter, I argue against a cinematic manhood that renders sexual and gender domination as its most privileged criteria without accounting for its injury to others.

Asian American heterosexual male forays into pornography do not confront the constraints upon sexuality adequately if filmmakers fail to imagine their characters' own identity and fantasies beyond a victimized subject position. Lack remains for heterosexual Asian American men when they become more deeply embedded in problematic relations with women and queer men. In defining manhood in terms of their distance from the power they covet in heterosexual phallic manhoods, they uphold the very hierarchy they protest. I emphasize this point by reading David Mura's essay "A Male Grief," which reflects on his addiction to pornography, as a testament to how Asian American manhood doesn't have to happen this way. I conclude by pointing to various works where Asian American men attend to the complexities of their sexualities, including the scene most vilified in straitjacket sexuality: the position of the bottom in homosexual sex acts. By looking at Hoang Nguyen's *Forever Bottom!* (1999) and other works, I identify an ethics of power in the form of auto-eroticism that confronts cinema's and society's classification of race and sexuality as humiliating for queer

Asian American men. In the chapter's conclusion I bring this classic work of queer cinema that embraces the pleasure in bottomhood in conversation with important new works in Asian American cinema: the festival-hit *Dick Ho*, a film that plays with the impossibility of an Asian American male porn star in the seventies; *Asian Pride Porn*, Greg Pak's ridiculing of Orientalist fetishism in pornography; and the blog of Keni Styles, the first Asian man to be celebrated in the U.S. heterosexual pornography industry. I do so in order to give a sense of the ways Asian American men work with pornography to break apart the lack-versus-domination analytic frame.

We will see that lack is defined not uniformly but in different ways in works by Asian American queer, transgendered, and straight men who foray into pornography and related media. Others acknowledge the oppression they experience as men in relation to race and ethnicity as well as queer subjectivity. Asexuality/effeminacy/homosexuality, which falls under the diagnosis of lack in the logic of straitjacket sexuality, is not a crisis of racialized manhood but an opportunity to explore men's being and their relations to others, including women and men—straight, queer, and in-between—especially if they acknowledge their unequal access to what Kaja Silverman calls the dominant fiction of conventional masculinity.

Silverman argues that male aspirations to mastery are undermined at many junctures—including race, class, and ethnicity—but this does not preclude the embrace of lack as a defining act of viable manhood.[3] In effect, she argues that men of all persuasions need to live with lack as women do, with the knowledge that the phallus is a fiction. "Lack is at the heart of all subjectivity." If we "unbind . . . the coherence of the male ego . . . [we] expos[e] the abyss that it conceals."[4] Following Silverman, this chapter explodes the fiction of conventional masculinity as a coherent being—a concept that haunts the manhood problems of Asian American men as articulated in their ventures into the genre of pornography. The chapter brings together a wide array of works by Asian American men who engage sexual acts in pornography as consumers, actors, and producers, each articulating a relationship to lack for Asian American men that differs from those in Hollywood movies.

Ultimately, I aim to illustrate how claiming lack makes manhood accountable to an ethical self and to others who must live with the kinds of manhoods men form. Building from the literatures on race, men, and masculinity on and off screen, I engage concepts that define a crisis of masculinity for men of color. I argue that the shattering of the self in the ecstasy of sexual encounter is an important moment where men are given the opportunity to disassemble and reassemble themselves in how their freedom, as defined through sexual acts and identities, relates to the domination of another. As Leo Bersani asserts, "the self which the sexual shatters provides the basis on which sexuality is associated with power."[5] Thus, the crucial act of reflecting on the shattering of the self, where the organization of one's identity unravels at the loss of control of the body in sexual vulnerability, can be very productive. One can learn from the relationship to lack— whether in embracing its pain and struggle or in rejecting it—and work with it toward building an ethics of manhood through pornographic and other representations.

Screens of Straitjacket Sexuality:
Hamamoto and Hou's Racial and Sexual Victimization

In 2004, University of California, Davis, professor Darrell Hamamoto completed a short film that garnered the attention of mainstream media in prime time and late-night shows hosted by Jon Stewart and Jay Leno, along with Hollywood industry newspapers such as *Variety* and other news outlets such as the *Los Angeles Times*.[6] In these national media venues, Hamamoto came a step closer to fulfilling his plans to become an Asian American Larry Flynt, one who would fund other Asian American filmic political projects with profits from his full-length pornography project titled *Skin on Skin* and other works.[7] The more politicized, short video version of *Skin on Skin*, *Yellow-caust: A Patriot Act* (2003), features a professional Asian American woman porn star, Leyla Lei, and an amateur Asian American man, Chun Lee, performing explicit hard-core sex acts that range from caressing, kissing, fellatio, and cunnilingus to coitus. Following the conventions of other gonzo films, or professional-amateur pornography—the most popular form of contemporary pornography today—the sex acts are shot from a variety of angles in the standard motel-room setting. However, unlike the traditional gonzo form, in *Yellowcaust* the filmmaker is not the featured actor. Hamamoto does insert himself into the sex acts via the documentary *Masters of the Pillow* (James Hou), which narrates and sets the scene for the making of the porn film. Hamamoto "wanted to [create] pure unadulterated physical pleasure between a Yellow couple to cut against the grain of our common history rooted in U.S. imperialism and the systematic acts of genocide that have been inflicted upon us in order to sustain that social order."[8] Thus, Hamamoto calls *Yellowcaust* his political "remix." His film's visual representation of Asian female–Asian male sex argues for a return to same-race love and desire as the "natural order" of things.

What is distinct about *Yellowcaust*, beyond its goal of representing Asian-on-Asian sex—not typical in the multibillion-dollar porn industry—is the framing of traditional gonzo porn sex acts with intertitle text that describes the personal histories of the actors (Korean American male adoptee and female Cambodian American), along with a litany of wartime atrocities committed against various Asian countries and peoples by the United States. While we see the unfolding of conventional sexual acts between the man and the woman—including kissing, cunnilingus, and fellatio on a sofa followed by missionary, cowgirl, reverse cowgirl, and doggy-style positions on a motel-room bed—we hear the ghostly wails of a massacre while we read about the "kill[ing] of 200,000 Filipinos at the dawn of the twentieth century . . . yet in the eyes of the colonized, every American soldier is P. Diddy or Brad Pitt." The money shot, or the visible evidence of male ejaculation, appears with intertitles too, declaring the importance of sex between Asian Americans as a "reclaiming [of] pleasure. . . . The joy of Yellow bodies will not be denied by the state. . . . Despite all efforts of eradication . . . Yellow people endure." The text privileges not only sexual reproduction for Asian Americans but also the importance of heterosexual racial identity within the context of state racism and genocide. As a film made by a Japanese American man, *Yellowcaust* does not account for co-ethnic exploitation, such as Japanese atrocities against Filipinos and Koreans or the long history of strife between Chinese and Japanese. After the money shot, the male actor shifts his gaze from the woman to the camera as she examines his ejaculation on her belly. The film ends with a close-up of his face, with a thoroughly happy smile. The movie suggests that Asian American sexual problems can be solved by achieving Asian American male pleasure within an Asian American heterosexual coupling.

Together, *Yellowcaust* and its making-of documentary *Masters of the Pillow* toured extensively across the United States and Canada and was screened at various festivals and numerous college campuses for about three years, from 2004 to 2007. Galvanized by the issues identified in the film, students and festival programmers organized panels of scholars, filmmakers, and activists to accompany the screening, opening public conversations about race, sexuality, gender, and representation that focused on the problems of Asian American men. As documented in the media by blogs and festival websites, many faced controversy and "tedious" bureaucracy to get the porn event funded and sponsored.[9] The filmmakers, Hamamoto and Hou, indeed succeeded in opening up large-arena discussions of the pain, anger, and frustrations of Asian American men who "lack the success of Asian American women . . . in interracial relationships—a sensitive fact" of Asian American gender relations.[10] However, this attempt at what Viet Nguyen calls "remasculinization"—the process by which men aspire to gain the patriarchal power and heterosexual privilege that has been historically denied them—falls short.[11]

Although years have passed since the two films' national tours, I take up these twin projects in order to identify the patriarchal aspirations that are central to and still persistent in approaches to solving Asian American manhood's sexual and representational problems. In these works, the role of women is as a fetish to replace the phallus lost in social castration. Premised on the belief that Asian American men have been victimized by the *repressive* power of sexuality and racist regimes of representation, both films propose a patriarchal heroism for the filmmakers and a heteronormative prescription for sexuality that renders women as bridges to male pleasure and power. That is, to use Kaja Silverman's words, "women are exchange objects that confer symbolic privilege upon the male subject."[12] The sexual encounter with the Asian female occurs within the social context of her hypersexuality and hypervisibility and the male's asexuality and invisibility. The sex act in *Yellowcaust*, then, is the confrontation of this difference. However, male subjectivity is privileged as the one in need of care, which is very similar to issues in black sexual politics as described by Patricia Hill Collins as the "den[ial] of the existence of sexism" or its relegation as a derivative issue to race and by Kimberle Crenshaw as a "single-axis framework."[13] His is an unpleasurable and unwanted position for which her fetishization as the white male object of desires serves. Race, as the force that gets in the way of Asian American male phallic identification, justifies his possession of her. For Silverman, the use of women to define men as the producers and representatives of their social fields is the most rudimentary articulation of the law of the father that governs our dominant fiction.[14] Hamamoto and Hou do not recognize that rendering women differently would provide another opportunity to resist hegemonic masculinity. Instead, the problem remains as a kind of incarnation of a Frank Chin approach in which the racial empowerment of men often equals the misogyny and the exclusion of sexism in their analysis of gendered racism. My concern is not to condemn pornography as a vehicle for addressing racial, gender inequalities but to forge representations that won't aggravate the subjugation of women but also won't elide the needs of men. To compete well within systems of machismo seems to persist as central to the game of securing manhood within normative criteria—rather than changing the terms of our understanding manhood. I imagine the embrace rather than abhorrence of lack as a political and powerful approach to achieving viable manhood that goes beyond accepting one's denigrated and disprized status.

The sexual labor and gendered acts within Darrell Hamamoto's *Yellowcaust* focus on the sexual victimization of Asian American men while treating Asian American women as bridges for securing conventional manhood. I argue that this strategy actually further embeds Asian American men in lack and strengthens the gender and sexual hierarchy that the filmmaker attempts to critique. Straitjacket sexuality remains a powerful disciplining mechanism in the alternative formations that attempt to address Asian American male sexual problems. Why is the eunuch best countered by the sexually dominant heterosexual man? Why is the fetishized female best replaced by a servile being-for-(racialized)-men? We need to re-imagine and re-image Asian American masculinities without reinforcing heteronormativity and gender hierarchy. These films articulate male aspirations toward phallic (symbolic) and penile (literal) power in ways that ultimately do a disservice to the formulation of socially viable, ethical masculinities for Asian American men.

The Racial and Gendered Context for Pornographic Speech, or "I don't care if you laugh or think I'm evil, someone had to do it"[15]

David Eng employs psychoanalysis, with its emphasis on sexuality as the primary mechanism for identity and loss, to help us understand Asian American masculinity as, according to Richard Fung, "Asian" = "Anus."[16]

Eng reviews Freud's main essays on fetishism, sexuality, and civilization to discuss how the civilized depended on the primitive to define itself. In this work, he concludes that sex has always been racial in psychoanalysis. The primitive—the darker skinned—to whom no unconscious can be ascribed, is much closer to savage sexuality, and hence excluded from heterosexuality, normal sexuality, and civilization. When those excluded attempt to enter the system from which they are barred, a psychic, social, and historical struggle ensues within the self. Therefore, psychoanalysis is useful for understanding Asian American masculinities.

Eng indicates that our identities are actually formed by various social mirrors, such as in the various historical and political encounters and pressures Asian American men and women face in the social world. An example to illustrate this brilliant framework is the popular teen movie *Harold and Kumar Go to White Castle* (2004) by Danny Leiner. Harold and Kumar's encounters with the perceptions of others shape and determine their journey to the full citizenship and manhood that White Castle represents. They deal with this fragmentation of their identities differently. At the beginning of the film, Harold is bullied by his white co-workers but by the end of the film, he not only fights them but also wins over a crew of racist surfer thugs. Harold moves away from the model minority interpellation and along the way, his friend and consummate pot-smoker Kumar changes his disavowal of his medical/surgical family career trajectory. In this process, they find themselves confronting the various versions and interpretations of their identities in the social world and make choices to achieve their manhood and citizenship. Similarly, David Eng asks us to question whose judgments about sexual identity shape our self-identities. We need to interrogate the fear of queerness in defining Asian American masculinity as a form of racism. In this way, we can address the pain of Asian American heterosexual men's subjection as feminine or queer without assailing Asian American women or condemning homosexuality as deviant.

A salon.com article by Harry Mok describes Hamamoto as defining Asian American sexuality as "damaged by years of colonialism and racism that has turned Asian women into a sexual fetish and Asian men into eunuchs. Asian-Americans have internalized these attitudes . . . causing a rift between the genders and perpetuating the stereotypes."[17] While Mok describes the intense sexual subjection of both Asian American men and women, Hamamoto assumes that women have power and that it is men who are victimized by their sexual racialization. In Hamamoto's interview on *The Daily Show*, he describes the futile search for Asian American men in the unnamed pornographic film *World's Biggest Gang Bang*, which he says shows Asian women's prowess in pornography.[18] While Asian American men were present among the hundreds of male participants, in the use of this example, he neglects to mention that this "classic" porn film is the famously controversial gang bang starring the Asian American actress Annabel Chong. In this film, she uses pornography as a feminist platform in response to the accusation that women who have sex with multiple men are sluts while men who have sex with multiple women are studs. Hamamoto's search for an Asian man in this production and his subsequent problem statement about their absence restricts Asian American women to same-race couplings and presents these as the proper and privileged relation while ignoring the complex project Annabel Chong embarks upon in this work.[19]

In his 1998 essay "Joy Fuck Club: Prolegomenon to an Asian American Porno Practice," Hamamoto describes Asian American racial colonization through the controlling mechanism of sexuality and offers a solution that ultimately pines for access to heteronormativity and gender hierarchy. As established by queer scholars Michael Warner, Eve Sedgwick, Gayle Rubin, and Adrienne Rich, heteronormativity assumes that heterosexual identity is the norm in social relations, and it exerts powerful pressure to adhere to this normalcy in the most intimate realm of self-perception. That is, belonging is contingent upon heterosexuality as the natural, normal, and ideal sexuality so that any non-heterosexual desire makes one doubt one's legitimacy.[20] *Yellowcaust* is the result of a promise Hamamoto makes in the essay, to make an "anti-colonial porno." In the essay, he promotes a totalizing, absolute-power understanding of how sexual images work. Supposedly, they dominate Asian American spectators' most private fantasies and make them desire whiteness and despise themselves. For Hamamoto, colonialism at the level of sexuality and love compels and warrants an Asian American pornographic practice. He defines Asian Americans and Asian American spectators as undergoing a kind of "self-alienation that has its material source in a sex/race/power regime *so total in scope and depth* that it reaches into the unconscious, shaping the stuff of erotic imagination."[21] Hamamoto's solution to this problem is achieve a kind of social liberation by creating videos representing sexual liberation.

James Hou, a former student of Hamamoto and director of *Masters of the Pillow*, concurs: "The general consensus is we're stereotyped in a way that dehumanizes our identities as men and especially in terms of our sexuality, it's never displayed on screen or explored. It's always repressed."[22] In such a uniform analysis of male subjection, all Asian American men are affected in the same way, without accounting for different relations to heteronormativity as I have mapped in this book so far. Within this context, which places importance on Asian American men defending their sexual power and viability in sociality, their films attempt to unbridle the repression of sexuality.

In *Yellowcaust*, the hard-core sex is juxtaposed to the sounds of atrocity and suffering meant to symbolize Western imperialism. Hamamoto describes its "dissonance" with sexual pleasure as "political theater."[23] Dissonance usually describes conflict; in social psychology, cognitive dissonance describes the process of recognizing the presence of conflicting ideas in the self, such as in the experience of pleasure during pain or the possession of two identities in conflict. Thus, this moment of dissonance in the Asian American man's sexual act—where he recognizes his stereotyping as asexual while experiencing the physicality of a sexual act—for Hamamoto is political. But how? Is the sex act political for the Asian man because he is no longer sexually absent? But what comprises his sexual presence?

In the *Sacramento Bee*, Hamamoto reveals a celebration of a kind of "bad boy" narcissism and the dominance of the repressive hypothesis in his problem identification. The article by Dorothy Korber, which appeared on November 2, 2003, characterizes the professor as

> both racial provocateur and unabashed pornographer. He aims to make a social point with his short film—and to turn a handsome profit with a 50-minute, pure porn version of it.
>
> If that makes people squirm with outrage, all the better. Hamamoto embraces controversy, revels in being the bad boy of academe.
>
> "I refuse to allow Asian Americans to be passive victims," he said.[24]

The process of making porn asserts heterosexual coupling as the norm to which we should aspire. Hamamoto points to a passive victimization to which he responds via pornography in order to assert dominance through heterosexual coupling that also naturalizes same-race pairing. This is also an uncritical assertion of presence in opposition to absence. Deviance and absence are central to Hamamoto's problem identification. Moreover, pornography seemed to promise more than the professoriate in terms of impact and reach: "I've written thousands of words, whole books about our exclusion from American culture. . . . I began to realize: Nobody's listening to me. . . . This project has done more to draw attention to these issues than all my other efforts combined."[25] In his interpretation, the self is centered as the victim that must rise up, speak its pain, and claim its power. It is a solid identity that is gained. In this solution, any visibility is viable. Dissonance is feared. In contrast, I assert the importance of embracing the shattering of the self. If the identity of asexuality is countered by sexuality in the act, it is a moment that requires reading and close analysis, for it is not identity stability that is gained in that encounter but identity instability, and possibly even shattering! As such, an opportunity to disassemble the self within racist regimes can be taken up in a new self-assembly rather than an aspiration to white patriarchal manhood.

This is precisely why I take up these specific films that privilege hegemonic masculinity. They are made in the context of and in response to, according to their authors, Asian American culture's repression of sexuality as well as the effeminization and desexualization of Asian American men as part of a racist regime. For Hou, Hamamoto asserts a voice within this silencing context. Hou says it is "difficult for Asian Americans to take huge risks because of cultural baggage. . . . That's why I applaud Hamamoto for taking a risk. Put your opinion out there, make it known and see where the chips fall."[26] To declare unbridled male desire becomes an occasion for celebration if the problem is understood to be the need for access to heteronormativity and gender hierarchy. It is to place Asian American men in a position of victimization that garners male admiration for "following the courage of his convictions"—despite the cost to others.[27] So the position of victimization does not account for how Asian American men can and must emerge with masculine identities that account for their complicity and conflicts with domination.

In *Masters of the Pillow*, James Hou begins with a shot of Hamamoto's essay "The Joy Fuck Club" where he argues Asian Americans share "the collective sexual imaginary dominated by whiteness." Hamamoto introduces himself—"I am a Ph.D., professor of Asian American Studies at UC Davis"—while we see him on campus, in his office among books by Asian American feminists, such as *Dragon Ladies* by Sonia Shah, and anti-censorship scholar Nadine Strossen's *Defending Pornography*. We see him among young Asian American students in the classroom as he discusses how Asian women in porn movies are always paired with white, European-American men and how he will bring together Asian American women and Asian American men: "a very fine sister here and a fine looking Asian male," he says, "filming them having sex." Following this scene, Hamamoto's image is intercut with an interview with a young media activist who supports his claims and who assesses the context for such images: "A lot of Asian girls, screwed by everyone and their cousin. When you do find an Asian man, he's gay and he's a bottom." In this discussion, Asian women are objects for male play and ownership. They do not have sexual agency; they do not express desire but are simply used by men, and this is an indication of Asian American male victimization by white men. Gay Asian manhood and the bottom position are similarly rendered as undesirable and powerless.

Through representation, we see how Asian American men can simultaneously experience stress, pressure, and pain as well as demonstrate their complicity in the domination that produces their subjectivities not only in relation to women but in how they define viable Asian American manhood as the opposite of lack. Asian American men as desexualized and effeminized in representation are differently racialized from Asian American women, who are hypersexualized and hyperfeminized. The difference occurs in how women, as I argue in *The Hypersexuality of Race*, engage their interpellation by negotiating its misnaming and recasting it with their concrete experiences in representation. The risk for men comes in countering their misnaming with another if they do not acknowledge their existence as agents of power and violence. Rendering oneself as victim does not achieve a proper accounting of the self. If the problematization of power is so severely flawed so as to miss men's possession of gender power, the practices recommended do not reflect the possibilities of formulating responsible, ethical, and sexually desirable manhoods, on and off screen. Rather than deriving lessons from a concrete project—the pairing of an Asian American man and woman—the lesson is already decided. We are shown what needs doing rather than what can be remade and imagined anew through exploring what Kath Albury describes as "possible sexual stories that can be tried on for size."[28]

This is why James Hou's documentary is important to assess: how can the practice that emerges from the problematization lead to an ethical heuristic for Asian American manhood? A bad boy Asian American manhood needs to confront questions of responsibility and ethics. Wesley Yang, in a recent cover article in *New York Magazine*, writes about his feelings of "estrangement" from his face.[29] He has an Asian face—which he describes as "a pancake-flat surface of yellow-and-green-toned skin. An expression that is nearly reptilian in its impassivity." This self-loathing extends to a self-pitying diatribe that lauds the choice to live a life opposite to that of the stereotype of the over-achieving Asian American. Part of his goal is to document exemplary Asian American academic performance and the subsequent lack of success in the highest echelons of corporate America. In his blog written immediately after the publication of Wesley Yang's article, cultural critic Jeff Yang provides a smart critique of the unproductive life lauded in the *New York Magazine* article: "celebrating your inability to engage with the world and its rules doesn't automatically make you a genius—in some cases, it just makes you a misanthropic asshole."[30] Jeff Yang goes further when he criticizes the lack of women's voices and the "solipsism" that undergirds Wesley Yang's perspective: "A dead giveaway is his failure to interview any Asian American women for the story—which, perhaps, is due in part to his embrace of the idea that sexual success can be conflated with financial/professional/ontological success."[31] Similarly, a self-pitying narcissism that drives Asian American women deeper into the bind of hypersexuality informs Hamamoto's premise. Indeed, solipsism, misanthropy, and self-pity characterize the male malaise of straitjacket sexuality that binds the manhood forwarded in both Wesley Yang's "Paper Tigers" and in Darrell Hamamoto's *Yellowcaust*.

If we try Hamamoto's solution of presenting Asian American men the opportunity to display their sexuality, what do we learn and discover about what Asian American men want and need? Jay Leno describes Hamamoto's critique as follows: "Asian men experience low self-esteem" and thus need representation in porn to alleviate this pain. This comedic reading offers precise analysis. The pornographer's privileging of conventional masculinity reveals a lack of security, or a kind of peace, in manhood outside that norm. However, the critique falls away when *The Tonight Show* created a spoof where Asian American men and women attempt to get it on but Godzilla interrupts them and chases them naked down the street. The audience laughs and laughs. Ouch! Leno says it was fun to shoot.

Back to *Masters of the Pillow*, we see Hamamoto going to pick up his star at the San Francisco airport, but he can't find him. The camera follows as he moves from the lower level arrivals to upper level departures while talking on a cell phone: "Where are you? What do you look like?" Unsuccessful, Hamamoto finally meets his actor at the car, all loaded up and ready to go. This subtle ridicule of Hamamoto contextualizes his presentation of the movie's goal: "making a porn sends a message that this is the actual order of things—Asian man and Asian woman together—Asian American man and Asian American woman together." This claim is immediately followed by an interview with his considerably younger girlfriend, Funie Hsu, who when asked about their age difference says her twenty-something peer group finds him "easy to talk to. . . . He acts immature—not 50." The description of immaturity from his closest collaborator, Funie, bookending his declaration makes Hamamoto's manhood part of the unfolding story. Showing analytical blindspots, he then goes on about how white male supremacy in a patriarchal society determines who can choose sex partners, as if women cannot act as agents against their interpellation. His platform identifies a system of sexual colonialism that leads to Asian female outmarriage to the master race. "A white male sex complex won't permit" Asian male competition, he claims. In this sequence, Hou establishes Hamamoto as a laughable as well as an easy-going guy. Hsu concludes her part by describing Hamamoto as into "popular culture and he won't judge you." Hou then interviews a set of established and respected intellectuals and cultural producers who provide contextual information that ultimately and (seemingly) unwittingly supports Hamamoto's claims regarding Asian American male sexual problems.

Tony-award-winning playwright David Henry Hwang, prominent film festival director Chi-hui Yang, celebrated film directors Justin Lin and Eric Byler, and renowned Berkeley Asian American feminist professor Elaine H. Kim comment on Hamamoto's project of proposing the solution to Asian American men's sexual problems through pornography. They confirm the lack of Asian American male representations in the media: Lin critiques the racially fetishized presence of Asian Americans in the media; Byler diagnoses the lack of Asian American power at the site of film reception; and both Kim and Hwang attest to racism in filmic representations, but question the appropriateness of porn as a solution. Through the editing, they contribute to the documentary in order for Hamamoto to declare, "given [the problems mentioned by those above] why wouldn't Asian people have an alienated consciousness." For him, no one has come out with an agenda for regaining Asian American wholeness and his pornography project is an actual agenda for confronting Asian American sexual domination by white racism.

Hou's critics have commented on how his documentary demonstrates a "reluctance to question Hamamoto more on his controversial opinions and methods, which occasionally makes the film feel as though it's a de facto endorsement of such beliefs."[32] The racial heteronormativity in *Yellowcaust* takes the form of male narcissism that centers the penis and the phallic economy, exemplified in the representation of male orgasm as emotional and political joy. Whom does this catharsis serve if it leads to a compulsory heterosexual demand that Asian American women be a sexual object for men? Is this dominant heterosexuality for men good if it is a fearful heterosexual response to the attribution of queerness and male effeminacy to Asian American men? To probe these questions, I accompany my close readings of the film with ethnographies of the viewing process and an analysis of the blogosphere and other web reviews of the films and their reception.

In response to the criticism of Hamamoto's porn-is-the-answer approach, he declares, "If it takes producing erotica to get some crucially important points across concerning White power, U.S. colonialism, and anti-Asian racism, then I cannot but accept the challenge of meeting this obligation."[33] The masculinity forged by this philosophy or rationale leads to a filmmaker-as-hero perception, in which suddenly the filmmaker is now an "icon himself."[34] In response to conservative criticism of his film, Hamamoto recalls the overall reception of the film screenings as "more than favorable. For at every screening that I have attended, the reaction to *Masters of the Pillow* has been overwhelmingly positive and enthusiastically in favor of the goals I have set forth."[35] As a spectator in at least two of the large venues where the documentary screened, my experiences differ significantly.

At the 2004 San Francisco Asian American International Film and Video Festival, the large San Francisco Kabuki Theatre was packed with a few hundred people for a sold-out screening of Hamamoto's *Yellowcaust* and Hou's *Masters of the Pillow*. There, the most enthusiastic praise came from male members of the audience. I sank in my seat after the film ended, as a crowd of men empowered by the film stood up, hollered, and rolled their arms vigorously in the air while whooping in triumph. During the question-and-answer session, cheers rang out at someone's interpretation that through this "Yellow" coupling the Asian American man emerged as a sexual agent. On his blog, Tad Doyle reports on October 9, 2004, that the screening he attended featured a panel discussion with "mainly guys asking questions. . . . One woman spoke about the attempt to blame women for the denigration of men when women partner with other races."[36] Similarly, at the screening I attended, I became more keenly aware of the male audience's desire for something else beyond affirmation of their masculinity on screen—the chance to find themselves in the role of consumer and possessor of Asian female sexuality.

At the question-and-answer session in San Francisco, a woman spoke about the heterogeneous history of anti-Asian violence in war in the intertitle text. She pointed out that the undifferentiated violence against Asians represented in the film ignored interethnic atrocities. This female audience member commented on the fraught histories of Asians fighting against each other, such as in the Japanese occupation of the Philippines, as an example of antagonisms within the Asian community not captured in the binary presentation of the on-screen text. Hamamoto's response was dismissive in a way that privileged racial identification without acknowledging interethnic colonialisms as well as the interethnic domination of the brown woman by the yellow man in *Yellowcaust*. Similarly, according to an online critique:

> Darrell Hamamoto . . . is very concerned that the yellow man is emasculated, he wants things the natural way. You know a yellow man with a yellow woman. He thinks the way to do it is for Asian American men to "star" in pornography. . . . He even produced an amateurish video with a Korean American ingénue and a Cambodian-Thai pro. A yellow man with a brown girl.
>
> Hashimoto explains that since Layla [sic] Lei feels that she is yellow she is. Gee, what happened to the "little brown brothers" (Filipinos) and what American vets affectionately called LBFMs [little brown fucking machines]? Is Dr. Hamamoto also re-writing history? Or is he just selectively color-blind?[37]

Like the woman at the San Francisco screening who criticized homogenizing Asian American colonial experiences and silencing interethnic exploitation, this critic points out how the film privileges race and assumes that all Asian experiences are uniform, when clearly that is not the case, especially across gender.

The discussion of this film by other Asian American male critics, such as William Nakayama, echoes the privileging of male pleasure and the servile role women must assume in the male's pursuit of that goal. Nakayama writes, "Chun's arousal and Leyla's accommodating mouth and loins are passably documented from [a] number of vantage points."[38] The performances of the actors reflect such inequity: the man occupies the role of privileged recipient of the woman's sexual labor. The dynamic of amateur man and professional woman is apparent in his anticipation of her decisive moves. Having experience with shooting sex scenes in pornographic films, Leyla Lei moves her body in relation to the camera and Chun's body as he is seated on the sofa. Unlike typical gonzo porn wherein the male-professional and the female-amateur dynamic showcases her potentiality as a star, *Yellowcaust* flips the roles so that it is the road for the Asian American man's entry as a porn actor that is paved. Chun is in a difficult position, however, as his performance is interrupted by Hamamoto. Moreover, we see Chun resist in asking the filmmakers of *Masters of the Pillow* to leave the set for the rest of the scene. However, his role is as a privileged recipient—rather than a passive recipient like the Asian male bottom discussed in gay films.[39] That is, the gay Asian male bottom role is seen as passive in a negative way. Here we see the act of receiving pleasure is not passive. The men in the audience cheer because they see Asian American

FIGURE 18 Hamamoto's subjectivity as a director is under gentle scrutiny in *Masters of the Pillow*. *Masters of the Pillow*. Dir. James Hou. Avenue Films, 2003.

men in a macho position of holding power over women. In this scene, the Asian American male reads as dominant because an Asian American woman occupies a position of servility.

I saw *Yellowcaust* for a second time at the Stanford University Asian Film Conference in May 2006. As an audience member and a member of the panel of filmmakers presenting Asian American sexualities on screen, I asked Hamamoto about the dynamics of casting a professional woman and an amateur man for his film. Another viewer added to this question by describing how the sexual acts reflected this uneven positioning so that the male seemed relatively passive and the woman's experience as a sex worker became prominent. As such, the Asian American male's empowerment comes to be borne by the professional woman porn actor. In this example of uneven professional experience of the actors, *Yellowcaust* privileges Asian American male sexuality and sexual subjection in ways that do not recognize Asian American women's different sexual racialization. If Asian American men are made to be sexually abnormal through their popular perception as being less desirable, and Asian American women's constructions suffer from excessive sexual availability, does her servility in *Yellowcaust* forward or worsen her situation? And does her ubiquity compared to Asian American men's invisibility necessarily mean she is in a position of power, or does this kind of diagnosis further marginalize her as part of a larger production of her objectification? The feminist response to his work is indicated in another article where Hamamoto's colleague and professor of sociology Laura Grindstaff drives the point home: "In his focus on Asian men and their oppression, what is he saying about Asian women? Does this feed into stereotypes of her as the sex kitten prostitute?"[40]

In a film meant to undo the female misrepresentation and male invisibility of Asian American sexualities, the professional-amateur gender dynamic, where a privileged man is served by an aggressive woman, actually reproduces the stereotypes of Asian male passivity and Asian female sexual power. Hamamoto seems to mistake pleasure for empowerment. Furthermore, closing on the ecstatic face of the Asian American man shows how the film is profoundly male in its interests. It celebrates male orgasm as standing for group emancipation. This occurs in the professional and servile hands of a woman relegated even more severely to a sexually limited role. The solution lies in the man's climax, not in the physical or emotional aspects of the encounter between the man and woman. Leyla Lei seems to sense her role in the story here, as she indicates her desire to start her own production company as well.

In reading closely the sexual labor depicted in the film and its performers, the overall character of the man is that of the eager sexual virgin. His sexual retardation is helped by the professional woman who initiates him into the sexual world that Hamamoto describes as boundless in its oceanic pleasures.[41] The emotions of the sex acts arise from these clearly delineated roles determined by the casting. An online review comments, "The interaction between the adult actors seemed dull because [the male actor] Chun's nervousness is so evident" while Lei takes charge with a professional calm.[42] At some point she suggests missionary, doggy style, spoon, and reverse cowgirl to Hamamoto, who tries to catch up. She is also tender and kind, rather than domineering, contributing to an assured stance that Funie Hsu comments on as a kind of confidence and professionalism.

How does this confident and assured Asian female sexuality and anxious and nervous Asian male sexuality produce a gender dynamic in *Yellowcaust* and *Masters of the Pillow*? A review in *Asian Week* offers a harsh critique by asking, "Why does [*Masters of the Pillow*] fall limp?" The critic Philip W. Chung demands more from the filmmaker, focusing on the compelling figure of Chun Lee, the amateur actor. Why did Chun Lee agree to "sex with a stranger?" What did his family and friends think of his "foray into porn?"[43] Chung points to the emotional centrality necessary for us to understand the Asian American male's history beyond a superficial registry of his presence as a Korean American man. Where is his particularity in the scene, beyond the intertitle text, which simply lists his background as an adoptee? How are he and his sexual specificity narrated and his bodily image dramatized?

If *Masters of the Pillow* presents an inadequate telling of the sexual problems Asian American men and women face in terms of racialization, Chung expresses a related dissatisfaction with *Yellowcaust* as well. He finds it "just plain boring. . . . Lee and Lei engage in the standard sex found in adult films but there is no energy, no joy, and nothing would suggest this as a revolutionary act in any way. It's devoid of all sexiness. It feels as passionate as someone mowing the lawn."[44] What is revolutionary about *Yellowcaust*, according to Hamamoto, is that it shows "the natural order of things" or the achievement of racial belonging and recognition that same-race partnering supposedly enables. But we don't see it. Instead the story told about the sexualization of race is male bewilderment and female expertise. The story of the confusion, pain, joy, and happiness of the racial experience is unengaged. What is missing from Hamamoto's work is a scene of complexity in the process of racialization, such as the cojoining of pain with pleasure in dramas of race and sexuality. In my comparison of the work of Kip Fulbeck with that of Stuart Gaffney in the Introduction, we have seen this same lack, and we will see it again later in this chapter when I analyze the work of Hamamoto and Hou against that of Keni Styles and Hoang Nguyen.

In my work on race and pornography, I find that spectators expect Asian American actresses to play a particular version of the Asian woman; resistance to this stereotyping occurs in performances that deliver the unexpected. For example, pre-1950s white women in yellowface costume and makeup established a particular standard—both visible and performative—that Asian women have continued to fulfill and enact. In Hamamoto's film we see the gendering of race in the form of female servility and male domination, albeit through inaction on his part. Moreover, in *Yellowcaust*, sexuality is defined without careful consideration of gender and its varying inflections for men and women; therefore, the possibility that what is sexually empowering for men may be disempowering to women is not considered.

The emergence of the male Asian American as sexual actor in representation seems to essentialize or totalize sexuality rather than indicate the production of identity as complexity and infinity. This production of an ethical identity—a sensitivity to others—is crucial in crafting from pornography a politics that escapes the totalized representation of manhood we see in Hamamoto's film and strives for the infinite possibilities in representations of manhood such as we will see in the work of Keni Styles. In an article in which Hamamoto defends himself against his critics, he defines sexuality as "the sheer majesty and oceanic pleasure that lies in potential within this boundless realm of human expression."[45] Such a definition relies on sexuality as intrinsic, transcendent, and based on a natural drive rather than a force that is shaped by the dialectic of subject formation in the interchange of both individual (internal) and social (external) forces.

Instead, Hamamoto frames Asian American male sexuality as coherent and victimized. He says that "Asian American sexuality . . . [is] warped by Euro-American colonization, occupation, and genocide in Asian countries; exclusion, expulsion and incarceration in the United States."[46] Such a definition of sexuality is not only simplistic but restrictive. It disallows the complexity of desire, including heterosexuality, and unequal relations across different categories and experiences as well as the use of different sexual acts to remake ourselves, our pasts, and our future worlds of desire. Sexuality is inherently neither racialized negatively nor positively but is a living social force that requires individuals to act and interact to make its meanings. Thus, Hamamoto's solution to the misrepresentation and invisibility of Asian American men in pornographic roles ultimately leads to stereotyped logics of racial representation. Positive images cannot simply undo the negative, especially when they do not uniformly affect Asian Americans. It is at the site of gender that this inequality in Hamamoto's work is most glaring.

The theory of representation under which *Yellowcaust* operates—equating positive and negative images—misses the complex way sexuality works on Asian American men. Can any positive or negative image do justice to the wide variety of experiences of sexuality of Asian American men on and off screen? How does the sexual fantasy offered by *Yellowcaust*, tinged with genocide and racial atrocity, exceed group identification? That is, Hamamoto's definition of sexuality is so limited it does not re-imagine power. It is simply about sexual liberation on screen as social liberation in scene. But even our desires and pleasures can involve subjugation, or its agent, and cannot simply be taken as a given, but must be brought into engagement with the binds of power and domination. So it seems that Hamamoto actually unwittingly demonstrates this through the film's gender dynamics. Does the film ultimately desire for Asian American women to occupy traditional roles, but only for Asian American men? Must the remasculinizing act assert Asian American men's ownership of Asian American women?

In "Queering Asian American Masculinity," Crystal Parikh describes the "incomplete incorporation" of Asian American men into heteronormative definitions of masculinity.[47] This exclusion allows for the "possibility for redefinition" of a feminist and queer-friendly, even heterosexual, masculinity or what she broadly calls an "alternative subject formation."[48] The lack of representation of Asian American men in heterosexual pornography indeed represents such an opportunity. That is, Asian American men's invisibility in heterosexual pornography actually provides another opportunity for them to redefine their images in popular culture. They could appear in pornography in a different way, as in Greg Pak's *Asian Pride Porn* (2000), a fake commercial that features playwright David Henry Hwang marketing an Asian American porn series—which I will analyze below—that empowers Asian American viewers through its reclaiming of stereotypes.

Although Hamamoto's work focuses specifically on Asian American presence in pornography, because Asian American men have so few opportunities to establish their own representations, the field for redefining existing
roles must remain wide open. More precisely, the direction in which Hamamoto takes us enables us to think more deliberately about two important
questions: what is the role of race in eroticism, and how can we think about
representation as not only articulating historical inequality but leading to
productive outcomes as well?

According to Hamamoto, because sexuality in representation has disciplined Asian American men, the solution to their subjugation must also be
found in sexual representation. Thus, Hamamoto strives to create his own
socially significant Asian American pornographic empire to address the lack
of sexually affirming images by showing Asian American men having sex
on screen. His formula for undoing sexual damage through sexual heal-
ing seems similar to my approach in *The Hypersexuality of Race*.[49] However,
while both works focus on sexuality, they differ in gender-object priorities.
Indeed, whereas my *The Hypersexuality of Race* shows how the sexual subjection of Asian American women finds its undoing in sexual representations
by Asian American women who use the tools of their subjugation to recast
and rewrite their roles, in *Yellowcaust* men use tools of domination that assign women the role of sexual object, and male power over women becomes
the basis for establishing the male racial self. Thus, Hamamoto's project
forces us to take seriously how the sexualizations of Asian Americans differ
according to gender.

While Hamamoto's definition of sexuality and representation remains
organized by a binary framework that does not account for existing alternative practices, he does provoke and widen what I consider a productive
debate. He also opens up the space for me to articulate the urgent need for
new methods of both sexual and moving-image literacy. *Yellowcaust* certainly accomplishes an important goal of concretely identifying how sexuality is a key issue in the gender formation of Asian Americans and how
sexuality, especially sexual acts, and practices in representation and in everyday life are under-studied sites in Asian American studies. His definition of
sexuality in moving-image representation, however, simplifies the complex
and unwieldy operation not only of desire and fantasy but of the multiva-
lent possibilities of interpretation present in the consumption of any image.
Ultimately, Hamamoto comes up with an equation "so total in scope and

depth" regarding sex/race and cinema that sociality and sexuality are simply reduced to subordination and domination.[50] Such an analysis oversimplifies the complexities of Asian Americans' representation and of their sexual object choices and experiences. For example, both Jessica Hagedorn and Peter X Feng describe viewing practices that reject the narrative lines of Hollywood movies that present Asian American female characters as simply bad.[51] Rather than following the lesson filmmakers may be teaching regarding Asian American subservience or malevolence, spectators have the power to turn away, reject the moral, or invent alternative fantasies. Pornography is met by people who can and do make their own meanings from these works and perspectives. The film *Yellowcaust* operates under the assumption that representation has the power to dictate sexual and social realities, or that the meaning of representation is unidirectional, but it does not directly account for how cross-race allegiances and intimacies can be part of antiracist and multidirectional spectatorial practices as well.

We need a map of sexuality in terms of race that accounts for the unwieldy dynamic of the subconscious ways we make sense of our sexual realities as well as an understanding of representation not simply prescribed as good and bad images. The terrain of representation in terms of fantasy, consciousness, and the unconscious can be explained via Kaja Silverman's theorization of what she terms the "dominant fiction," and here I will emphasize its production in terms of the social categories and experiences of race, class, gender, and sex. Silverman theorizes the process of consent in terms of Gramscian hegemony. She argues that "the ideology of a particular class cannot simply impose itself upon a socius; in order to command collective belief it must intersect with the society's 'reality,' which does not 'belong' to any class."[52] Society's reality is determined by individuals and group epochs—this is clearest when Silverman defines the dominant fiction "as [consisting] of the images and stories through which a society figures consensus" and as "significantly inflected by the ideologies of gender, class, race, and ethnicity."[53] Silverman argues that the "dominant fiction calls upon the male subject to see himself, and for the female subject to recognize and desire him, only through the mediation of images of an unimpaired masculinity. It urges both the male and female subject . . . to deny all knowledge of male castration by believing in the commensurability of penis and phallus, actual and symbolic father."[54] Here we see that the coherent self or the "unimpaired masculinity" is prized in our ideas of manhood and masculinity in ways that require a denial of the softness that the penis may possess or the in-process nature that manhood can be.

This book pays attention to the specific ways representations function with identity categories so as to identify the in-process work of constructing our understanding of racialized manhoods. Through this lens, even the declarations of power in macho and in sexual virility and prowess can reveal lack. In *Yellowcaust* heteronormativity is claimed as a right. While the exclusion from heteronormative standards of masculinity creates a great deal of pain, we need to think about how racial anger about masculinity can produce an aesthetic that holds up identities that require the subjugation of others. In an essay on the comic series *Secret Asian Man*, Tasha Oren describes how anger can be a powerful and useful emotion if part of a productive critical project—wherein content also shapes the form in a fashion so original as to shock our assumptions of what emotions are proper to Asian American men. Hamamoto's film does not achieve this. After a screening of *Yellowcaust*, Philip W. Chung wrote:

> At a post-screening Q&A session, Hsu [Darrell Hamamoto's girlfriend and a *Yellowcaust* cameraperson] said simply seeing an Asian American man and woman having sex is what makes the project revolutionary. That's like saying simply seeing two Asian American leads in a feature film is enough to make it revolutionary. But I like to think quality still matters even in the world of porn. If the revolution is going to be televised, it has to be worth watching.[55]

Beyond visibility, quality and content matter—as does form. How will these actors contend with their problems, whether racial, sexual, or gendered? Moreover, how will these heterosexual figures converse with queer people and others whose subjectivities and futures are entwined in terms of group identity and individual relations?

In the interviews in the documentary *Masters of the Pillow*, the cultural producers David Henry Hwang, Justin Lin, and Eric Byler all insist upon the achievement of great art. Hwang proposes that any stereotype must be countered by three-dimensionality. Lin and Byler insist that a work must be compelling—defining good art as necessary to political work in representation. Part of that political work, according to Hamamoto in *Masters of the Pillow*, is showing that "Asian men definitely have it. No doubt about it—even as it's been repressed, suppressed, and denied." The repressive hypothesis appears as the wounding of Asian American manhood that shapes sexual practices in Hamamoto's project. Byler says: "We need to retrain Asian American men to have sex, to retrain Asian Americans how to have sex. Not just 'I want to be your friend' but [to] just ask women to go out." Byler seems to be implying that Asian American men should refuse their assignation and play in the heterosexual game—in order to participate, raise your self-image. In this vein, Hamamoto insists on the evolutionary step of his work—to push the discourse to a much higher level through his porn project. David Henry Hwang expresses skepticism and asks if what we will see in Hamamoto's porn transcends regular porn or is it simply two bodies. What do we learn about Asian American bodies entwined here? This is the question that needs asking, rather than simply accepting the sight of Asian American heterosexual coupling as a correction to Hamamoto's assessment that "we are more than we are made out to be." Hamamoto then shares his dreams in a close-up: "Someday I hope to be the Asian Ameri-

FIGURE 19   Hamamoto speaks directly to the camera regarding sexual hierarchies of women that he hopes to resolve by becoming an Asian American Larry Flynt. *Masters of the Pillow.* Dir. James Hou. Avenue Films, 2003.

can Larry Flynt—to have stores, a website, DVD, products, everything. I want to buy the *Hustler* building—occupy that building with my name up there as Hamamoto Enterprises Worldwide." He also often repeats that the response to his work is "overwhelmingly enthusiastic from everyone in their early 20s to mid-70s," that it's a project that's long overdue. "Asia is the most densely populated part of the world. Asians are the masters of the pillow," the film concludes. Here the film ends not with what we discover through the sexual acts between the Asian American man and woman but with Hamamoto's articulation of his desire for the phallus—to achieve symbolic and literal power of conventional and dominant manhood in the form of capitalist ownership within the pornography industry.

Hamamoto's demand that Asian American men be considered viable pornographic subjects and his goal of achieving visibility involve narcissism, defined in the simplest terms as the assertion of the self as central, important, and as a love object.[56] However, I argue that narcissism is not the right solution for the ethical dilemma of Asian American sexual problems, but instead what is needed are care and concern for the self and others. Indeed, the political act of demanding social recognition by those without access to it requires a self-centralizing frame. However, narcissism can lead to the repression of others, in this case non-heteronormative subjects or practices, and the return of the sexually powerful/servile Asian American woman. Placing Asian American men in a forum, in this case porn, where they are not represented fulfills the search for oneself in representation, but when that representation is not problematized for its marginalization of others, then it becomes an affirmation of a desire for the way things are. If, as Crystal Parikh argues, ego-erotics are present in all identity politics, how then do we assess the necessity or prevalence of narcissism and its possible cost to others?[57] That is, if narcissism is essential for Hamamoto to assert the importance of Asian American male heterosexual representations in pornography, is it acceptable to settle for individual self-love and to forsake love of one's racial community, including women in that community? Ultimately, Hamamoto rejects Parikh's identification of the potential power of alternative masculine subject formation in redefining Asian American masculinity. Instead, he chooses a form of compulsory racial heterosexuality that ultimately aspires to serve the self, or to fulfill a form of male narcissism that forsakes others within the very racial group for which the case of inequality is made. Moving away from narcissism and the concern for the self at the expense of others, we now explore works that attend to the shattering of the self in sexuality so as to figure a manhood that goes beyond the self to care for others.

The Shattering of the Self in Sex: Lessons from David Mura's *A Male Grief*

An ethical form of manhood uses intimacy as the opportunity for reflection and representation as a process of exploration, rather than an imposition of fantasies and identities. Ethical manhoods are formed in the shattering of the self through intimacy as sites for disassembling and reassembling one's identity. This occurs only with reflection in the work of sexual representation. If the sexual act witnesses the shattering of the coherency of the self in jouissance—what Juliana Chang translates from Jacques Lacan as the simultaneity of enjoyment and trauma in the racial scene of subject formation[58]—it offers in my study the opportunity for evaluating the self in relation to another and the world. The formation of manhood is authored by the self in the moment of intimacy, in the context of one's conditions, and affords the opportunity to reflect upon the meaning of the sex act and its implications for and beyond the self.

The conditions for developing Asian American manhoods on screen include the social forces of gender, race, and sexuality mapping the ways individuals arrive at moments of sex as the opportunity to form an ethics of manhood. If we use this rubric, of asking how individuals understand their subjectivity as both capable of discipline and action, we can see how the gestures and acts performed by the men on screen formulate Asian American masculinities that are good for Asian American men as well as conducive to the social relationships contextualizing their subject formation. The experience of masculine anxiety, that unsexy male malaise, can lead not only to the upholding of phallic power and gender hierarchy but to the more unwieldy place of imagining and creating new worlds that directly confront and critique hierarchies of masculine subjectivities.

To help make sense of the impact of an unethical heterosexual manhood in Hamamoto, I use the problematic definitions of gender and sex in *A Male Grief: Notes on Pornography and Addiction* by Japanese American sansei and heterosexual male writer David Mura, whose work as a poet, essayist, and novelist engages race, gender, and sexuality. Winner of the Milk-weed Creative Nonfiction award, Mura creates in this chapbook a work of art that meditates on the making of manhood through pornography. Upon the undoing of straitjacket sexuality, as a manhood that must be upheld and to which men must aspire, I attempt through the work of Mura to decenter the Asian American man as a victim of sexuality, a banner too often raised to justify the subjugation of others in making one's racialized manhood.

In his chapbook, David Mura describes a psychic experience in consuming pornography. To engage in its pleasure is to call up one's history. Mura expresses the intensity of pornography and male addiction to it as a "grief" that shows us the pursuit of the body in "vertigo, a fearful exhilaration, a moment when all the addict's ties to the outside world do indeed seem to be cut or numbed. That sense of endless falling, that rush, is what the addict chases again and again."[59] Here, pornography is a site of fantasy where a psychic entanglement and disentanglement occurs in the physical experience of pleasure. Pornography allows flight from one's location and bodily image as a castrated Asian American man and articulates fantasy as desire. It is a position of incoherency in David Mura's description. Mura's definition enables me to show the problem in Hamamoto's and Hou's prominent examples of Asian American male engagement with pornography where they enter the scene already set on taking the dominant position, a position of coherency that must be achieved for masculinity by territorializing others. For Mura, pornography and addiction to it are about experiencing a release from the self and its structuring desires.

Pornography requires a physical response. According to Mura, the experience is not pornographic if the response is without passion or not "strong sexually."[60] Mura engages male addiction not only to pornography but to a larger set of what he calls "sexual 'highs'" that include "affairs, visits to prostitutes, anonymous sex, exhibitionism, voyeurism, etc."[61] In writing that allows no admission of guilt for the author, he sets up addiction as a possibility, not a fact, and therefore a premise for exploring the meaning of pornography and its consumption by men. In *A Male Grief,* Mura identifies how the "psychic pain" inflicted by cultures of violence and abuse as one becomes a man is drugged by pornography into a "numbing."[62] To be addicted to pornography is to be enslaved by it and its philosophy of privileging sexuality as the main sense, the primary category of identity that measures one's own as well as the other's worth. Mura says, "Any element

which questions the illusion that sexuality is all encompassing, must be denied."[63] All other factors, categories, and lenses of analyses disappear and are
subsumed under sexuality. One becomes stupefied by sexuality.

I believe this critique of sexual overdetermination helps to illuminate
Hamamoto's definition of fantasy as limited and inadequate in identifying
the needs and problems of Asian American men. His pornography does
not do justice to the actual experience of sex as an arena that ropes in one's
history, emotions, and complex psyche. The sexual experience is not reduc-
ible to the flesh in the body of the woman or even the man. In Hamamoto,
to use Mura's words, "each gesture, each word, each image is read first and
foremost through sexuality. Love or tenderness, pity or compassion, become
subsumed by a greater force . . . reduced to a single common denomina-
tor."[64] Sexuality is the primary force in pornography and it is this privileged
definition that limits Hou's and Hamamoto's visions of viable manhoods
unbridled by racial oppression.

While Mura finds convincing the feminist antiporn argument that pornography is abusive to women, arguing that the master, like Sade, requires a
victim who has no choice, I find his definition lacking theorization in terms
of the dialectics of power and consent. He makes this claim of women's injury by pornography so as to prove that men also abuse themselves through
viewing the world "pornographically."[65] Men become their own victim, Mura
argues. What porn cannot address, according to Mura, is male pain from
abuse learned and experienced as a child in the process of becoming a man.

The pain and suffering of men—what he calls male grief—is learned
from childhood and the experience of enduring adults who are in charge
of defining the world. Children learn frameworks and attitudes from their
parents—what is called in psychoanalysis as the law of the father. In Kaja
Silverman's work on Althusser, she identifies the primacy of the family as the
original wound that structures the child's perspective. She says "it is through
ideological belief that a society's reality is constituted and sustained and that
a subject lays claim to normative identity. . . . Dominant fiction or ideological reality solicits our faith above all else in the unity of the family and the
adequacy of the male subject."[66] For Mura, the world the parents provide is
the only one children know. If the world of abuse comprises what children
understand to be love, this is a testament to the power of adults to overwhelm and determine the worlds of their children. Even if the child resists,
the adult can refuse the child the right to resist. In other words, according to

Mura, the adult can refuse the child's assertion of childhood and abuse the child. It is a mighty lesson to learn abuse as love. Mura defines the consequences in the child's definition of sex: "the exertion of power by the stronger over the weaker . . . the denial of feelings . . . is fear and secrecy . . . [and is] how I can make others pay attention to me."[67] In this scenario, abuse leads to pornography as self-abuse, for it acts as a repository of unexpressed rage and displaced affection. Parents are responsible for making sure their children know their right to say "no" and to express their feelings. He notes that "facial expression and body posture can tell a child what to express" and parents can reproduce lives lived in alienation if unexpressed, so that the "victim has disappeared in the conspiracy of silence" because he or she "lack[s] knowledge of another way of acting."[68] Adults must make available to children especially the tools to speak!

In speaking, the child unleashes the power of feelings that help in knowing and navigating the world. Feelings, Mura describes, "tell us how the world moves beyond our control, beyond whatever boundaries or categories are set up by our intellect. In a sense feelings are prior to language, closer to our animal being." As such, for Mura, "the language of the body communicates neither ideas nor facts but the feeling self."[69] Through Mura, I argue that the "feeling self" is what is missing in Hamamoto's definition of pornography—within the sex act and the representation of sexuality. Hamamoto uses the actors in *Yellowcaust*—both the man and the woman—to illustrate an addictive sexuality whose political lessons are very limited.

The difference between addictive sexuality and intimate sexuality is crucial in defining Asian American manhood. When Hamamoto directs the couple to gaze upon each other's object status as *beautiful woman, sexy man,* what is missing is the intimate sexuality that leads to and exposes the multi-layered meanings at work in the sex act. In Hamamoto's work, sex acts are finite and predictable lessons about manhood and not an opening into infinity and the unpredictability of the body and the psyche when engaging another. Mura helps me to define how it is through intimate sexuality that we can witness the ethical formation or the ethical turn of manhood. He precisely describes this opportunity in the sex act:

> Intimate sexuality believes that sexuality can contain not only the other but also one's emotions, history, fallibilities and possibilities. Such an acknowledgment though is extremely frightening: it is an affirmation of all we do

not control, a letting go of our defenses. It admits the knowledge of the pain we bear.[70]

In this passage, I identify the shattering of the self in the sexual act where the power of sexual experience can lead us to embark on a process of ethical reflection and recognition. Pornography sets off a trembling inside Mura that resonates today in scenes such as his wife arriving to find him bending down in shame about his sexuality.[71] Men endure a lot of pain in this area of inquiry, but Hamamoto and Hou focus on it as a victimization that can be solved by aggressive masculinity. They ignore the intimate as a site of recognition for male vulnerability as well as lack and the process of over-coming that lack via connecting with the other as a form of care for the self.

Hamamoto's work encourages Asian American men to be conscious of their victimization, but not their power, or the larger worlds where Asian Ameri-can men confront the intimacies of the accusations of asexuality/effeminacy/queerness as lack. In his recent work, Viet Nguyen describes this process as a violent remasculinization of those deprived of manhood in American cul-ture.[72] This is helpful in showing how Hamamoto's film does not go beyond identifying men as the object upon which power operates. I argue that this is not enough to attend to the problem of sexuality for men, for a man must also recognize himself as the cause for and the agent of power through his own actions. To escape a racial narcissism that may be good for one person or constituency, but not for others, one has to decenter oneself and account for one's role in the encounter of power in and out of cinematic representation.

Conclusion: *Forever Bottom!*, *Dick Ho*, *Asian Pride Porn*, and Keni Styles' Porn Star Blog

The future is promising for Asian American men to use pornography as a venue for showing the multiple manhoods available between the poles of lack and domination in sexual representations. I conclude this chapter with a sprinkling of works that explore the politicizing of the bottom, in Hoang Nguyen's classic videowork *Forever Bottom!*, a film that eroticizes the posi-tion assigned to Asian gay men as the bottom in sexual and social relations of power; the absence of Asian American men in the 1970s porn industry, in Jeffery Lei's *Dick Ho: Asian Male Porn Star*, a spoof of 1970s porn and Asian

American male heterosexual prowess and stardom; and finally, the emergent stardom of an Asian American male, in the blog of the Adult Video News Award-nominated porn star Keni Styles, British Asian a heterosexual actor who blogs avidly about his work in the global porn industry. These works expand the repertoire of Asian American male sexualities from a myriad of positions and particularities.

In the queer classic video *Forever Bottom!* (1999), Hoang Nguyen shoots himself first in the privacy of his own home as he supposedly is anally penetrated. His camera acts as the penetrator as his legs frame the screen. Refusing to hierarchize the position of bottom as one without power, Nguyen positions his body to actively receive and respond to the penetrations by the camera (and by the spectator) in a wide array of spaces that move on to the public sphere, whether in the car or the beach. In each, he gyrates and shrieks with the efforts of generating self-pleasure. An assertion of insatiability for the pleasurable position of the bottom in gay male sexual practice, the film demands recognition and protection of pleasures we deem right for ourselves in the face of their classification as undesirable, powerless, and colonizing. In *Asian Pride Porn* (2000) by Greg Pak, the playwright David Henry Hwang advertises a fake pornography series called "Asian Pride Porn" that claims to enable sexual pleasure that won't contradict one's progressive politics. It features scenes such as a Chinese American delivery person bringing not only food but sex as the woman gives the camera knowing looks. *Dick Ho* (2005) by Jeffrey Lei asserts the hidden history of a fictional Asian American male heterosexual porn star in the golden age of pornography in the 1970s. Porn legends such as Annie Sprinkle and Sharon Mitchell testify to his skills as a sexual actor, including his martial arts training, as well as the size of his penis. We see him as a Chinese food delivery man, a monk of sorts, and in other roles with a variety of women in and out of coitus. The film directly confronts the absence of Asian American men in the porn industry by inserting this fictional character in history, humorously. It does not assert a need for Asian American men to be in porn, but comments on their absence by establishing as believable the function of stereotypes in the language and grammar of pornography.

Keni Styles, the first Asian heterosexual actor to receive recognition in the American porn industry, blogs about his life and work as a "Lucky Asian Guy" on www.kenistyles.com, where he declares a humble mission to document his luck in scoring a career in porn. As a youth, he emigrated from

Thailand to England, where he grew up. As a professional porn actor, he lives where his work and porn-star life take him. He describes the blog as follows:

> I started this blog so that I could look back and remember how lucky I've been. I also wanted to show you guys a real insiders [*sic*] look at this fantastic, crazy, exciting and sexy life in the world of porn! Making this blog exercises the few parts of my brain that aren't controlled by my dick! I'm trying my best not to evolve into a just 'that' hired piece of meat! Anyway, don't take me too seriously, I'm just having a bit of fun! I've designed and written it all by myself and it's my first crack at this web stuff so yes of course I am super proud!

Written in an approachable and light-hearted voice, the blog presents a persona of an easygoing, typical, and everyday guy who happens upon the porn industry. Styles comes from a military background and has a lithe and strong physique, which is prominently displayed online. He describes his encounters with young stars with whom he is shy at first and then makes a concerted effort to talk with before their sex scenes, so as to get to know them and to overcome his shyness before their intimate encounter. He emerges as a nice guy who is quite aware of his classification but won't present himself according to it. He understands that he meets his sexual partners as individuals and attempts to alleviate the social awkwardness in the artificial nature of pornography's sex with strangers by connecting with others and attempting to experience pleasure with other people. Sex is an activity entailing pleasure and it is a social and intimate practice he addresses with care in order to emerge with experiences worthy of evaluation and celebration as part of a fully lived life. As such, his blog is full of quotations from the marketing of his films: the brash, hunky, sexy—and enjoying it as a phenomenon outside himself.

My analysis of Keni Styles' blog focuses on a particular instance so as to illustrate the forms of masculinity he deploys to compete in macho manhood games. In his entry "In Love with Cindy Hope For a Day . . . ," posted on May 21, 2009, Styles describes in detail his meeting "the ridiculously hot chick Cindy Hope." His definition of hotness resides in not only her physical beauty but her ability to relate to others as "cool, funny, friendly and smart. She definitely has her head switched on and seems buzzing with energy and enthusiasm about everything." Most important in this description is his attribution of consciousness to her personhood. Within the setting of porn, his observation regarding her as "switched on" points to an awareness of self in the industry of producing sex on screen as an important act one does consciously. His description further illuminates the awkward relationships that need to be navigated within an industry where sex is a guaranteed enterprise for the actors who are just meeting each other. Keni describes his self-consciousness as well in acting "ridiculously distant and awkward" as he plays with his iPhone, and demonstrates awareness of his being "tongue-tied and not knowing where to look, or what to make small talk about." In this description, we see lack in the sense of questioning one's existence and being as qualified to compete for her attention. He plays with her dog instead until he does "man up," meaning he could no longer "avoid her eye contact," and comes face-to-face with the knowledge that sexual contact is certain—he introduces himself and asks to film her for his blog. She responds positively and he expresses surprise. In a conventional mode of heterosexual courtship, she actually awaits his moves to reveal her knowledge and awareness of him, his blog, and their mutual friends. In this scene, we see that they both understand and comply with male and female gendered social choreographies and perform accordingly. He says he falls in love at that moment (for a day). This description is crucial—he notes her touching him and his feelings of confidence that result from her desire and affirmation. He questions his own responses—"I even nervously and slightly creepily strocked [*sic*] her HAIR!? WTF was I thinking? . . . erm anyway she didn't scream and run off so I was smiling from ear to ear like a Cheshire cat!" He then follows her around somewhat obediently "like a lost puppy." He describes himself pointedly, in contrast to those whom he describes as "smelly alpha male types. Over brimming with testosterone on set, they gotta touch everyone up, grabbing or drooling over anything that moves. It's horrible and sleezy [*sic*], almost painful to watch sometimes. I'm always conscious never to come across like that." In this way, we see his formulation of an alternative that depends on consciousness and awareness.

No manhood is unaffected by the normative standards of what makes a man. In Keni Styles' work as a porn star, we see the ultimate criterion by which to judge viable manhoods: awareness of others and oneself in encounters of intimacy where recognition and connection are possible. It is crucial not to use each other, but for an actual exchange to occur. "I'm not arrogant but I am not the quiet grey man in the corner who does his best, pops a load and slides off home without anyone even remembering his name either."

Styles attempts to experience sex as a man who follows the choreographies of manhood—the requirement of strength, aggression, and action.

> We come to the kissy bit. Well, there is no way I'm not gona [*sic*] let her know I'm the man here in this one so I look her dead in the eye, hold her hand with one hand and the back of her head with the other and move in for a kiss. I pressed my lips firmly but not forcefully and I enjoyed the smell of her lipstick and the softness of her lips on mine mmmmm.

Key to following the choreographies of gender in sexual relations is the delivery: Keni Styles knows to offer care, affection, and pleasure and to receive the same in mutual recognition. He demonstrates an ethical manhood in explicit representations of sexuality in pornography and beyond.

This chapter focuses on the genre intent on arousing pleasure, particularly studying a wide array of Asian American male engagements with pornography and explicit sexuality, for in it we see crystallized the powerful search not only for the penis but a specific kind of wrestling with phallic power's elusiveness. As I have already noted, Asian American men are largely absent from the U.S. porn industry, yet, as Richard Fung argues, there is a prominence of Asian American bottoms in gay porn. At first glance and in the literature, the framework of asexuality/effeminacy seems a precise diagnosis for Asian American men in this multibillion dollar industry of representation. However, pornography tells us not only about the power of cinema in relation to fantasy but also about the centrality of the body and the penis to our ideas about manhood and alternatives to those ideas, as we in the work of Hoang Nguyen, Greg Pak, Jeffrey Lei, and especially Keni Styles.

In the next chapter, I show that the sex of pornography is not the only sex available to Asian American men in the movies. Asian American men have been having sex in the movies for decades. I rewind fifty years to the work of Hollywood heartthrob and dreamboat James Shigeta, whose handsome looks and dashing demeanor as leading man in 1950s and 1960s Hollywood films drew legions of female fans, and explore how his movies especially in terms of the actualizing and problematizing of romantic love between white women and Asian men at the dawn of the Civil Rights era in the United States. In his films, we see the Asian American man grapple with what it means to be the object of love by white and Asian women and what it means to be the lead in someone's eyes and on screen. His roles and performances negotiating gender and racial power as well as class and sexuality can be in effect a lesson from the past in building an ethical manhood for today. I also bring Shigeta's work into conversation with that of Jason Scott Lee, who made several films as a leading man in the 1990s, approximately forty years after Shigeta. To capture both their wielding of power over others and their bearing of lashes by others is a special subject position from which a theory of ethical relations may emerge. From my interview with Lee and my reading of his works involving fantasy characters in inter- and intra-racial romance, I formulate an ethics of masculinity that is embodied in a calm manhood that emerges from the cranky male malaise subjecting Asian American men in the movies. Evaluating James Shigeta and Jason Scott Lee, along with notes on John Cho and the minor characters who populate current mass media, highlights the options available and still changing for Asian American manhoods in U.S. popular culture.

FIVE

Unbinding Straitjacket Sexuality

The Calm Manhoods of
Asian American Male Hollywood Stars

In this chapter, for the sake of the future, I call back from cinematic history two Asian American actors who counter the amnesia regarding Asian
American male romantic leads in the movies: one a 1950s heartthrob and
the other a 1990s sex symbol. Critical performances by James Shigeta in
1959–1961 and Jason Scott Lee in 1993–1994 challenge the representations
of Asian American men as repudiated figures when they become idealized objects and subjects of love, desire, and sex in Hollywood films. As
romantic leads, they confront dissonance with ideality, which is the position of acknowledgment and acceptance as a man, usually unavailable to
Asian American men within U.S. industry representations. In their films,
these Asian American men struggle with their racializations in the realms
of love and sex. They face obstacles in accepting the position of deserving
love object as well as grabbing the central role of the subject, specifically,
the one with power to confer recognition on others. Their roles fulfill and
exceed what film theorist Kaja Silverman calls "political ecstasy," or the
amazing ability of cinema, in the face of limited frames in which Asian
American male actors exit, to move spectators away from their own structural location to a place where they can identify with the disprized other.
Rendered impossible and fantastic even as they move from undesirable
to desirable and desiring subjects, Asian American actors can nonetheless
produce ethical examples for how to be a man in the face of racial, sexual,
and gendered pressures.

Theorizing the Ethics of Inter- and Intra-racial Relationships of Love and Sex

Kaja Silverman argues in the context of psychoanalytically theorizing love in the movies, that "ideality is the single most powerful inducement for identification; we cannot idealize something without at the same time identifying with it. Idealization is therefore a crucial political tool, which can give us access to a whole range of new psychic relations."[1] In effect, to idealize— to assign value and desire—generates empathy, essential for understanding another's circumstances. For Silverman, this process is not conscious and is often "textually steered. We consequently need aesthetic works which will make it possible for us to idealize, and, so to identify with bodies we would otherwise repudiate."[2] Here, film possesses the magnificent potential to make subjects aware of others who occupy concretely different bodies and that then shapes not only the subjects' experiences but the availability of choices in life.

Silverman advises us that any identification across difference occurs "excorporatively rather than incorporatively, and, thereby respect[s] the otherness of the newly illuminated bodies. It is equally vital that we be brought to a conscious knowledge" of our own agentic role in that learning.[3] To clarify her concept of political ecstasy, though a rapturous feeling of transcendence, it does not negate the very real confines of identity and body. It's not a matter of becoming the other, or uniting with the other's body, but of learning from proximity, so as to invest in the other's future and well-being. In this, Silverman assigns immense responsibility to the viewer: "The eye can confer the active gift of love upon bodies who have long been accustomed to neglect and disdain."[4] For Silverman, it is in the location of the spectator in the act of any viewing that we can see the potential to transform our culture. When we fall in love with or identify with difference, we have the opportunity for changing our ability to care for those considered abject. She especially encourages the embrace of "spectatorial self-estrangement" when we watch a film that counters previously held beliefs.[5] The projecting within the "bodily parameters" of femininity, masculinity; within the privileged, the homeless; the straight and the gay in each other's shoes is a site of potential transformation with important social ramifications.

This method would "eroticize this identity-at-a-distance (or the separation one feels from another subject), and, so, make it the source of new and intoxicating pleasures."[6] As such, film, as another subject, is particularly the "privileged potential vehicle for . . . political ecstasy" because of its "propensity for abducting the spectator out of him- or herself."[7] In this chapter, I show how we can see this dynamic—what I call the shattering and reassembly of the self—by the spectator indeed, but also by the actor. I am specifically interested in how James Shigeta, one of the very first Asian American romantic leading men in major Hollywood films and forty years later, Jason Scott Lee, one of the most sexualized Asian American men in screen history, show us the workings of political ecstasy and its limits.

When films present these characters as impossible—where Shigeta's Joe Kojaku in *The Crimson Kimono* simply imagines racism and where Lee's characters occupy unrealistic and unworldly roles as men—the effects of political ecstasy are curtailed. What I am concerned about is that the seemingly sympathetic representation of derivative subjects can actually be strange, as I will show in my analysis of Shigeta's and Lee's works. So while films can certainly expand our ideas about others, they can also shut them down. Using this framework of understanding the power of cinema, I consider the production of Asian American manhood in terms of a sexuality that limits not only ideality but identification itself. If the fruits of political ecstasy are based on a fleeting image, an anomaly that occurs only once every forty years or so, what will be the long-lasting effects of its politics? I interview Jason Scott Lee to better understand the constraints he faced as an Asian American actor in leading romantic roles as a sex symbol—a transitory phenomenon that leads him to another place, what I call a calm manhood, building from what Emmanuel Levinas refers to as "peace-with-self."[8]

James Shigeta, Asian American Romantic Lead

A rather dapper Dan with heartthrob good looks, James Shigeta was cast as a romantic lead in four major Hollywood films from 1959 to 1961. The films *The Crimson Kimono* (1959), *Walk Like a Dragon* (1960), *Flower Drum Song* (1961), and *Bridge to the Sun* (1961), for which he won Best Newcomer at the Golden Globe Awards, featured Shigeta in roles that intensely engaged the meaning of heterosexual courtship, love, and marriage across racial difference. This is especially so in *The Crimson Kimono*. Shigeta played roles that reflected rapid and tumultuous change in social relations during the era stretching from the end World War II, through the rise of the Cold War and the emergence of the Civil Rights movement, to the Vietnam War: a Japanese ambassador to the U.S. at the beginning of World War II in *Bridge to the Sun* (1961), a Chinese worker during the California Gold Rush in *Walk Like a Dragon* (1960), a second-generation, college-aged Chinese American fraternity boy in *Flower Drum Song* (1961), and a Los Angeles-based Japanese American detective in *The Crimson Kimono* (1959). I focus on Shigeta's character in *The Crimson Kimono* as one who problematizes love with a white woman to recast interracial love as an ethical relation and a fantasy.

The *Crimson Kimono* must be contextualized in the Cold War, specifically U.S.-Japan relations, and domesticity. In *Orientals*, his book on Asian Americans in popular culture, Robert G. Lee argues that liberalism makes racial equality the idealized law of the land in an era of miscegenation where the "Oriental [was transformed] from the exotic to the acceptable."[9] Lee describes how World War II "unraveled the Yellow Peril" and how the Japanese bombing of Pearl Harbor and the incarceration of Japanese Americans in internment camps in the United States "brought into sharp focus the contradiction between their exclusion as racial subjects and the promise of their assimilation as ethnic citizens."[10] Similarly, historian Naoko Shibusawa traces U.S. popular culture's interest in presenting Japanese Americans as an important ally in both literature and film. Intermarriage between Asians and (white) Americans came to be looked upon as deserving of not only "focus" but indeed sympathy.[11] According to Elaine Tyler May, the national embrace of marriage by "postwar Americans [revealed an] intense need to feel liberated from the past and secure in the future."[12] In the context of anticommunism and fear of larger social forces, the "home" came to be the site for "domestic containment" or the place where social problems could be alleviated.[13] Within these pressures, the family and couple came to be the site for gender ideology, national politics, and social anxiety about racial difference. That is, love became a battlefield for social relations. These historical events informed and made possible Shigeta's roles such as in *The Crimson Kimono*, which explicitly acknowledges and centralizes what it means to be a socially disprized subject in giving and receiving love. Through him, we access what it means to form an identity as a racialized man competing against a less-than-ideal interpellation. Social assignations organize the character's self-perceptions and self-identities, demanding action and choice—even if the film ultimately pathologizes his understanding of race and racism as imagined.

The Crimson Kimono (1959)

In Samuel Fuller's noir feature *The Crimson Kimono*, Hawaiian-born Japanese American actor James Shigeta played his first leading role as a Japanese American police detective named Joe Kojaku, a man at the center of a racialized love triangle between him, his partner Charlie and a key witness named Chris during a murder investigation. His best friend and fellow police detective, a white man named Charlie with whom his bonds stretch back to their wartime brotherhood, falls in love with a "pretty blonde," Chris, who actually loves Joe. In *The Crimson Kimono*, the racialized male other wins the love of the woman. Nevertheless, he experiences this success with a kind of racial and gendered melancholy, a concept I will discuss in the context of Asian American critique. The film shows how his attainment of the desired object of love entails the loss of a male friendship that he then mourns. A form of romantic grief ensues, which he must break to unleash his own desires.

The film's portrayal of racial melancholy, a term theorized by Anne Anlin Cheng, and David Eng and Shinhee Han, exceeds the examples of effeminate and emasculated manhoods vilified in popular representations.[14] What choices does Joe Kojaku have to make his manhood worthy of love? He negotiates a larger field of social relations where there's a difference not only between desirable and undesirable ways of being but also courtship rituals and other practices. In my analysis, Joe recognizes his place in a hierarchy of manhoods. While he has the opportunity to chart relations anew, he does so with hesitation. Cheng asks, "How does one master the world at large on the one hand and sustain difference as identity on the other? What kind of mourning enables social survival and what kind disables communal relations?"[15] I find this helpful in my evaluation of Joe Kojaku, who understands his romantic crisis to be a racial crossroads for terrains of both friendship and love.

Joe and Charlie live together as friends and establish what Eve Sedgwick calls a homosocial bond, as the two men very apparently share a great comfort in each other.[16] The homosocial bond is the "affective or social force, the glue" that holds men together in an important relationship.[17] Women allow for a bond to develop between men in sexual terms. In competing for women, men who are not allowed to express desire for each other direct their energies into a love triangle in order to relieve the forces that bind them.[18] The love triangle in *The Crimson Kimono* reveals the asymmetrical ways gender is constructed for these differently racialized men. Joe and

Charlie compete for and approach Chris differently in terms of their court-ship practices.

Film scholar Richard Dyer posits the problem of representing (white) male sexuality as the default sexuality—the opposite of perverse and abnormal sexuality: "Even when not looking at male sexuality, we are looking at a world within its terms of reference."[19] Moreover, when we see "routine" aspects of sexuality in cinema "they feel almost natural, just the 'way things are done' . . . so obvious and inevitable, we can lose sight of the fact that what they are actually representing is a particular sense of male sexuality with its own history and social form."[20] In Charlie's case, he looks upon Chris with desire, which he expresses in a matter-of-fact aggressive and forceful manner. He kisses her, grabs her—and she surrenders. As spectators, we then recognize them as typical romantic hero and heroine where the man pursues the woman and declares his intent through sexual aggressiveness. Following Dyer, this coupling occurs in the story to reaffirm male sexuality in conventional ways. Dyer asserts that narrative filmmaking "reinforces a notion of male sexuality . . . to see things from a male point of view, and moreover to see things through a particular sexual sensibility."[21] Dyer cites Nancy Henley's *Body Politics* to point to conventions in "heterosexual exchanges" that occur as follows: "Men stare at women, women submit to being looked at, or at most steal a glance."[22] She occupies a position of "vulnerability" in relation to men where "we are invited to relate to the heroine through this version of heterosexual male sexuality." Indeed, this is what distinguishes the men in the movie from each other. Strong and aggressive Charlie pushes himself onto Chris—while Joe exposes both the power of his love for her and his own vulnerability in their relationship.

Alone after dinner, Chris inquires about Joe's cultural background by observing: "Charlie tells me you're quite an expert at kendo." Joe translates that this martial art is like monks wearing baseball catcher outfits. Here, he describes the cultural practice humorously and in a way that's very American, citing the national sport. He gauges her interest for "after dinner music" and she takes this opportunity to plead with him to play the piano. His playing of the children's song "Akatombo," or red dragonfly, moves her. She expresses interest in him with questions that dig deeper. "What made you become a policeman?" she inquires. And he tells her how his father, as an artist, found "utopia in painting" while he found detective work more reliable. In this conversation, racial difference becomes unthreatening. She affirms his attempt to provide her the reassurance of his normalcy against his more obvious racial difference. Her response is to declare that she already knows that about him. Here we note that she establishes romantic interest in her statement of recognition.

Next, Joe demonstrates their compatibility based on shared interests. He gives Chris feedback on her artwork, which she appreciates and makes her even more interested in him. It becomes apparent that she desires to be with him, for the next thing she asks is if he has a "girl." He replies no, saying "I'll know at first glance if the right girl comes along." Suddenly, the conversation takes on a sexual energy. "Do you feel people fall in love who've never heard of love?" His obscure question meets a grounded response in her, which identifies the feelings between them. "You can't fight natural feelings." This line authorizes him to approach her from behind, leaning in to smell her hair as she relishes his closeness. "Let's not trigger a bomb" he says. At this point, she realizes that he won't kiss her, won't acknowledge the intense attraction they feel for each other.

Their conversation—intellectual and informative—differs from her carnally driven pairing with Charlie earlier in the film. Joe and Chris withhold the consummation of a kiss as they relish its possibility. He connects with her by talking about their shared interests. Unlike Charlie, Joe does not

FIGURE 20   In the conversation that ignites an intense bond between Joe and Chris, they almost kiss. *The Crimson Kimono.* Dir. Samuel Fuller. Columbia Pictures, 1959.

use sex to achieve intimacy but rather talks his way into that place. His is a different form of masculinity, for it approaches femininity differently. It is premised on her making a choice to be with him in the context of competing masculinities vying for her attention. His position is imbued with sensitivity and emotion. These emotions are multilayered beyond his courtship—for he tangles with his position as a sidekick, an interloper, and an outsider whose emotions and subjectivity are usually peripheral to love and friendship in everyday life and in the tradition of the cinema. In claiming his position as her lover, he struggles with moving to the center, or taking the lead of the movie's narration.

In the next scene, we indeed discover the racial reasons why Joe won't move forward with Chris. He discloses to Mr. Yoshinaga, an elder of the community, that he's "got a problem. A girl . . . she's Caucasian. I love her. . . . I'm all mixed up, I don't know what to do. I didn't look to fall in love with her, it happened." His love is presented as a problem of crossing social boundaries that his emotions did not recognize and he does not know how to overcome feelings that do not follow racial borders. The term "mixed up" indicates the confusion he feels. To "mix," when added with the word "up," can also mean his fear of making a mistake. His confession to Mr. Yoshinaga includes his understanding of the mismatch, precisely because of their racial difference: "How do I meet a girl, like Chris? Me, Joe Kojaku. It would be wrong . . ." In his previous encounter with Chris, we recall that he asserts his background and does not hide it. He emphasizes their common interests: his ability to speak of her art as the son of a painter and his Americanness in negotiating a description of kendo in relation to baseball. Now that he is at the threshold, with the opportunity of accepting her love, he presents their racial ethnic backgrounds as a problem that not only tests social mores but his intimate sense of self. He questions his ability to let his love for a white woman out and fears the implications. Joe experiences sexuality not as mastery, but as a refusal and as a source of anxiety.

In cinema, film scholar Richard Dyer says, "male sexuality is said to be goal-oriented; seduction and foreplay are merely the means by which one gets to the 'real thing,' an orgasm, the great single climax."[23] We already see Charlie heading toward the goal of claiming Chris as a prize while Joe refuses her, the willing object of his desire. Joe prioritizes Charlie, for the sake of maintaining their friendship. In this sense, Joe's decision comes to be a refusal of the position of the "central protagonist—[as the one] who make[s] things happen and who move[s] the narrative along. . . . The drive to a climax is so bound up with the promise of a woman at the end that all stories seem to be modeled on male sexuality."[24] Thus ultimately, Joe refuses the woman, the heroic role, and male sexuality to become the friend—and deprive himself of joy.

Joe considers his emotions secondary in prioritizing his friend Charlie's subjectivity. For this, Joe enters into a state of mourning—what Freud defines as the loss of one's love object and more (ideals, country, and freedom).[25] Eng and Han describe mourning as "a psychic process in which the loss of an object or ideal occasions the withdrawal of libido from that object or ideal."[26] Indeed, Joe's character withdraws into himself—he is on the verge of shriveling. Charlie, in contrast, barely contains his frustration with Joe. "What's the matter with you? You feel like a zombie." The frustration, rather than exploding, gives way to affection. Charlie dismisses Joe's mood rather than unleashing himself in violence. Charlie withholds violence because of his affection for Joe. And Joe prioritizes his friendship and chooses Charlie above his own desires. They love each other in a way that is different from the usual understanding of male relationality. Between these men, a kind of beautiful care exists in their homosocial relations, away from the penis and the phallus. Charlie even defends Joe against Chris, whom he misinterprets as using a racial slur against Joe. Between men, we see relations of tenderness.

In relation to Chris, Charlie's representation is of the phallus—the man in power, dominant, and commanding in his approach. What we see in the presence of Joe in the romantic lead is the offering of a different manhood in the form of calm and restraint. He won't press Chris and make her fit into a way of relating that preexists for men and women, but instead invites her to rewrite power dynamics as they work against the classification of wrongness in their pairing. His meeting normative standards enables his alternative manhood to succeed: financial stability, height, fitness, good looks, and perhaps too, that deep baritone voice. But Chris must counter the friendship between Joe and Charlie, sealed by blood during wartime, by asserting an aggressive femininity. Chris moves away from the white male possession of her subjectivity to become a desiring figure in her own right when she declares her choice of Joe. While the traditional role for the woman is ruptured, the homosocial bond between Joe and Charlie threatens to unravel in the next scene through violence.

When Charlie and Joe combat in kendo, they fight for the opposing "Caucasian" and "Nisei" schools. When Joe violates all the rules to beat on Charlie, he gets booed. So Joe's masculinity can also be violent. From the unnatural demand of holding oneself back from self-centrality—he explodes. When Charlie awakens from Joe's beating, the latter confesses his relationship to Chris: "I'm in love with her and she's in love with me. And that's how it is." Joe declares this with a wave of his arms, as if driving home how he cannot do anything about it. "On account of you, I never even touched her. I wanted to hold her in my arms, I couldn't. It's not normal to keep my feelings bottled up. It's out, it hurts, there's nothing I can do about it." Here we see that the alternative manhood Joe presents to Chris is actually shaped by his derivative status vis-à-vis Charlie. He chooses to act more like Charlie when he "clobbers" him on the kendo floor. Like Michael in *Charlotte Sometimes*, he represses his feelings. Unlike Michael, he unleashes his rage on the other man and decides he deserves to express his desires. Cathartic for Joe is the recognition that withholding his love out of deference to Charlie means preventing himself from achieving normal sexuality. So Joe's confrontation and confession is an assertion of his own subjectivity.

In this way, Joe claims the central narrative as well as the position of hero, or rightful contender for carrying the narrative. The storytelling now comes from the possession of anxieties about what he deserves, what he can claim, and how he travels within the story to identify his wrongful subject position. It is a storyline his character dramatizes across social relations as he charts his manhood. However, the white protagonists, his best friend and his lover, question his perceptions of their racism. When Joe expects to encounter Charlie's rage at losing Chris, instead he meets a bizarre response. Charlie says, "You mean you want to marry her?" Joe interprets this statement as an affront, that Charlie considers him undeserving of Chris—as if they are not equal competitors in love due to their racial difference. In an extreme close-up that the camera settles on for some time, Joe claims that Charlie wouldn't have asked him that value-laden and disdainful question if he were white. So the homosocial bond is threatened by racial difference after all. Joe accuses him, yelling: "What burns you is you lost her to me. The thought makes you sick to your stomach. Look at your face!" But Charlie's face is ambiguous. It's hard to discern if he expresses disdain or devastation over losing Chris. The film represents Joe as confused when looking at his relations through a racial lens. Both his friend and lover question his use of this perspective.

When Joe returns to Chris, he explains that Charlie's response was "not just plain normal jealousy. That's why the words came out of me." Chris, believing the homosocial bond, rather than racial hierarchies of manhood, is responsible for Joe's anxiety, disagrees with him. "You only saw what you wanted to see," she says to Joe. But Joe further explains he recognizes the look on his best friend's face. "He doesn't have to mean it, or say it, it's there all the time. It's . . . behind every word, every look." The confrontation with Charlie enables Joe to articulate what he suspected for a long time regarding his friendships and his work: that racism shapes their disregard. But the object of his love, the one for whom his feelings lead to these discoveries, won't acknowledge his perceptions either. She challenges what he deems to be the truth of his own point of view in understanding racialized, gendered, and sexual relations. For him, it is a social problem and for her, an individual one. So if he is asking for racial recognition, she won't give it. She sees the issue differently.

Here is where the question of political ecstasy enters, away from spectatorship but into the relation of intimacy itself. Joe reminds Chris of the space between them because of their racial difference: "You gotta be in my shoes to know what I'm talking about." When she says, "I do know," she confidently asserts that she understands his way of being and how she recognizes him. I am curious if she identifies with this situation in individual and/or social ways and if she acknowledges the racial reasons that shape his perceptions and encounters. He sits down next to her and delivers a meditation on the impossibility of identification, even in love. He points to the great gap separating two subjectivities within an intimate entanglement of attraction and desire that do not merge, but remain apart despite their proximity.

> You can't feel for me unless you are me. Take a good look, Chris. Do I look different to you than I did yesterday? Did my face change? I've got to say it. I never felt this in the army or in the police. Maybe it's 5,000 years of blood behind me bursting to the front. For the first time, I feel different. I taste right through every bone inside me. I catch myself trying to figure out who I am. I was born here. I'm American. I feel it, live it, love it. But down deep, what am I? Japanese American. American Japanese. Nisei? What label do I live under? Chris, you tell me.

In his speech, Joe invests in Chris to recognize that there are differences that exist between them and exceed their particular historical moment. And the power of love does not resignify the meanings of race for him. He presents the gnawing power of racialization that precedes their relationship. Joe wants her to recognize his marginality when he asks: "Did my face change?" Interracial love, according to Joe, leads to a history larger and longer than his or her individual history. In this powerful monologue, he historicizes the length of his experience in formulating this racial perspective. The history of that racial otherness precedes even his subject formation. As David Eng and Shinhee Han state, "despite the fact that they may be U.S.-born or despite however long they have resided here, Asian Americans are continually perceived as eccentric to the nation."[27] Kojaku feels the force of that history palpably—in the very physical description of the blood he tastes inside him. This is how he describes his contention with social definitions of his personhood as well as his own individual desires that counter historical assignation. That is, his love for Chris leads to the identification of his status as a marginalized man.

Indeed, the lovers contradict each other—in this speech, he asks her to consider the gravity of his psychic and social crisis. In concluding with an apology, he engages the contradictions of his gender privilege as a man even in terms of his racialization. He says, "I'm sorry, honey. Why am I taking it out on you?" She reassures him in a way that is gendered female, but also cognizant of her own multiple positioning, including as a racially privileged subject: "You're hurt and it's the kind of pain I can't wipe out." She acknowledges his ability to hurt her and his position of pain. Her response here reveals an understanding of race and racial experience particular to him and to her as something she cannot undo or erase from their situation. At the same time, she won't delete its truthful force from his and her life. Accepting her position as a recipient of his pain is an indictment of male privilege as well as her gendered female role. For Chris, as the film ultimately advocates interracial relations, love becomes possible when the lovers' privileges and disadvantages are identified.

It takes more to convince Joe, who tests both if their love can work because of his experience with Charlie and the limits of his friendship: "[My racial difference] was on [Charlie's] mind. The cracks he made when I wasn't there." But the declaration by Chris that Joe can expect "everything" from her because she loves him counters the traditional scripts not only of the peripheral minority man but the white woman who asserts her own desire. She reminds him of their situation as an opportunity to recast previous relations before them and outside them. She says, "What you see in my face is what you want to see." She demands that he look at her face, so as to connect with her subjectivity as infinity, not totality. Together, from her perspective, they can chart new terrain as an interracial couple in love. She attempts to educate him on the concrete reality of her identification with him, that she is a white woman who fights for his consent, across their racial difference, to fall in love.

What does it mean to fall in love or fall into what Kaja Silverman calls "an identificatory alignment with the socially disprized?"[28] Throughout the film, we see Shigeta's Kojaku contend for the role of leading man with his smoldering looks and handsome face, centered on screen as the subject of love and the object of desire. We actually are enabled to occupy a position of political ecstasy through our identification with Chris—who herself falls in love with a repudiated subject in sociality. The film presents Joe's suspicions to be wrong when Charlie confesses his allegiance to him despite losing Chris. When Chris refuses to give Joe less than a full-fledged commitment when he questions her choice to love him, the film problematizes what it means for subjects usually handed vitriol to be given love.

The film concludes with Charlie and then Chris confronting Joe about his judgments against them. Charlie says, "You threw me off guard when you told me about Chris. It was a look of hate on my face. Normal, healthy, jealous hate." Joe won't respond for he recognizes that Charlie regards him as an equal in the male competition for women. Chris joins in the intervention. She's there to "do anything I can to convince you how wrong you are." The white protagonists attempt to demonstrate their faith and devotion to Joe. The only way Joe succumbs is when he solves the murder. Miss Wilson, a Caucasian wigmaker, confesses to killing a stripper, Sugar Torch. As Miss Wilson suffers from the gunshot by Joe Kojaku, she confesses that she felt insecure about herself when she encountered Sugar Torch's normative beauty. It was an illusion that killed her, for her lover never even looked at anyone else. Only now does Joe recognize his own mistake when he hears her confession. Miss Wilson portends to know what men want: Sugar Torch's body. Similarly, Joe realizes that Chris does not want the conventional leading man Charlie. She wants him, he realizes, Japanese American or American Japanese or Nisei. What is to blame, in this post–Cold War film on interracial relations, is the perception of racism that is ultimately untrue. The lesson: refuse your interpellation if it gets in the way of your centrality. For this film, the primacy of hero, lover, and sexual being is claimed for Joe when the movie ends with a passionate kiss with Chris in the streets of Little Tokyo in Los Angeles. As Joe confronts Charlie, he senses Chris running toward him from behind. He turns to her and in front of the cityscape, twirls her around and lands a huge kiss as they face each other, eye-to-eye.

The Crimson Kimono dramatizes how an Asian American man wrestles with his racialization in terms of love. He wins the woman by demonstrating an alternative and more tender masculinity that does not depend on sexual aggression. The film does not privilege machismo, or gender domination, but the complexity of particular entanglements with specific others who confront the meaning of interracial desire. The subjectivity before Joe entails difference—racial and gendered—that comes to complicate the sexual encounter uniquely. The encounter wells up with power and possibility—enough to move the self to action and change, specifically in terms of an ethical relationship that exceeds one's own subjectivity. For the character to recognize his need to assert his specific and unique subjectivity to win love is to achieve self-centrality without further marginalizing others. And

FIGURE 21   Through this kiss with Chris, Joe finally acknowledges his role as lover and hero in *The Crimson Kimono*. *The Crimson Kimono*. Dir. Samuel Fuller. Columbia Pictures, 1959.

for spectators to identify with these problems and positions is to expand the concept of who is acceptable in society.

Speculation as to why James Shigeta no longer found work as a romantic lead includes the dawn of the Vietnam War as the fall of the idea of the U.S. as a savior, a white knight. Asian American men could no longer be seen in the role of a romantic lead who engages in a complex romance with white women. The role of a lover is a powerful one—it is a position of centrality, of importance, indeed, but also one where choices and actions can show us a manhood we can learn from: how to love, how to defy interpellation, how to create one's own mirror, how to own the terms of one's misnamings, and move beyond them, to laugh at them. To attend to the archive of James Shigeta in terms of his offering of an Asian American ethics of manhood within the context of heterosexuality rectifies some of the amnesia about Asian American men on screen as not having access to romance, love, and desirable man-hoods. I identify Shigeta's rich performance that problematizes race relations in love. Romance, sex, and manhood become available in the roles played by Shigeta like never before in the careers of Sessue Hayakawa and Philip Ahn, and even yellowface actors like Richard Barthelmess. While Shigeta's romantic leading roles were momentary, he surely mined ethical Asian American man-hoods—responsible to self and others. Claims of the absence of Asian Ameri-can men in leading romantic roles need to shift—what enabled this small window to open in 1959–1961 so that James Shigeta could smolder on screen? I acknowledge his work, though short-lived, for destabilizing the claim that Asian American men never kissed and never got the girl. Not only did Shigeta make movies as a romantic leading man, he fashioned an alternative mas-culinity that made white masculinity look less attractive for its brutality as a form of power. I now move to the most recent Asian American leading man in Hollywood, with his collection of films that made available a serious wres-tling with Asian American male sexuality for new generations.

The Pono Manhood of Jason Scott Lee

Jason Scott Lee burst onto the Hollywood film scene playing the lead in a romantic triangle with a white man and a mixed-race Native American woman. A French film, *Map of the Human Heart*, features an indigenous manhood as portrayed by an Asian American actor. Soon thereafter approached to play the iconic role of Bruce Lee in *Dragon*, which I discuss in an earlier chapter, Jason Scott Lee then starred in *Rapa Nui* and *The Jungle Book*. All of his movies involve interracial romance and celebrated sex scenes—as well as the opportunity to provide an alternative manhood especially against brutish white male sexuality. Since then, Jason Scott Lee has embarked on a different kind of role—as a man living close to nature in Hawaii (where he was raised), residing on a working farm, and living for a long time without electricity. I examine Jason Scott Lee's fantasy roles as racially ambiguous men with strong sexual currency—roles I read as fantastic in terms of his ideality as a figure to love and desire. Jason Scott Lee plays indigenous men in *Rapa Nui*, *Map of the Human Heart*, and *Jungle Book* as well as Bruce Lee in *Dragon*, films that share an other-worldliness. I first analyze his work as a romantic leading man in films made in 1993 and 1994, arguing that they present a racialized manhood that is intensely sexualized as the characters Jason Scott Lee portrays struggle with power and the importance of demonstrating accountability to others. The emphasis in Lee's performances and in his own manhood off screen is not on aggression but rather a calm manhood that is not simply reactive. Instead, the characters evaluate their creative contributions to the world in an ethical determination of their actions within a wider web of social relations.

Map of the Human Heart (1993)

Map of the Human Heart tells the story of Avik, a European and Inuit mixed race boy who grows up to become an aerial photographer in World War II and ultimately disintegrates into a drunken old man in his hometown in Arctic Canada after he gives up his mixed race lover, Albertine, with whom he fathers a daughter. Avik and Albertine consummate a passionate affair in what Roger Ebert calls "two of the most astonishing romantic scenes I've ever seen in a movie—one on top of a barrage balloon, the other inside the hollow of the Royal Albert Hall."[29] The sex scenes are allegories of the obstacles the couple faces. In the first sexual encounter, in the dome, the two come together as a bomb explodes. She grips Avik with fear that then turns to arousal. Among ashes, they kiss—he becomes elated. But Albertine then tells him that she dreams of marrying a white man, thus relegating their relationship to a temporary liaison. His elation dissipates as she silences his pain with her fingers on his mouth. In the latter scene on the balloon, he strips her. When she reveals her chest, he kisses the long scar that is also revealed—reminding him of their shared physical ailments that led their hospitalization as children. We see an extreme close-up of his mouth on her chest as the shot dissolves to reveal their naked bodies on the balloon. In this way, the sex scenes are magical and out of this world—impossible physical feats of lovemaking in very high places. Indeed, it is a prelude to the failure of their love.

FIGURE 22   Albertine attempts to silence him with her touch, also an expression of her sexual desire. *Map of the Human Heart*. Dir. Vincent Ward. Australian Film Finance Corporation (AFFC), Les Films Ariane, Map Films, 1993.

FIGURE 23   Avik touches Albertine's scar and the shot dissolves to the impossible and fantastic sex scene on the barrage balloon. *Map of the Human Heart*. Dir. Vincent Ward. Australian Film Finance Corporation (AFFC), Les Films Ariane, Map Films, 1993.

When Avik's last mission as a crew member on a bomber results in a crash that only he survives, he becomes overwhelmed with guilt and retreats from both society and Albertine, to become a drunken native among the new generations of European travelers in his hometown. The film ends with his daughter with Albertine seeking him out to invite him to her wedding. He dies tragically in an accident en route, imagining a romantic reunion with Albertine as he drowns in the freezing water. In these last moments, he finally recognizes what is possible apart from the social death he lives, but it is too late. We see Avik dying intercut with the scene he intended to attend: Albertine waiting for him at their daughter's wedding. The film ends tragically, for Avik chose a manhood that retreats rather than contends with his racialization. Unlike Joe Kojaku, Avik retreats from the possibility of achieving self-centrality. The film at the same time offers promise in presenting the first Asian American sex symbol in Jason Scott Lee. What does such a sexualized cinematic presence achieve for Asian American men?

Rapa Nui (1994)

In his next film, *apa Nui*, Jason Scott Lee plays another fantastic and mostly naked indigenous character. Easter Island, according to the opening titles, is where some "1,500 bands of Native people settled . . . lost to the rest of world . . . in warring clans . . . [and lived in increasingly] barren, treeless lands [where] ancestor worship [ruled. They believed they were the] only people left on Earth." The story is told in the format of a love triangle involving two forbidden camps: the elite Long Ear and the servile Short Ear tribes. Jason Scott Lee plays Noro, the prince of the Long Ears, who loves Ramana, played by the mixed race actress Sandrine Holt, a Short Ear beauty whom he asks to marry him. She has also captured the devotion of Make, a Short Ear man played by the Chicano actor Esai Morales. The Long Ears enslave the Short Ears, demanding they build icons to the bird gods. The Long Ears then battle among themselves in a kind of biathlon of running and swimming to another island to capture a bird's egg, which then determines the next chief. The only way Ramana and Noro can marry is if he wins the contest. As part of their protest, the Short Ears declare that Make can also compete for the position of chief as well as for Ramana's hand. If he loses, he must die. When Noro wins, the evil priest demands Make's death. Make resists and kills the priest, touching off disorder that leads Noro and his pregnant wife Ramana to flee the island. Make regrets the loss of order, despite their new freedoms, as he witnesses the Short Ears cannibalize the Long Ears in ways that defy their humanity.

We see Jason Scott Lee in memorable scenes of intimacy in both *Map of the Human Heart* and *Dragon*, which *Rapa Nui* adds to in its display of passionate relations between brown-skinned and nude Noro and Ramana. The film begins with an incredible setting for an intimate encounter. The couple lie together on a cliff, both wearing minimal clothing. In the golden light, he lies on top of her and asks her to marry him. She is not just a sexual being for him. Although she is a Short Ear, he regards her with respect and dignity. In another scene, when his grandfather asks why Noro does not just sexually exploit Ramana, he explains he loves her. He intends to win the biathlon and earn permission to marry her according to the law of the tribes. The couple works within the constraints of the social order. She, through her own perseverance, earns the right to marry by enduring confinement in a cave for six months. This purifies her skin, a criterion of importance

FIGURE 24   Noro realizes her resolve to endure the pain of the cave for his love. *Rapa Nui.* Dir. Kevin Reynolds. Majestic Films International, 1994.

imposed by society. From both sides they hear: "Why can't they love their own kind?" The pressures from the outside strengthen their resolve. They meet at their tree, and in another tender love scene she cups his face in her hands to affirm their love.

In *Rapa Nui* we see Noro's and Ramana's as well as Make's struggle for dignity. Noro and Ramana love each other and attempt to work with their elders in order to earn the right to marry and secure their rightful place as adult members of society. Make, similarly, protests the order that does not allow him to participate in the biathlon so that he and his tribe may have the opportunity to become chief. Make attempts to chip at the discriminatory roles, recognizing in his work as a sculptor of gods—a skill only the Short Ears possess—that he can find dignity through aggression. While Ramana does not favor him romantically or sexually, he will impose himself in the marital arrangement if he wins the position of chief. Noro demonstrates a kind understanding for his former friend, refusing to engage his demands but instead recognizing the frustrations of the Short Ears within the hierarchy of men. The character Jason Scott Lee plays is sympathetic in terms of being a compassionate man and an idealized manhood—upright, ethical as well as sexually viable.

Rapa Nui, and its celebrated sex scenes like those in *Map of the Human Heart*, corrects the amnesia regarding Asian American men's sexual practices in Western cinematic representations but adds the strong dimension of sexual presence for the Asian American actor. The sexualized hero—strong, kind, handsome, and honorable—is an exceptional and rare role that somehow tells us that different manhoods are available in impossible scenes, only in cinema that imagines other places and times. So while this film shows notable sex on screen for Asian American men, it also tells us of the exceptional status of the subject. These are not real Asian American men—as if there is no place for Asian American male ethical heroes in films set in the here and now.

The Jungle Book (1994)

Continuing in the vein of portraying indigenous fantasy characters in a kind of timeless place but with even more nudity, Jason Scott Lee plays Mowgli in *The Jungle Book*. A young Indian boy travels with his father to transport a white British officer to his new post. Lost in the jungle as a child, the adult Mowgli (played by a very fit Jason Scott Lee) encounters the adventurous Kitty, his childhood friend (played by Lena Headey, a classic brunette beauty whose fully dressed body provides a contrast). Though she is under no threat, her suitor, a pale military officer, Captain William Boone (played by handsome blonde Carey Elwes), defends her against Mowgli. The suitor deems him an animalistic long-haired creature, barely dressed and showing off a golden and muscular physique. He calls Mowgli an "animal in need of lessons in manners. I'll protect you!" The animals come to protect Mowgli in the confrontation with guns. Mowgli remains innocent in the face of civilization's weapons and classifications of savagery. When Kitty's family adopts Mowgli, he learns English and "civilized" manners from a tutor (played by funny man John Cleese). As he learns the ways of the Western world, Mowgli becomes alienated from the jungle. When he recognizes that Kitty is not available to him as a romantic partner due to the exclusions by racism in the segregated organization of society, he decides to return to the jungle. He is followed by Kitty's fiancé, who want to get his hands on the treasures—whose location only Mowgli knows—buried in the jungle. Betrayed by her fiancé, Kitty realizes the desirability of Mowgli's manhood as they kiss under a waterfall.

In key scenes, we recognize Mowgli's alienation from society. Mowgli teaches Kitty about life in the jungle, where "with animals, every look and sound has meaning. The jungle speaks to me and I learned how to listen." In contrast to this idyllic scene, he is attacked physically and verbally by a cohort of young officers at every chance they get. He learns about concepts like hate from his rival, Captain Boone, who attempts to find out where Mowgli got the bejeweled sword that Boone envies. Mowgli discusses with Boone the difference between laws of man and laws of the jungle, and declares his preference for animals rather than humans: "You kill for sport and anger and treasure. The jungle law says to kill to eat or avoid getting eaten." We see a competing manhood emerge in contrast to the lying, cheating, and aggressive Boone: a considerate, calm, and careful Mowgli.

When Mowgli discovers Kitty's engagement to his rival, he is told that "she belongs to him." When further bullied by Boone's entourage, Mowgli confronts Kitty, expressing his unique position as between man and animal. He leaves for the jungle, where Boone follows, betraying Kitty's father's orders, and working in cahoots with other greedy men, both Indian and white. A mythical tiger attacks the greedy men when they attempt to locate the treasures hidden in the jungle. Kitty and Mowgli come to recognize and affirm their love for each other and her father accepts him as a good man, unlike his rival, who steals and kidnaps.

In *The Jungle Book*, Jason Scott Lee's Mowgli is an attractive character who offers a worthwhile masculinity when the alternative is the aggression and violence of the other (white) male suitors. When Boone and his cohort accost Kitty's father, we see that they offer a manhood fueled by selfish aggression. Mowgli imagines a better world—not of hate but of love, which Kitty ultimately embraces. The last scene of the film features her finding him in the jungle surrounded by wild animals and seeking to kiss him. And throughout the movie, Jason Scott Lee's body is displayed—bathing, frolicking, running in the jungle, riding animals as one with nature, and fighting fully dressed men to embody a thing of beauty.

In these films, Jason Scott Lee portrays an intensely sexualized yet caring brown manhood against an aggressive and domineering white one. His characters in *Map of the Human Heart*, *Rapa Nui*, and *The Jungle Book*—and my discussion of *Dragon* in an earlier chapter—offer manhoods that refuse to dominate others as they stand up for their own principles, in direct contrast to their competitors. Within a hierarchized field of social relations, theirs is a degraded but noble manhood. What's most interesting, then, is that the women—Albertine, Ramana, and Kitty—choose not the traditional form of white macho masculinity but one of tenderness, strength, sensitivity, and calm in the form of brown men with whom they can have physical pleasure. Indeed, Jason Scott Lee's cinematic archive collects images that exceed normative standards of physical beauty. What did the sexualization make room for? In terms of political ecstasy, films can certainly expand our ideas about others; they can also shut them down when the representation of Asian American men is too fantastic. Using this framework of understanding the power of cinema, I consider the excessive production of Asian American male sexuality to limit not only ideality but identification.

Regardless of whether their romances are considered successful, manhood is still in process for Jason Scott Lee's characters. Avik remains fraught with guilt, making his way around his homeland, negotiating his vast knowledge and lowly rank. Despite this position of denigration, we see through his eyes the recognition of a world that unfairly relegates him to this position. And we do not identify with those who discriminate against him. Instead, in a form of political ecstasy, we sympathize with his position as the one degraded unfairly and made to suffer immensely at the tremendous loss of family and social regard. His is a manhood, even with social failure, honored by the movie in his achievement of clarity while enduring unfair punishment. His noble manhood invites empathy. In *Rapa Nui*, Jason Scott Lee's character Noro must find another way, and he too embraces expulsion from society. Unlike Avik, he risks familiarity in search of a dignified manhood—with a wife and a child in tow. The film celebrates this as the right decision, though we don't know what meets them as they flee the violence of Easter Island. While we identify with Noro's struggle to win the biathlon, we are uncertain of his future. What will happen to him in the outside world? Will he face new forms of discrimination as he maintains his dignity away from the greed and violence of their old home? His predicament is out-of-this-world so that the lessons we extract from such a far-fetched scenario are so limited—though a pleasure to watch. In *The Jungle Book*, Mowgli gets the girl, but recognition in a colonial society remains elusive. The coming together of the white woman in her puritanical garb and the brown man in his naked beauty stays a fantasy of waterfalls and friendly wild animals. With their extraordinary physicality and beauty, the manhoods performed by Jason Scott Lee are similarly incredible: gentle and strong, just and right and also dream-like as the indelible sex scenes on screen. His career as a romantic leading man stopped soon after these set of films from 1993–1994. What happened to the actor who portrayed these characters?

FIGURE 25   Against waterfalls and among wild animals, Mowgli and Kitty kiss. The interracial pairing occurs in a fantasy land with no certain future. *The Jungle Book.* Dir. Stephen Sommers. Walt Disney, 1993.

Living Pono: An Interview with Jason Scott Lee

In the mid-1990s, Jason Scott Lee's stardom indicated the possibility for Asian American men to play in cross-racial roles as sexually desirable and desiring beings. However, after these films, the opportunities to play these types of lead romantic roles dried up and he was offered roles in action films that did not cohere with his vision. Currently, Jason Scott Lee lives in Volcano, on the Big Island of Hawaii, on a farm where he grows taro and sweet potato in a life committed to sustainability and lessening the impact of human life on the environment. His work is featured in the documentary *Toward Living Pono* (2010) by Rick Bacigalupi. "Pono" translates to living closer to the land with accountability to it in the resources one uses.[30] In the video, Jason Scott Lee introduces us to his farm, which is named Pumu after the two Chinese characters for "simplicity" and "nothingness." We see his hands pulling out roots in his "cloud forest" as he tells the long history of the harvest in Hawaiian culture. He started out "not knowing anything about agriculture or anything about growing food [when he] began to return to nature, simplify his life." He describes "living pono" as "living righteously" or to "respect, honor and have reverence for the land and oceans." In this philosophy, Lee provides a unique and literal example of a manhood that is responsible to himself and others. Yet he describes the lack of understanding he felt from people in "giving up his career" when returning to nature.

The documentary-in-progress *Toward Living Pono* shows us "Jason Lee," healthy, happy, and living on his own terms in a house that uses only what is necessary. He has become a farmer who exists in a place of beauty including a pretty outhouse, which he shows us while laughing. He swims among friends in an idyllic existence. And every once in a while we hear his voicework in *Lilo and Stitch*, or we see him in the occasional action film such as *Nomad: The Warrior* (2005). We also see him speak out on Native Hawaiian issues and Asian American causes online. He says, "When needed, I participate." As of May 2011, Jason Scott Lee's homepage—authorized by Lee—received 172,679 hits since it was put up in 2000.[31] What he does with this legacy is chart a manhood away from phallic narcissism, introducing the importance of holding out for a thousand possibilities and not just one heroic stance.

On May 7, 2010, I described to Jason Scott Lee how I saw the problem of Asian American men in the movies as a collection of hardly flattering images. Within this context, Jason Scott Lee's work and contributions help. I wanted to better understand his place in modeling how to create better manhoods for Asian American men using the power of the movies. Creation fuels him and sustains him. He told me that acting is a way of expressing oneself and that creativity is an act that sustains through the "emotional ride of performance." For Lee, acting is "intellectual creativity" where one "create[s] without real tools" but just "one's body, voice, and mental capacity to conjure up things with your imagination and translate [that into] story-telling using the power of gestures and the face." Acting, according to Lee, requires using one's individuality and history as well as one's desire to contribute in this fashion. However, he also talked about the opportunities to act as a historically situated phenomenon. He got the chance to play Avik at the age of 24. And ideas embodied in *Map of the Human Heart*, his "first established role where it was a positive lead," were actually very different from "U.S.-based ideas of roles for Asian actors." Because the film was made by an "international group of artists, filmmakers, and technicians," it "broadened my horizons for what was possible in film." He discusses the opportunity the director afforded him to create as an actor:

> He encouraged me to go very in-depth as a researcher, to read a great deal of books and watch archival footage to get you into that space. He dropped me in this village of 300 people called Lake Harbor in the Arctic, in an Inuit village and left me for seven or eight days. I flew in by myself and entered with no relationship. I had a host family and we spent the time fishing and hunting. I watched them carve soap stone. There's a lot of interpretation of a role in a period piece or playing an indigenous character in observing how they move through the snow and how excited to be in it waist deep and what their expression is when turning to the wind. Little things like that, picking up on breathing and the breathing rhythm.

In describing the act of learning about others, Lee details what he had to do to capture different ways of moving, such as how to be an old man in a bar or walking into to a dancehall to discover your love betrayed. He describes how acting requires a certain "humility" in terms of having to engage roles where one is perpetually an immigrant and where one does "not really have a choice" when it comes to available roles.

Moreover, off-screen racisms can inform the on-screen racisms one encounters. For example, he and another actor were standing in front of the hotel in London where the big dance hall scene in *Map of the Human Heart* was filmed "and a big fat Winston Churchill–looking man came up to me saying, 'Boy, walk and get me a paper.' It was an interesting and shocking moment." This informed the feelings he used in the dancehall when he feels "under pressure like a fish out of water. When Avik realizes Albertine is with someone else, he walks away—that's the only person he knows in the world. He asks himself, how did this happen? I thought she felt the same way as me. He knows a stronger connection with her, on a primal level." When playing the older Avik at the bar, "after years of alcoholism, stiffness, from age, comes into play. He has witnessed a lot." As an actor, he uses his background to help inform the scene. "For me, even in Hawaii, the broken hearts I see. It's sort of like the depressed situation of Native American reservations. For Avik, everything is cloudy, nothing is the same. He does not know well what to do. Almost similar to the Japanese American 442nd, when they came back, they were heroes when they came back, to a repressive state. They were not given any respect." Jason Scott Lee's commentary links Native American and Japanese American manhoods—the betrayal, injustice, and disrespect they encounter. Here, he speaks from his perspective as a racialized man who empathizes with other racialized men in preparation for his portrayal. He uses his background to enrich the characters in a small form of authorship despite the limited parameters of the role.

I asked Jason Scott Lee about portraying sexual relations and sexual characteristics in the movies. He talks about strange experiences off screen, such as being approached by a man asking Lee to have sex with his wife. These are scenes he prefers to avoid, though he finds them interesting to study in terms of how they reveal different sexual cultures and practices. He analyzes his own cinematic sex scenes too. In his relations with Albertine, Avik comes from a very playful place that also appreciates the rawness of the encounter. Lee also tells of the practical considerations of filming sex scenes, even ones celebrated by critics.

> The sex scene in the barrage balloon [for *Map of the Human Heart*] was incredibly frustrating. The wind was blowing in the English countryside and I am holding on to a tether I have wrapped around my hand behind her so we don't roll off. We only have a three foot area to play with and it was very cold. . . . I want to do this shot! It had to be close, he pulled away when he was in close because it was so cold my ass cheeks were shaking. Both of us were butt naked and he said, "Jason is there any way to stop your butt cheeks from shaking?" Anne [Parillaud] and I tried our best to stop laughing about it!

Lee describes sex as part of the dramas of everyday life—where each character performs acts that reveal their understanding of their particular cultures and identities. His descriptions also show the constructed nature of the production of sex in the movies, as, for instance, where he helps the actress cover up during the shoot in a respectful dynamic that reminds me of Keni Styles' own approach in his recollections of shooting sex scenes.

For Lee, performing certain acts and gestures reveals character—such as the "cat screech and cat scowl that [Bruce Lee] utilized and found effective—only for the movies [rather than off-screen fighting]." These sorts of performances taught Jason Lee about his own manhood. He trained for playing Bruce Lee by becoming very physically fit—he found the "best thing [to do] is to create character (and to ask) what muscles were developed that [Bruce Lee] developed in order to understand his movements." The more he understood the training technique and the relaxation between movements the more he understood Bruce Lee; "those were the things that allowed me to get inside his mind. The body will follow the mind. The mind has to be free enough in that relaxed flexibility mode the way his did." As such, he achieved a physical likeness to Bruce Lee through understanding his bodily movements and level of fitness.

Emotionally, he played Bruce Lee with much more compassion than was expressed in the "charisma and kinetic energy, a meanness—a raw sort of thing" that the original possessed. He says Hollywood movies idealize characters for the sake of identification. For example, Mowgli in *The Jungle Book* is raised by wolves. "The history of kids raised by animals requires a bizarre rehabilitation into civilization. The accounts are not going to be roses and waterfalls." Similarly, in terms of playing Bruce Lee, "there is a romantic version of him in the movies. As an actor, one can only do so much in terms of your abilities to play the character. Once again you are limited. It's like being the son of a famous person. You try to emulate your dad, but no way! His experience is deeper and more involved that you can ever imagine. Let's shape out an impression that's not a biographical character."

In terms of learning about manhood from conducting research on playing Bruce Lee, Jason Scott Lee describes him as

> quite the rooster—very hip, sexy clothes, tight shirt, bell bottom pants—he had [a] very impeccable appearance. For Bruce, it was very important, his hairstyle and fashion. He was very self-confident being an incredible, virile fighter. He exuded something from fighting. You would feel something

when he enters the room. You would turn around and it's Bruce. Those are
the things that in a universal sense are very attractive—Bruce cultivated an
animal magnetism.

Jason Scott Lee describes this as very particular to Bruce Lee's "very driven"
character. And extends this to how his "supporters wanted me to push
towards that and go down the same road." But he understands that way of
being as different from his own.

> That was Bruce's path. He had something to prove and something to
> show. I don't have the kind of drive to do that. There's a side of me that's
> closer to nature and close to the ocean. I like to experience rawness and
> power of a very different world. What Bruce cultivated through entertain-
> ment is to have power in society. My path I feel is a lot different . . . so I
> stepped out of the venue. I feel my life more in a non-discriminating way.
> I wanted to diversify my mind. See other vocations and ask what brought
> me to this place.

He adds that it is "attention, sensitivity and awareness" that he finds important in developing within society and within history. Jason Scott Lee says,

> A lot of what I've done in the last twelve years of trying to experience that
> and try to test that is the ability it takes to have perseverance and strength
> of character to push myself to the test of man versus nature. I am not in
> competition, in that context, with macho-ism or a whole society's percep-
> tion of what is sexy or what is a man. When you strip down face to face
> with a 14-foot tiger shark, it doesn't matter if you are black, white, female,
> or male. That creature doesn't discriminate. When you're around nature
> more often, you lose discrimination in your own mind, which is what
> Bruce is trying to go for. A fighting system with no style, as your style is no
> form as form. I get to that realm to do what is necessary for the moment
> and what for you is all you can do.

Rather than celebrate Bruce Lee for his ability to dominate others, Jason
Scott Lee honors the form of manhood that seeks a kind of peace with
oneself.

In terms of social and political life, Jason Scott Lee says he's mapped
out a way to use his position and at the same time question the terms of
the debate about representation and politics. Rather than accept the terms
of others, external forces such as the industry, Jason Scott Lee now charts
the terms of his own existence by following his own unique desires, which

reflect his particular history. He explains his philosophy of forging his independence:

> All culture stems from agriculture and that brings them close to nature and a large degree of empowerment. My food source is independent. It gives me a small sense of freedom. This is an experience in nature for the firehorse to run free, to have creativity and resources to live on that canvas. Like for me the movies have been great but nothing like creating that canvas.

He prefers the creativity he discovers when working on the land. In deciding to live a creative life close to the ground, he shares his wisdom about the limits of Hollywood as a creative and life-sustaining force. The opportunities available to him led to larger questions about what is worth pursuing in life.

> What I realize about Hollywood is that they try to pigeonhole you. I sat with all these execs who offered me three-picture deals. They want to get to know you. Siphon all the words down, they just want me to be Jean Claude Van Damme or Steven Seagal. I could do that, but I had to look at myself—is the reason to do this just to make a lot of money? If I need to speak to my principles, why did I get into this anyway? It's not about business, it's about inspiration. I want to inspire myself. The material for me is not out there, I will shoot myself in the foot. The truth of it all is to be honest with yourself that it's not what you want to do. I've been ridiculed for it. Even my parents say "Don't ruin your opportunities, strike while the iron is hot! You have the abilities, you should be out there doing this thing." Everyone looks at it and if we sit down and talk about it, what is the real problem? What is the real issue? *Let's not band-aid our problems with a superhero for all of us to adore.* [My emphasis.] Will that motivate us to change our whole lives? . . . For making films, I will always have the ability and talent, but it's up to me to what degree I want to cultivate it. You don't want your slow death, pining at the bit with no jobs. The shape of the industry has changed over twenty years. That's always the case, even now they are not writing anything empowering for Asian male roles. They are putting them in background roles. I want to raise imagination so it goes through the roof!

Jason Scott Lee expresses concern with how one keeps cultivating oneself to find the most effective way to contribute and to create a world where one uses one's talents and intelligence. He asks what else can be available apart from and along with the known paths and goes forth to what I have lauded in this book as open-ended and bold infinity rather than the fixity of totality.

The Calm Manhood of Jason Lee

In my interview with Jason Lee, he reflects on his life and work to present his understanding of movies, movie-making, and manhood that concretely inform my thesis of an ethical life. He evaluates the larger social map and positions himself in a place where he possesses the power to transform his existence, to benefit others beyond himself in both his acting and his work on the land. What we take from the interview, which we don't necessarily get from the films themselves, is the recognition of power in his acting work and his wrestling with the potentiality to make a significant impact on opening options for Asian American men in Hollywood and beyond. His is an ethical dilemma that accounts for power and responsibility in crafting his manhood. I am especially taken by his refusal to be the man who occupies a position of macho—a hypermasculine and hypersexual phallus who rides in to save the day—as if this one kind of manhood can redeem the projection of lack for Asian American men. Moreover, he presents a thoughtful meditation on what he learns from the opportunities presented to him.

Yet, Jason Scott Lee reminds us of the dearth of viable roles for Asian American men in the 1980s and 1990s when he says most roles were small bit parts and how even those dwindled away. The larger social field determined the limits of roles available for Asian American men. For Lee, acting is an incredibly powerful vehicle not only for self-expression but also for self-inspection. Despite Lee's marginalization as a minority actor, his role as Avik in *Map of the Human Heart* allowed Lee to step into a completely different culture from the position of one who has the power to represent radically underrepresented people—a position that is rarely available. Here power and constraint describe his location, one where few people have the opportunity to wield the transformative power of film and performance.

Jason Scott Lee describes the skill required to observe and to portray as powerful. What he calls research is really an ethnographic approach of occupying a position of nearness in order to learn something about the other. He had not only to see but attend to a totally different way of life, which he describes as learning how to breathe anew and how to walk in new circumstances. The body learns a new way of occupying the world in the walk of Avik, Bruce, Noro, and Mowgli. More than all aspects of Jason Scott Lee's research, the work of physically shaping his body to the fitness of Bruce Lee is key to his performance. He describes the confidence that discipline and work brought to Bruce Lee's carriage and bearing. In his discussion of Bruce

Lee, Jason Scott Lee also reveals the incredible way the original actor demonstrated a sensibility for moving the widest possible audience. The ambition and drive that Bruce Lee's way required is not what Jason accesses in is own trajectory. When Hollywood offered him roles in the Steven Segal and Jean Claude Van Damme vein, he refused and instead pursued the life-and-death struggle of confronting a shark in the water and learning how to raise his own crops as part of living responsibly on the land. He embarked on a transformation of his manhood as one closely linked to the natural world that nonetheless won't deny his history as an actor of major Hollywood movies. He demonstrates a calm confidence in his power as an actor and his ability to do more beyond that work. In conclusion, the lesson to take away is that we cannot look for the next James Shigeta or Jason Scott Lee—that hero we all would adore for the "band-aid solutions" he would supply. Instead, we should look for masculinities that find different places across the map of representation and of history where individual men like Jason Scott Lee chart their own way as productive members of society. Looking out on the horizon, the map of manhoods in the movies should be vast, multiple, wide-ranging and not limited to one kind of hero—instead, what is needed are characters who care for others beyond themselves.

The exciting thing to witness in revisiting the numerous filmic representations of Asian American men in the last fifty years is how they navigate their way in and out of a gender and sexual order that precedes them. What legacy do they leave behind so that we can account for their work as we envision manhoods for the twenty-first century? In *Straitjacket Sexualities* thus far, I pay attention to subjects who encounter others as opportunities for charting manhood. These encounters, especially in the choreography of the eye-to-eye, face-to-face, and the power of touch, represent opportunities to establish relations that form the basis of an ethical manhood that cares for self and others. This is a mapping of masculinity that the asexuality/ effeminacy/homosexuality as lack assessment, what I call straitjacket sexuality, ignores, especially in the work of Asian American actors who actually played leading roles in Hollywood films in ways that should not be forgotten, for they dramatized so well the entanglements of race, sex, and love.

At this moment, we see a number of Asian American actors in all kinds of media—the movies, television, and the internet. In film, John Cho, Kal Penn, Leonardo Nam, Aaron Yoo, and Ken Jeong play characters in major Hollywood and independent films that include romantic interests in hit teen summer movies such as *Sisterhood of the Traveling Pants*; pot-smokers in the seminal and massively profitable franchise *Harold and Kumar* series; a goofy gangster/crime lord who's in on the joke in *The Hangover*; and confused American-born second generation youth in *The Namesake*. On television, we see Masi Oka and others in *Heroes*; B. D. Wong in *Law and Order*; Harry Shum, Jr., Darren Criss (though they call him "vaguely Eurasian"), and others in *Glee!* In new media, we hear from Keni Styles the porn star, the Angry Asian Man, the Secret Asian Man, and we see George Takei of *Star Trek*'s Captain Sulu fame, roast his co-star Captain Kirk and combat homophobia and heterosexism in short videos gone viral on Youtube. May a million manhoods thrive out of straitjacket sexualities and may they demonstrate responsibility to self and others, setting new criteria for unbinding Asian American manhoods into new paths and on new terms.

Claiming the Power of Lack in the Face of Macho

Asian American Manhoods in the Movies

Perceived by critics as actor and director Clint Eastwood's apologetic response for playing ruthless and unforgiving white male characters across the entirety of his career, *Gran Torino* (2008) features Asian American male characters pitted against each other and portrays a number of racialized manhoods. Rapacious and brutish gangsters, both Hmong and Mexican American, go against an innocent and childlike Thao Vang Lor (played by Bee Vang)—the lead character—who represents an adopted son of Eastwood's Korean War veteran, the racially intolerant Walt Kowalski. While this film may be analyzed as the further embedding of Thao into a castrated boyhood by a white man, I argue that he claims his lack—whether imposed or innate—and deploys it to critique hypermasculinity. To refuse absolute power over others is itself an alternative form of power in Bee Vang's performance. The character Thao Vang Lor enables me to conclude with the presentation of lack as a viable form of male power—so effective that it moves the white man to himself embody an ethical manhood. While Bee Vang looks back on his role as one that further effeminizes Asian American men in the movies, I show that the character illustrates an infinite subjectivity or one full of possibility. To dismiss Thao as castrated, infantilized, and ridiculed falls into the trap of straitjacket sexuality in envisioning Asian American manhood.

Clint Eastwood directs and plays the lead role in *Gran Torino*. As a military veteran, he perceives Asians, including his Hmong neighbors, as "gooks" with whom he fought in the Korean War. Considering his status as an old-timer in the auto industry of Michigan, his character also recalls Ron

Ebens, the man who beat and killed Vincent Chin in the 1980s and whose lack of jail time led to massive organizing by the Asian American community into a national movement.[1] When Walt hails Hmong into the subject position of unwanted foreigners, he fails to recognize them as refugees in the United States. He simply resents their moving into his neighborhood. This resentment is part of a larger rage expressed in growls and squinted eyes as he murmurs irritation at consumers not buying American cars or as he glares at the population of non-white doctors, nurses, and patients at the hospital. He hates that the nurses cannot pronounce his name and he takes time to adjust to his young Asian American female doctor. His anxiety about the changing demographics of the United States manifests itself in a cranky old white manhood suspicious of others—including his family and neighbors. He holds on to an imaginary past of ethnic homogeneity and a conservative and conventional manhood that shows no weakness and no need for others—including his son, whom he never learned to relate to or know. His estranged son is similarly confused and unable to connect with him. On Walt's birthday, the son suggests his father move into a nursing home. His father explodes mightily at the idea. Overall, his life is a male malaise of discontent.

The philosophy of an absolute and infallible patriarchy emerges in his continual maintenance of his prized car, a 1972 classic Gran Torino. He considers this car, which he himself worked on in the assembly lines of the auto industry, a symbol of a fleeting American masculinity as he encounters men who are not men he respects, but mere boys who steal rather than work and who harass rather than honor women. These man-boys are not only Asian, but also black, and even include his own son. Other men of his generation similarly covet the car as a symbol of their passing American manhood. When Walt meets Thao, the patriarchal manhood he holds onto dearly loses its value when he receives and provides care from and for his new young friend.

Masculinities and Misrepresentations

In "*Gran Torino*'s Boys and Men with Guns: Hmong Perspectives," Louisa Schein and Va-Megn Thoj prioritize the lens of cultural misrepresentation that this film performs. They employ what Schein earlier calls an "ethnotextual" approach that prioritizes a contextualized knowledge as crucial to the process of interpretation.[2] Or in other words, it prioritizes a particular group's history as it reads its representations by others. Using such an approach, Schein and Thoj present Clint Eastwood's character Walt Kowalski as one who "liberate[s] [Thao] from the effeminacy apparently imposed on him by his domineering mother and sister" and argue that "eventually, Walt becomes more and more of a white savior striving to intervene to keep the boy from a gang."[3] In Gina Marchetti's study of the representations of white men and Asian women, she defines the "white knight" as one who "promises salvation from any number of woes ranging from simple lack of self-esteem, boredom and sexual frustration to poverty, oppression, or the stifling confines of the family." Essentially, the racial (and gendered) other is a passive subject chosen by the heroic white knight as someone who must be saved, as part of a myth that justifies Western colonial attitudes and "moral righteousness" toward primitive others.[4] While this is an important critique that rightly identifies the importance of communities to grab cameras and represent the complexities of their own cultures, such an assessment of Walt's character oversimplifies his development as well as his relationship with the subjectivity and the contributions of Thao himself beyond a "passive subject" who wishes to be saved. That is, missing in this analysis is how both Walt and Thao transform, as we can see in the shooting style itself, which prioritizes the subjectivities of other men beyond Walt.

In reading Louisa Schein's interview with Bee Vang, who reflects on Thao's failure to achieve a dignified manhood, I conclude this book with a final illustration that argues how the discourse of misrepresenting a community needs to be split from the critique of asexuality/effeminacy/homosexuality as lack for Asian American men. The representations of Asian American men as failing to achieve sexual consummation are not necessarily a psychic, material, and social castration. By looking closely at the specific scenes of the film where Thao asserts lack as an alternative to macho, I show how his character compels the white man to transform. The severity of straitjacket sexuality prevents us from mining the powerful ways Asian American manhood transforms self and others.

By paying attention to the form of the film, I argue that straitjacket sexuality dominates even the actor Bee Vang's own analysis of his performance, which is key to the promising manhood ultimately produced in *Gran Torino* for the young Asian American man. In an interview published in the *Hmong*

Studies Journal in Spring 2010, Vang outlines his understanding of Thao's manhood as lacking. He argues that while his character is especially essential to Clint Eastwood's Walt Kowalski and his triumph, yet "we fade out in favor of his heroism. I felt negated by the script and by extension in my assuming the role. It's almost like a non-role. Strange for a lead."[5] In attending to the specific problem of assessing masculinity in terms of heteronormative sexuality and gender hierarchy, my reading of Thao and his formulation of a viable manhood in the film differs from actor Bee Vang's assessment of his role. I conclude my book with Thao's forging of a manhood that does not prioritize macho and its dependence on sex. In *Gran Torino*, the young Asian American man refuses persistent macho judgments in an embrace of lack that leads to a new embodiment of a dignified manhood.

Gran Torino (2008)

In *Gran Torino*, Thao uses the power of his gaze to resist interpellation by others as merely a deferential, bowing boy. In the beginning of the film, he will not look at the Mexican gangsters when they taunt him. The opening scene shows us Thao alone, walking in a desolate area while intently reading a book. Mexican gangsters in a car threaten him with rape while driving alongside him. We fear for Thao but then notice that he, a mere pedestrian, represents an exceptional man. He is deemed effeminate and homosexual in the taunts by the gang, who supposedly cannot tell if he's a boy or girl. They then relay the situation that if they were in the penitentiary, they'd fuck him. But Thao keeps walking. He won't look at them. He won't express fear. Instead, he smiles. He courageously laughs them off and refuses to give them the power of his acknowledgment despite the frightening taunts.

Indeed, the film shows him resist across multiple sites: in a scene in a barbershop, he defies Walt with his speech—when he won't follow the script he's directed to speak by the other characters as part of his training into manhood. Or when his mother and sister force him to work, we glimpse the rage directed at Walt, blurting out his wish not to work for him. His bowed head betrays a refusal to show Walt his face in the basement, to discuss his love interest, the beautiful and charming Youa. But the actor Bee Vang undersells his contribution when he says, "I reinforced the image of effeminate Asian guys who are wimps, geeks and can't advocate for themselves."[6] His character, however, maintains his look away as part of a tradition of the colonized who "learn . . . to look a certain way in order to resist."[7] Perhaps Thao deploys what little power is available from the subject position of a youth without "a job, a girlfriend and a car" or to express his lack of investment in macho as a queer youth.

Unlike Thao, other Hmong American men participate in the logics of macho. A Hmong gang drives by to "save" him from the Mexican gang bullying him. The two gangs pull guns on each other. The Hmong gang's big gun leads the Mexican gang to drive away while vowing to return. Thao's cousin Spider, one of the gang members, shakes his head and calls Thao the one "who flies solo"—or one who must be protected by other men in the name of the clan. It's as if going his own way threatens the stature of a larger brotherhood. In the Hmong gang's logic of macho, Thao now owes them and must pay them back as an acknowledgment of their powerful manhoods. Like the Mexican gang, they wish Thao to express deference and to participate in their male competition. Thao wants to refuse but the gang approaches him relentlessly, finding him at home several times and following him on the streets on his way from work. Within these very limited constraints where his manhood is policed by gangs, Thao more than ever needs to find a way out of the macho judgment of his manhood as lacking.

I find Thao's way of being—flying solo in the face of hypermasculinity—a most promising embodiment of manhood. He looked macho in the eye and refused it—when invited by the gangs and even when initiated by Walt into rituals of manhood Thao does not understand, he stood apart and calmly evaluated his options. Bee Vang considers Thao unable to "grow" in the film, seeing instead that he is supposed to relent to the "shameless macho" of the gangsters and white manhood.[8] Vang does not buy how his performance, of head "hang[ing] down and absorb[ing] abuse . . . could bring any change to Walt."[9] I argue that it is precisely this assertion of lack as power that teaches Walt to sacrifice himself for the sake of opening a better future for Thao and his sister Sue, whom Walt similarly becomes close to. While it may be a shortsighted imperialist gift on the part of a self-centered Walt, as Schein and Thoj argue, it is nonetheless motivated and inspired by the manhood Thao uses to counter the limited constraints of macho surrounding him.[10]

Lack includes recognizing the importance of others and expressing need for their well-being as crucial to one's own. To use the framework of bell

hooks, who counters black cinematic figures' prioritizing of white protagonists' futures in lieu of their own, this kind of lack is evident in the film
The Bodyguard (1992), which portrays the sacrifice of a valued white life for
racial others.[11] I follow a similar vein of identifying a kind of love in the
unexpected sacrifice by Walt for Thao and Sue. I now proceed to two close
readings that emphasize the forging of both Walt's and Thao's manhoods as
part of a transformative mutual recognition—a phenomenon I am deeply
concerned with in all of my studies of intimate relations across difference.

Close Readings

The Hmong gang sets their sights on Thao because they frame him in terms
of lack and consider his recruitment important to their brotherhood. They
tell him he has to steal his neighbor Walt's "nice ride." When Thao tries to
steal the 1972 Gran Torino, however, the gun-wielding Walt discovers and
almost kills him. Shamed by the attempt to steal, the family insists Thao
pay Walt back with his service. Thus, a mentorship and friendship begins
where Walt helps Thao get a job, advises him on girls, and tutors him to
talk and walk like a man. From here, we see their manhoods transform
when Walt witnesses Thao struggle to make his way, such as in his desire to
get a job when no other options seem available or putting in work in order
to repay his debt. In one scene, they attempt to carry a heavy appliance
from the basement, arguing about who gets to be on top. Thao wins, despite Walt's whining. Thao acknowledges his power in this moment, telling
Walt he's tempted to let go and crush him. It's a joke. With a beloved wife
recently dead, a great loneliness dawns for Walt. His vulnerability is exposed to Thao gradually, and especially when Walt coughs up blood. When
he witnesses this evidence of certain illness, Thao expresses sympathy and
insistently advises him to seek help. It is a concern that moves Walt. When
he observes that "I have more in common with these gooks than with my
own family," he invests in them, prioritizing the worthiness of their lives
and futures before his own life. In the conclusion of the film, Walt uses
violence to defend others. He does so with the conscious acknowledgment
of his masculinity as already tainted by violence—unlike Thao, who is only
beginning to develop as a man. Not only does he teach Thao the importance of keeping calm and thinking his responses through, he protects him

from the logics of illogical warfare where death is certain. It is a bargain with violence that results in Walt's own death, as a sacrifice for the future of his friends.

While the actor Bee Vang may protest Eastwood's particular direction as a method that naturalized him into an essential Hmong identity, I find that as a director myself, work with actors can be streamlined and does not always involve a process of disclosure but of keeping information away—as a method effective in capturing performances from both trained and untrained actors. A lack of opportunity to develop characters psychologically is not uncommon and is not straightforward evidence of castration of an actor by a director. However, in *Gran Torino* the camera movement reveals how the film also centers the internal lives and struggles of the non-white characters rather than Eastwood's Walt alone.

In a later scene, the camera stays with Thao as Walt nags him to become a better man—which means working on the pursuit of a worthwhile woman and speaking in a way that other men hear. In two matters, Thao's courtship of Youa and the scene at a barbershop, we see how Walt comes to care for his friend and realize a bond. The old white man changes and accepts others even late in life. He discovers belonging with others like him who at first seem so far away from him. And through this friendship, Thao is enabled to craft a manhood against the obstacles of macho. Walt provides him support and a community as he formulates his manhood. As the film progresses, we no longer see Thao head down toward Walt. And Walt no longer regards him with a suspicious glare, but looks to him as one he trusts with his Gran Torino to go on a date. At a hardware store, Walt buys him tools to enable Thao to take his new job as a construction worker. Thao appreciates his generosity and plainly tells him so. Walt turns to acknowledge him as coming into manhood. They stop in the aisle, look eye to eye and shake hands in mutual acknowledgment of the other.

Walt wants to tell Thao about the importance of romance to manhood. He may not be the most pleasant person in the world but he got "the best woman in the world" to marry him. For not noticing the beautiful Youa checking Thao out in the basement party, Walt chastises him: "You let Click-clack, Ding-dong and Charlie Chan walk out with what's her face. . . . You know why, because you're a big fat pussy." Despite these slurs, the camera stays focused on Thao as he processes this information, still slumped in the basement, on his way to being a man, in this context where he has to

F I G U R E 2 6   Walt and Thao shake hands, eye-to-eye and face-to-face in mutual respect. *Gran Torino*. Dir. Clint Eastwood. Warner Brothers, 2008.

defend even the pronunciation of his name. Bee Vang asks why the beautiful girl Youa desires his character Thao. In this instance, Vang repeats the puzzlement of his character Thao Vang Lor—who cannot fathom why a girl would look at him. It may be the pouting emo-boy look that contemporary youth find so attractive and totally adorable. Instead of appreciating that alternative masculinity, Vang finds his character to be a "dumb, passive, quiet, loner guy [who] can still get the best girl. It pained me that Thao let his masculinity suffer so badly over the course of the story."[12] But how exactly does his masculinity "suffer"? When using the criteria of straitjacket sexuality, he fails. We need to expand conceptions of manhood so that his success is not measured, according to Vang, simply by his kowtowing to Walt and moreover, failing to have a girlfriend.[13] Thao speaks to Walt eye-to-eye and face-to-face in crucial instances where he expresses concern for Walt's health or talks about finding a job. In this way, homosocial friendship across age differences, or even platonic love across gender differences such as noted in my study of independent films in an earlier chapter, can be part of our vision of a viable manhood. Perhaps heterosexual romance depends so much on the concept of male conquest of women that it's hard to decipher the pressures of heteronormativity and gender hierarchy, or straitjacket sexuality. Respect and alliance across racial lines and age divides should count for a substantial relationship and the shy, innocent and cute courtship between Youa and Thao can identify new terrains of manhood available today.

In a later scene, however, we discover that Thao eventually asks Youa out. They meet in Walt's backyard for a barbeque and Walt teases Thao for not asking Youa out. Youa shyly looks at Thao and announces to all that he actually did. Sue interrupts Wally (Walt hates this name she uses) and tells Youa not to listen to him for he is the "white devil." In this scene, not only do we see Thao exceed Walt's expectations but also demonstrate a quiet confidence as Youa looks at him adoringly. Here we trace the small ways large transformations of manhood occur for both Thao and Walt.

In the barbershop, Walt's tutoring of Thao continues, this time in manspeak consisting of retorts that hint at familiarity and humor from a longtime friendship between men. The barber greets them with derogatory terms for Polish and Chinese. And Walt introduces Thao as "the pussy kid from next door. I'm trying to man him up a little bit." They tutor Thao to speak like a man, which entails swearing, participating in the nuanced disparaging of others who are not present, and the mentioning of a car, job, and girlfriend—the emblems of manhood that lubricate homosocial bonds. Thao does not quite get it. He swears at the barber, and unwittingly refers to experiencing homosexual domination by his co-workers. The old men laugh. Thao's lack of understanding not only shows the ridiculous rituals of men but exposes how manhood is learned from others. Bee Vang reads this scene as disparaging and condescending to Asian men. As part of a team, he makes a spoof video called "Thao Does Walt," which portrays the latter as a wrongheaded "white savior" using a reversal device of punishing or "man-

FIGURE 27   Youa and Thao giggle about their impending date. Walt offers the Gran Torino for them to drive. *Gran Torino.* Dir. Clint Eastwood. Warner Brothers, 2008.

ning up" an older white man into the ways of caricatured Asian manhood.[14] But in *Gran Torino*, we see Thao employ what he's learned in this scene to help him get a job at the construction site. Explaining why he does not have a car, Thao uses the same language and style that Walt recommends so that he becomes familiar or legible—and heard or recognizable by the foreman who hires him. In these scenes, Thao learns to get a date and a job so that the film becomes a vehicle for audiences to learn how to become a man as well.

As Thao learns to "get a girl" in a way that counters macho and gets a legitimate job rather than steal, the Hmong gangsters will still not relent. When they fail to recruit Thao, they beat him up and steal his tool belt so he cannot go to work. They burn his face with a lit cigarette so that lack, in the form of a hole, appears on his face. When he discovers this assault, Walt attacks the lead gangster and brutally beats his face. Audaciously, this occurs in front of the gang's house. Bruises and blood mark macho manhood. The gang retaliates by raping Sue, treating women as objects for male warfare. The gang, which includes Sue's cousin Spider, drops her off at the house with her face bloodied and black-eyed, with the most telling evidence the overwhelming amount of blood staining her legs and thighs. With these incessant attacks and unrelenting punishments, Walt realizes Thao and Sue will never "have peace." He returns to the gangsters' lair and gets killed on their lawn as a sacrifice of the self so that Thao and Sue may be spared, in a truly epic scene for it recalls Bruce Lee's seeking of justice through death as a form of ethical manhood. The film ends with Thao driving away in the Gran Torino inherited from Walt. Is this a scene of castration? The gift that Walt bestows can be read as the passing on of a fleeting manhood but actually it is ultimately an ethical one that recognizes in Thao the potentiality to chart a path of his own.

In Conclusion

In his talks across the country, including the one I organized at Stanford University on May 9, 2011, Bee Vang wishes for his character the emblems of manhood. He says Thao should have a girlfriend, not just a dog and a car in at film's closing, for him to achieve a more redeeming manhood.[15] While the question that Thao may be queer is not pursued in this line of thought, the large victory of "lack as power" that moves the old white man to change exceeds these emblems. The film indeed ends with Thao as the only man alive, even if he is without the girl in the car. From here, Thao is full of potentiality to chart his own sexual course, which includes getting together with Youa or following another course, maybe even with a man. I suggest this possibility because his queerness may be why he lacks investment in the gangster culture of male rape as threatening and instead smirks at it in the beginning of the film. To conclude girlfriend-less, the film actually renders a broader manhood for Thao, including a meaningful brotherhood with an unexpected ally in the cranky old white man whose death opens future paths. As he drives away in the Gran Torino, his future is an infinity, in the Levinasian sense of unhinging as promise. He drives away not just from sex as conquest but from male power over women and the assignation of lack as weakness. He moves toward new horizons—deserving of our attention as he takes control of his own destiny as he moves into a future manhood, one that not only refuses macho but shows the power of lack to move others to change.

To close, I want Asian American men to acknowledge their privileges as men, instead of understanding their subject positions mainly through the lens of straitjacket sexuality. May the medium of film, and its special abilities to expose the process of how individuals choose to act and shape their destinies in the face of their hailing, help us to understand how Asian American men exist at the crossroads of power. Asian American men stand with the potential to forge manhoods that recognize the power that holds them down and the power they hold so as to free themselves from the fraught sexualities that cause anxiety and misery. As Thao drives alone to uncertain futures toward places and times better than what we have here and now, may Asian American men recognize the boundless dramas and pleasures of making new manhoods of service to self and others.

Notes

Introduction

1. Whitney McNally, "Anthropology: Gay or Asian?" *Details Magazine*, April 2004.

2. Chong, "Look, an Asian!"

3. Risheng Xu, "*Details Magazine* Sparks Protest," *The Harvard Crimson*, April 19, 2004.

4. Bhabha, "The Other Question."

5. Neal, *New Black Man*, 23.

6. Ibid., 27.

7. Cohen, Introduction to Emmanuel Levinas, *Ethics and Infinity*, 12.

8. Foucault, "Sexual Choice, Sexual Act," in idem, *Ethics*.

9. Connell, *Masculinities*.

10. Bersani, "Is the Rectum a Grave?" in idem, *Is the Rectum a Grave?*

11. Takaki, *Strangers from a Different Shore*; Ting, "The Power of Sexuality"; and Pascoe, *What Comes Naturally*.

12. Cohen, "Introduction," 13.

13. On social relations, see Corbett, *Boyhoods*, Connell, *Masculinities*, and Halberstam, *Female Masculinity*; on American social histories, see Bederman, *Manliness and Civilization*, and Kimmel, *Manhood in America*; on racialized masculinities, see Muñoz, *Cruising Utopia*, Eng, *The Feeling of Kinship* and *Racial Castration*, Harper, *Are We Not Men?*, Kim, *Writing Manhood in Black and Yellow*, Marriott, *On Black Men*, Neal, *New Black Men*, and Nguyen, "The Remasculinization of Chinese America"; on feminist approaches, see Carby, *Race Men*, and Collins, *Black Sexual Politics*; and finally, on queer masculinities, see Katz, *The Invention of Heterosexuality*, and Carter, *The Heart of Whiteness*.

14. Shimizu, "Master-Slave Sex Acts."

15. Butler, *Giving an Account of Oneself*, 9.

16. Levinas, "Signification and Sense," in *Humanism of the Other*, 12

17. Parikh, *An Ethics of Betrayal*, 3.

18. Lee, "Enemy Under My Skin," 643

19. Levinas, *Time and the Other*, 67.

20. Gabriel, "Teaching Third World Cinema," 60.

21. Levinas, *Otherwise Than Being*, 100.

22. Sedgwick, *Between Men*.

23. See Ono and Pham, *Asian Americans and the Media*; Marchetti, *Romance and the "Yellow Peril" Race*; and Xing, *Asian America through the Lens*.

24. Fung, "Looking for My Penis"; Nguyen, "The Resurrection of Brandon Lee"; Lee, "The Joy of the Castrated Boy"; Oren, "Secret Asian Man"; and Nguyen, "The Remasculinization of Chinese America."

25. In the vein of "race men" analyzed by Harper, *Are We Not Men*; Carby, *Race Men*; and Carbado, *Black Men on Race, Gender, and Sexuality*. On the diagnosis of effeminancy and asexuality, see Kim, *Asian American Literature*; Cheung, "The Woman Warrior Versus the Chinaman Pacific"; Bow, *Betrayal and Other Acts of Subversion*; and Kim, "Once More, With Feeling."

26. Ding, "Strategies of an Asian American Filmmaker."

27. Miyao, *Sessue Hayakawa*.

28. www.seaweedproductions.com/work/default.htm.

Chapter One

1. Chan, "Bruce Lee's Fictional Models of Masculinity," 371.

2. Fung, "Looking for My Penis."

3. David Henry Hwang, "Are Movies Ready for Real Orientals?" *New York Times*, Aug. 11, 1985: 21.

4. Prashad, "Bruce Lee and the Anti-Imperialism of Kung Fu."

5. Levinas, *Totality and Infinity*; Bernasconi, "The Truth That Accuses"; Bernasconi, "The Violence of the Face"; and Bernasconi, "Levinas and the Struggle for Existence."

6. Douglas, *Love and Arms*.

7. Paul Starr, "Hollywood's Ideal of New Masculinity," *New York Times*, July 16, 1978; Alexandra Trottier, "The Cycle of Masculinity in the Cinema: The Male Hero at a Glance," *(cult)ure magazine*, Jan. 31, 2008, www.culturemagazine.ca/cinema/the_cycle_of_masculinity_in_the_cinema_the_male_hero_at_a_glance_.html; and David Denby, "Out of the West," *The New Yorker* 86, 3 (April 18, 2010).

8. Weldon Johnson, "Mike Lee Hope for Rotsa Ruck: U Introduced to Gung Fu," *Seattle Times*, in Little and Lee, *Words of the Dragon*, 24.

9. Vincent Canby, "Green Hornet from Bruce Lee Series," *New York Times,* Nov. 28, 1974: 47

10. Von Eschen, "Globalizing Popular Culture in the 'American Century' and Beyond."

11. Ibid., 57, 61.

12. Jack Moore, "Superstar Bruce Lee? Who's He? Well, He's to Easterns What Ol' John Wayne Was to Westerns," in *Off Duty Pacific,* Nov. 1972: 149, in Little and Lee, *Words of the Dragon,* 149.

13. Michael Sauter and Ann Collette, "Exit the Dragon," *Entertainment Weekly,* July 17, 1998: 96.

14. Judith Rosen, "Bruce Lee Kicks into High Gear," *Publishers Weekly,* Nov. 6, 2000: 30.

15. Joel Stein, "Bruce Lee," *Time,* June 14, 1999: 118.

16. Ibid.

17. Shu, "Reading the Kung Fu Film in an American Context," 52.

18. Ibid., 53.

19. Ibid.

20. Bordwell, *Planet Hong Kong.*

21. Stein, "Bruce Lee."

22. Prashad, "Bruce Lee and the Anti-imperialism of Kung Fu," 54.

23. Ibid., 55.

24. Ibid., 57.

25. Ibid., 64.

26. Ibid., 57.

27. Thomas, *Bruce Lee.*

28. See Fujino, *Heartbeat of Struggle.*

29. Prashad, "Bruce Lee and the Anti-imperialism of Kung Fu," 63.

30. See Wong, "Denationalization Reconsidered"; and Koshy, "The Fiction of Asian American Literature."

31. Bruce Lee in a letter to Pearl Tso in September 1962 in Lee, *Letters of the Dragon,* 31.

32. Bruce Lee in Pang Cheng Lian, "Inside Bruce Lee," *New Nation* (Singapore), Aug. 14, 15, and 16, 1972.

33. Chan, "Bruce Lee's Fictional Models of Masculinity."

34. Bordwell, *Planet Hong Kong.*

35. Linda Lee, *Bruce Lee.*

Chapter Two

1. Stockton, *Beautiful Bottom, Beautiful Shame,* 7.

2. Ingraham, *White Weddings,* 151.

3. Ibid., 166.

4. Ibid., 166–167.

5. Edelman, *No Future.*

6. Sedgwick, *Touching Feeling,* 61, 64–65.

7. Ibid., 64–65.

8. Stockton, *Beautiful Bottom, Beautiful Shame,* 83.

9. Ibid., 87.

10. Ibid.

11. Levinas, *On Escape,* 63.

12. Ibid., 64.

13. Lowe, *Immigrant Acts.*

14. Sedgwick, *Touching Feeling,* 64.

15. Ibid., 72.

16. Muñoz, *Cruising Utopia,* 91.

17. Ibid., 88–91.

18. Ibid., 91.

19. Ibid., 95.

20. Chiang, "Coming Out into the Global System," 374.

21. Eng and Hom, *Q & A*; and Leong, *Asian American Sexualities.*

22. Eng, *Racial Castration,* 205.

23. Ibid.

24. Alison Macadam, "Long Duk Dong: The Last of the Stereotypes?" National Public Radio, Mar. 24, 2008, www.npr.org/templates/story/story.php?storyId =8859 1800 (accessed June 28, 2010).

25. Leonard Quant and Albert Auster (1992) describe a "film-based political vision" in Reagan's policies, and likewise, Michael Ryan and Douglas Kellner (1996) describe the high-minded discourse that covered "anti-democratic corruption" (as cited in Sheen and Davison, *The Cinema of David Lynch*).

26. Sohn, "Introduction"; and Palumbo-Liu, *Asian/American.*

27. Macadam, "Long Duk Dong."

28. Ono, "Re/membering Spectators," 145.

29. Bersani, "Is the Rectum a Grave?" 15.

30. Ibid., 24.

31. The Geeky Asian Guy Blog, "I'm Glad I Don't Live in Arizona," April 29, 2010, www.geekyasianguy.com/?m=201004. The blog ends with this disclaimer: "(By the way, I don't want anyone to think I'm down on Gedde Watanabe for taking the role. There just isn't that much work for Asian American actors. IMHO, he did the best he could with the script that he was given. Gedde went onto better things, including leading roles in the films *Volunteers* and *Gung Ho.*)"

32. www.amctheatres.com/sixteencandles (accessed April 30, 2011). The previews for new generations of audiences do not emphasize Long Duck Dong as a foreigner but one of her friends who parties excessively.

Chapter Three

1. Pascoe, *What Comes Naturally*, 153.
2. Ting, "The Power of Sexuality."
3. Pascoe, *What Comes Naturally*, 152; and Baldoz, *The Third Asiatic Invasion*.
4. Levinas, "On Escape," in idem, *On Escape*, 58.
5. Ibid., 55
6. Levinas, "Substitution," in idem, *Otherwise Than Being*, 80.
7. Abdul Ali, "After 13 Years, Love Jones Still Stands Out," *The Root*, Feb. 14, 2010, www.theroot.com/views/thirteen-years-later-and-still-got-jones (accessed May 30, 2011).
8. Raymond Fisman and Sheena S. Iyengar, "Racial Preferences in Dating," *Review of Economic Studies* 75 (2008): 117–132, http://faculty.chicagobooth.edu/emir .kamenica/documents/racialPreferences.pdf; and http://tierneylab.blogs.nytimes .com/2007/04/13/single-female-seeking-same-race-male (accessed Nov. 30, 2010).
9. Eric Byler in Oliver Wang, "Pushing Buttons," www.popmatters.com/film/ interviews/byler-eric-030508.shtml (accessed May 8, 2011).
10. Espiritu, "We Don't Sleep Around Like White Girls Do."
11. Eric Byler, on a panel moderated by Roger Ebert, "Saturday Night at the Overlook Theater" (extra features on the *Charlotte Sometimes* DVD).
12. If we follow Alfred Adler's "masculine protest," would Asian American men then invest in an intense patriarchy? R. W. Connell describes this singularly useful theorization by Alfred Adler in "Radical Psychoanalysis" as defined in *Masculinities*, 16.
13. Ibid., 253.
14. Early ethnocommunications graduates include Monteczuma Esparza, Billy Woodberry, Larry Clark, and Debbie Allen.
15. Kimmel, *Manhood in America*, 300.
16. Connell, *Masculinities*, 220.
17. Lee, *Orientals*; Liu, "Negotiating the Meaning of Access"; and Okada, "The PBS and NAATA Connection."
18. http://us_asians.tripod.com/articles-eric-byler.html.
19. www.variety.com/profiles/Company/main/2008619/Visionbox%20Media% 20Group.html?dataSet=1; and www.variety.com/profiles/Company/main/2124747/ Small%20Planet%20Pictures.html?dataSet=1 (accessed Jan. 27, 2010).
20. Levinas, *Time and the Other*, 67.
21. Ibid., 86.

22. Ibid.

23. Levinas, "God and Philosophy," in idem, *Basic Philosophical Writings*, 145.

24. Ibid.

25. Butler, *Undoing Gender*, 18.

26. Ibid.

27. Greg Pak, "Charlotte NOW: Three Reasons to See 'Charlotte Sometimes,'" May 1, 2003, www.AsianAmericanFilm.com/archives/000009.html (accessed Jan. 26, 2010).

28. Pigs and Battleships Blog, July 28, 2003, www.pigsandbattleships.blogspot.com/2003/07/charlotte-sometimes-byler-b.html (accessed Jan. 26, 2010).

29. Rick Curnutte, "An Interview with Eric Byler," *Film Journal*, www.thefilmjournal.com/issue8/byler.html (accessed May 21, 2011).

30. Ibid.

31. Levinas, "God and Philosophy," 140.

32. Levinas, "Substitution," 80.

33. Diane Weddington, "Nothing Overly Talky about Eric Byler's 'Charlotte Sometimes,'" *Oakland Tribune*, May 9, 2003.

34. Eric Byler, "Race, Sex and the 'Charlotte Sometimes' Controversy," IM Diversity.com, www.imdiversity.com/villages/Asian/arts_culture_media/archives/byler_charlotte_sometimes_hapas.asp (accessed May 23, 2011).

35. Oliver Wang, "Interview with Eric Byler," *PopMatters*, www.popmatters.com/film/interviews/byler-eric-030508.shtml (accessed Jan. 26, 2010).

36. Curnutte, "An Interview with Eric Byler," 5.

37. Kimberly Chun, "Why I Like *Finishing the Game* Director Justin Lin," *San Francisco Bay Guardian*, Mar. 13, 2007, www.sfbg.com/2007/03/14/sfiaaff-got-fangs?page=0,1 (accessed May 30, 2011).

38. A binarism and the rendering of Asian American women as traitors with more power than men persists. AsianAmericanFilm.com quotes from Byler's blogs on his PBS television pilot, "My Life Disoriented." He says: "Mainstream media and mainstream culture welcome and celebrate Asian American women as beautiful and exotic. But doors that are open for Asian American women are often closed to Asian American men, who are perhaps too closely associated with the wars of the 20th century and 'the axis of evil.' This leaves Asian American women in a quandary. Should they insist that doors of opportunity be held open for their Asian American brothers and risk having it closed on themselves? In *My Life Disoriented*, Kimberlee is offered the ideal doorway to acceptance and popularity at her new school. But, if she is observed hanging out with Char-lie [*sic*] and Naka, will she be branded as 'one of them' and lose her fragile status as 'one of us?'" www.asianamericanfilm.com/archives/001261.html (accessed Feb. 24, 2010).

39. Levinas, *Otherwise Than Being*, 95–97.

40. Ibid., 122.

41. In "Is Ontology Fundamental?" Emmanuel Levinas describes how relations between beings, who are "open" by virtue of their existence in the world and the dynamics and conditions that contextualize them, are "irreducible to comprehension" (5). Arguing against Heidegger's conception of the being as universal, Levinas says the self and the other are not "beyond the particular" (5). Levinas, "Is Ontology Fundamental?" in idem, *Basic Philosophical Writings*.

42. "Ontology is not accomplished in the triumph of human beings over their condition but in the very tension where this condition is assumed. . . . The comprehension of being does not presuppose a merely theoretical attitude but the whole of human comportment. The whole human being is ontology" (ibid., 3). Here, ontology is not a given being that exists as a universal essence but one that is felt, shaped, and performed as "contingency and facticity . . . an act of intellection" (3).

43. Ibid.

44. Ibid., 6.

45. Ibid., 18.

46. Ibid., 19.

47. Levinas, "Substitution," 81.

48. Ibid., 22.

Chapter Four

1. Oishi, "Bad Asians"; Shimizu, *The Hypersexuality of Race*.

2. Wallace, *Black Macho and the Myth of the Superwoman*.

3. Silverman, *Male Subjectivity at the Margins*, 52.

4. Ibid., 121.

5. Bersani, *Is the Rectum A Grave?*, 25.

6. *The Daily Show* aired the segment "They So Horny" featuring Professor Hamamoto. He appears as if in on the joke here, and on *The Tonight Show*, where his pornography work is mocked by host Jay Leno. Samantha Bee, "They So Horny?" with Darrell Y. Hamamoto, *The Daily Show with Jon Stewart*, NBC, Feb. 26, 2004.

7. Julie Kim, "X-Rated Film Shows Students the Reality of Asian Sexuality," *Daily Titan*, May 9, 2005, www.titanyearbook.com/archives/2005/2005-05-09.pdf. "The motive was accessibility: it's easier to make money in the multibillion-dollar porn industry, after which he planned to invest in works by other Asian-American moviemakers."

8. Amy Ikeda, "*Yellowcaust* Director Darrell Hamamoto Interviewed," VC Film Fest 2004, www.vconline.org/ff04/intervhamamoto.html (accessed May 23, 2011).

9. Kim, "X-Rated Film Shows Students the Reality of Asian Sexuality."

10. David Pierson, "Sex and the Asian Man," *Los Angeles Times*, May 12, 2004, http://articles.latimes.com/2004/may/12/entertainment/et-pierson12.

11. Nguyen, "The Remasculinization of Chinese America."

12. Silverman, *Male Subjectivity at the Margins*, 36.

13. Collins, *Black Sexual Politics*, 5; Crenshaw, "Demarginalizing the Intersection of Race and Sex," 140.

14. Silverman, *Male Subjectivity at the Margins*, 36.

15. Hamamoto as quoted in Kim, "X-Rated Film Shows Students the Reality of Asian Sexuality."

16. *How Do I Look?*

17. Harry Mok, "Yellow Porn," Salon.com, Oct. 10, 2003, http://dir.salon.com/story/sex/feature/2003/10/10/asian/.

18. John T. Bone, *World's Biggest Gang Bang*, 1990, DVD.

19. This interpretation of Asian American male and female sexual problems is not isolated. The widely screened Asian American documentary *Slaying the Dragon* (Gee, 1988) features an Asian American male critic decrying popular representations of white male–Asian female sexual and love relations, as they may influence Asian American women to pursue such relationships instead of same-race liaisons.

20. For example, in Jennifer Phang's short video *Love Ltd.* (2000), an Asian American family's dinner is the setting for the children's coming out as a gay man and lesbian woman. They do so unevenly. The man comes out with relative ease in comparison to his sister. However, both must battle their mother's expectations of heterosexuality as she incessantly interrogates her children about their love lives with opposite-sex partners.

21. Hamamoto, "The Joy Fuck Club," in Hamamoto and Liu, *Countervisions*, 60 (my emphasis).

22. Andrew Sywak, "Sunset Filmmaker Examines Asian-American Sexuality," *The Sunset Beacon*, www.sunsetbeacon.com/archives/SunsetBeacon/2004editions/May04/jameshou.html (accessed May 2, 2011).

23. Dorothy Korber, "Porn as Commentary: Film on Asian Issues Grabs Attention Stirs Debate," *California State University Daily News Clips*, Nov. 3, 2003, www.calstate.edu/pa/clips2003/november/3nov/porn.shtml (accessed June 6, 2009).

24. Ibid.

25. Ibid.

26. In Sywak, "Sunset Filmmaker Examines Asian American Sexuality" (accessed June 4, 2009).

27. Albert Lanier, "Mambo Italiano; Aragami; Yellowcaust; Refugee; Hotel Hi-

biscus; Masters of the Pillow; Drifters," *Ain't It Cool News*, Nov. 13, 2003, www.aint itcool.com/?q=node/16497 (accessed May 31, 2011).

28. Albury, "Reading Porn Reparatively."

29. Wesley Yang, "Asian Like Me" or "Paper Tigers: What Happens to All Asian American Overachievers When the Test-taking Ends," *New York Magazine*, May 8, 2011.

30. Jeff Yang, "My Thoughts on Wesley Yang's *New York Magazine* Feature 'Asian Like Me': What a Long Strange Trip," *Original Spin*, May 9, 2011, http://originalspin.posterous.com/52393496 (accessed May 31, 2011).

31. Ibid., 1.

32. Shuriken, YW Mafia, "From an Email Sent to Me by My Friend," *Yellowworld.org*, comment posted July 28, 2005, http://forums.yellowworld.org/showthread.php?t=23170.

33. Darrell Hamamoto, "On Asian American Sexual Politics," National Sexuality Resource Center, http://nsrc.sfsu.edu/article/asian_american_sexual_politics(accessed Oct. 1, 2008).

34. Korber, "Porn as Commentary."

35. Hamamoto, "On Asian American Sexual Politics." Amy Sueyoshi's article that surveys the scene of viewing the film contradicts Hamamoto's self-assessment. See Sueyoshi, "InnovAsian in Pornography?"

36. Tad Doyle, "*Masters of the Pillow* Screening Blog 1," 2004 APA Film Blog, posted on Oct. 9, 2004, www.apafilm.org/2004/2004Blog.php.

37. Purple Tigress, "Marrying Out into Bananadom," Blogcritics Culture, May 24, 2004, http://blogcritics.org/culture/article/marrying-out-into-bananadom.

38. William Nakayama, "Liberating the Asian American Libido," *Goldsea*, http://goldsea.com/Mediawatch/Pillow/pillow.htm (accessed Oct. 1, 2008).

39. See Fung, "Looking For My Penis"; and Nguyen, "The Resurrection of Brandon Lee."

40. Professor Laura Grindstaff as cited in Dorothy Korber, "Porn as Commentary" in *Sacramento Bee*, Nov. 2, 2003.

41. Hamamoto, "On Asian American Sexual Politics."

42. LeRoid, Review of "Masters of the Pillow," AA Rising: Da Asian Pacific American Entertainment Resource, http://aarising.com/reviews/oct2004.htm, Oct. 2004.

43. Chung, "Porn Losers Fail to Flesh Out Vision."

44. Ibid.

45. Hamamoto, "On Asian American Sexual Politics."

46. Ibid.

47. Parikh, "The Most Outrageous Masquerade," 860.

48. Ibid., 890.

49. Shimizu, *The Hypersexuality of Race.*
50. Hamamoto, "*The Joy Fuck Club.*"
51. Hagedorn, "Asian Women in Film," 74; Feng, "Recuperating Suzie Wong," 40.
52. Silverman, "The Dominant Fiction," in *Male Subjectivity at the Margins*, 29.
53. Ibid., 30, 34.
54. Ibid., 42.
55. Chung, "Porn Losers Fail to Flesh Out Vision."
56. Ellis, *Studies in the Psychology of Sex*; and Freud, *On Narcissism.*
57. Parikh, "The Most Outrageous Masquerade."
58. Chang, *Inhuman Citizenship.*
59. Mura, *A Male Grief,* 23.
60. Ibid., 3.
61. Ibid.
62. Ibid.
63. Ibid., 4.
64. Ibid.
65. Ibid., 6.
66. Silverman, *Male Subjectivity at the Margins,* 15–16.
67. Mura, "A Male Grief," 9.
68. Ibid., 11, 13.
69. Ibid., 14.
70. Ibid., 15.
71. Ibid., 16.
72. Nguyen, "The Remasculinization of Chinese America."

Chapter Five
1. Silverman, *Threshold of the Visible World,* 2.
2. Ibid.
3. Ibid.
4. Ibid., 227.
5. Ibid., 85.
6. Ibid., 93.
7. Ibid., 93.
8. Levinas, *On Escape,* 55.
9. Lee, "Cold War Origins of the Model Minority," in idem, *Orientals,* 146.
10. Ibid., 146.
11. Shibusawa, "Hollywood's Japan," in idem, *America's Geisha Ally,* 256.
12. May, *Homeward Bound,* 10.
13. Ibid., 14.

14. Eng and Han, "A Dialogue on Racial Melancholia"; Cheng, *The Melancholy of Race*.

15. Cheng, *The Melancholy of Race*, 95.

16. Sedgwick, *Between Men*, 2.

17. Ibid.

18. Ibid., 21.

19. Dyer, *The Matter of Images*, 111.

20. Ibid.

21. Ibid., 118.

22. Ibid., 119.

23. Ibid., 120.

24. Ibid.

25. Freud, "Mourning and Melancholia."

26. Eng and Han, "A Dialogue on Racial Melancholia," 670.

27. Ibid., 671.

28. Silverman, *The Threshold of the Visible World*, 2.

29. Roger Ebert, "Map of the Human Heart," *Chicago Sun Times*, May 14, 1993, http://rogerebert.suntimes.com/.

30. Bacigalupi, *Towards Living Pono*.

31. "The Jason Scott Lee Homepage He Knows About!" http://web.singnet.com.sg/shade/insight3.htm (accessed May 23, 2011).

Epilogue

1. Zia, *Asian American Dreams*.

2. Schein and Thoj, "*Gran Torino*'s Boys and Men with Guns," 9.

3. Ibid., 8

4. Marchetti, *Romance and the "Yellow Peril,"* 114.

5. Vang, "*Gran Torino*'s Hmong Lead Bee Vang on Film, Race, and Masculinity," 3.

6. Ibid., 5.

7. Hooks, "The Oppositional Gaze: Black Female Spectators," in idem, *Black Looks*, 116.

8. Vang, "*Gran Torino*'s Hmong Lead Bee Vang on Film, Race, and Masculinity," 7.

9. Ibid., 4.

10. Schein and Thoj, "*Gran Torino*'s Boys and Men with Guns."

11. Hooks, *Outlaw Culture*.

12. Vang, "*Gran Torino*'s Hmong Lead Bee Vang on Film, Race, and Masculinity," 4.

13. Ibid., 6.

14. *Lost Scenes: Thao Does Walt,* dir. Clint Yee-Vu, video, 2010, www.youtube.com/watch?v=dMaIOFMg64M (accessed May 29, 2011).

15. http://events.stanford.edu/events/268/26855/.

Bibliography and Suggested Readings

Albury, Kath. "Reading Porn Reparatively." *Sexualities* 12 (2009): 647. http://
sexualities.sagepub.com/cgi/content/abstract/12/5/647.

American Sons. VHS. Directed by Steven Okazaki. Center for Asian American
Media, 1994.

Asian Pride Porn. VHS. Directed by Greg Pak. Part of the "Avenue of Asian
Americas" digital shorts anthology. Asian American Filmmakers Collaborative,
2000.

Bacigalupi, Rick. *Towards Living Pono: With Jason Scott Lee*. Documentary. Bacipix,
2010. www.bacipix.com/livingpono/default.php.

Baldoz, Rick. *Third Asiatic Invasion: Empire and Migration in Filipino America*.
New York: New York University Press, 2011.

The Ballad of Little Jo. DVD. Directed by Maggie Greenwald. New Line Home
Video, 1993.

Bederman, Gail. *Manliness and Civilization: A Cultural History of Gender and
Race in the United States, 1880–1917*. Women in Culture and Society Series.
Chicago: University of Chicago Press, 1996.

Bernasconi, Robert. "Levinas and the Struggle for Existence." Pp. 170–184 in
Addressing Levinas, edited by Kent Still, Eric Sean Nelson, and Antje Kapust.
Evanston, IL: Northwestern University Press, 1985.

———. "The Truth That Accuses: Consciousness, Shame and Guilt in Levinas and
Augustine." Pp. 24–55 in *The Ethics of Postmodernity*, edited by Gary B. Madison
and Marty Fairbairn. Evanston, IL: Northwestern University Press, 1999.

———. "The Violence of the Face." *Philosophy and Social Criticism* 23, no. 6
(1997): 81–93.

Bersani, Leo. *Homos.* Cambridge, MA: Harvard University Press, 1996.

————. *Is the Rectum a Grave?* Chicago: University of Chicago Press, 2009.

Better Luck Tomorrow. VHS. Directed by Justin Lin. MTV Films, 2003.

Bhabha, Homi. "The Other Question." Pp. 66–84 in idem, *The Location of Culture.* New York: Routledge, 1994.

The Big Boss or *Fists of Fury.* DVD. Directed by Wei Lo. Golden Harvest, 1971.

Blue in the Face. DVD. Directed Wayne Wang. Miramax, 1995.

Bordwell, David. *Planet Hong Kong: Popular Cinema and the Art of Entertainment.* Cambridge, MA: Harvard University Press, 2000.

Bow, Leslie. *Betrayal and Other Acts of Subversion: Feminism, Sexual Politics, Asian American Women's Literature.* Princeton, NJ: Princeton University Press, 2001.

Breakfast at Tiffany's. DVD. Directed by Blake Edwards. Paramount Pictures, 1961.

Breakfast Club. DVD. Directed by John Hughes. Universal Pictures, 1985.

Bridge to the Sun. VHS. Directed by Etienne Perier. Cité Films, 1961.

Brokeback Mountain. DVD. Directed by Ang Lee. Alberta Film Entertainment, Focus Features, Good Machine. 2005.

Broken Blossoms. VHS. Directed by D. W. Griffith. D. W. Griffith Productions, 1919.

Bruce Lee: His Last Days, His Last Nights. VHS. Directed by John Lo Mar. W.W. Northal, 1975.

Bruce Lee: The Legend. DVD. Directed by Leonard Ho. Paragon Films, Ltd., 1977.

Bruce Lee: The Man, The Myth. DVD. Directed by See-Yuen Ng. Eternal Film Company, 1976.

Butler, Judith. *Giving an Account of Oneself.* New York: Fordham University Press, 2005.

————. *The Psychic Life of Power: Theories in Subjection.* Stanford, CA: Stanford University Press, 1997.

————. *Subjects of Desire: Hegelian Reflections in Twentieth-Century France.* New York: Columbia University Press, 1999.

————. *Undoing Gender.* New York: Routledge, 2004.

Carbado, Devon. *Black Men on Race, Gender and Sexuality: A Critical Reader.* Critical America Series. New York: New York University Press, 1999.

Carby, Hazel V. *Race Men.* The W. E. B. Du Bois Lectures. Cambridge, MA: Harvard University Press, 2000.

Carter, Julian B. *The Heart of Whiteness: Normal Sexuality and Race in America, 1880–1940.* Durham, NC: Duke University Press, 2007.

Chan Is Missing. DVD. Directed by Wayne Wang. New Yorker Films, 1982.

Chan, Jachinson. "Bruce Lee's Fictional Models of Masculinity." *Men and Masculinities* 2, no. 4 (April 2000): 371–387.

————. *Chinese American Masculinities from Fu Manchu to Bruce Lee.* New York: Garland Publishing, 2000.

Chan, Jeffrey Paul, Frank Chin, and Lawson Fusao Inada. *Aiiieeeee! An Anthology of Asian American Writers.* New York: Signet, 1991.

Chang, Juliana. *Inhuman Citizenship: Traumatic Enjoyment and Asian American Domestic Narrative.* Minneapolis: University of Minnesota Press, forthcoming.

Charlotte Sometimes. VHS. Directed by Eric Byler. Arts Alliance America, 2002.

Cheng, Anne Anlin. *The Melancholy of Race: Psychoanalysis, Assimilation, and Hidden Grief.* Race and American Culture. New York: Oxford University Press, 2001.

Cheung, King-Kok. "The Woman Warrior Versus the Chinaman Pacific: Must a Chinese American Critic Choose between Feminism and Heroism?" Pp. 234–251 in *Conflicts in Feminism*, edited by Marianne Hirsch and Evelyn Fox Keller. New York: Routledge, 1990.

Chiang, Mark. "Coming Out into the Global System: Postmodern Patriarchies and Transnational Sexualities in *The Wedding Banquet.*" Pp. 374–396 in *Q & A: Queer in Asian America*, edited by David Eng and Alice Hom. Philadelphia: Temple University Press, 1999.

Chin, Frank, et al. *Big aiiieeeee! An Anthology of Chinese American and Japanese American Literature.* New York: Meridian, 1991.

Chinese Characters. VHS. Directed by Richard Fung. Video Data Bank, 1986.

The Chinese Connection or *Fist of Fury.* DVD. Directed by Wei Lo. Golden Harvest Company, 1972.

Chong, Sylvia. "Look, an Asian!" *Journal of Asian American Studies* 11, no. 1 (Feb. 2008): 27–60.

————. *The Oriental Obscene: Violence and the Asian Male Body in American Moving Images in the Vietnam Era, 1968–1985.* Durham, NC: Duke University Press, 2011.

Chu, Louis. *Eat a Bowl of Tea: A Novel of New York's Chinatown.* New York: Lyle Stuart, 2002.

Chung, Hye-Seung. *Hollywood Asian: Philip Ahn and the Politics of Cross-Ethnic Performance.* Philadelphia: Temple University Press, 2006.

Chung, Philip W. "Porn Losers Fail to Flesh Out Vision." *Asian Week*, June 4, 2004. www.asianweek.com/2004/06/04/porn-losers-fail-to-flesh-out-vision (accessed Nov. 11, 2011).

Cohen, Richard A. "Introduction" to Emmanuel Levinas, *Ethics and Infinity.* Pittsburgh: Duquesne University Press, 1985.

Collins, Patricia Hill. *Black Sexual Politics: African Americans, Gender, and the New Racism.* New York: Routledge, 2005.

Connell, R. W. *Masculinities.* Berkeley: University of California Press, 2005.

Corbett, Ken. *Boyhoods: Rethinking Masculinities.* New Haven, CT: Yale University Press, 2009.

Crenshaw, Kimberle. "Demarginalizing the Intersection of Race and Sex." *University of Chicago Legal Forum* (1989): 139–168.

The Crimson Kimono. VHS. Directed by Samuel Fuller. Columbia Pictures, 1959.

Cvetkovich, Ann. *An Archive of Feelings: Trauma, Sexuality and Lesbian Public Cultures.* Durham, NC: Duke University Press, 2003.

Davis, Angela. "Rape, Racism and The Myth of the Black Rapist." Pp. 172–201 in idem, *Women, Race, & Class.* New York: Vintage Books, 1983.

The Debut. DVD. Directed by Gene Cajayon. Sony Pictures, 2000.

Dick Ho: Asian Male Porn Star. DVD. Directed by Jeffrey Lei. A Take Out Production, 2005.

Ding, Loni. "Strategies of an Asian American Filmmaker." Pp. 46–51 in *Moving the Image,* edited by Russell Leong. A Project of the UCLA Asian American Studies Center and Visual Communications, Southern California Asian American Studies Central. Seattle: University of Washington Press, 1991.

Douglas, Helen. *Love and Arms: Violence and Justification after Levinas.* New York: Trillium, 2011.

Dragon: The Bruce Lee Story. DVD. Directed by Rob Cohen. MCA Universal, 1993.

The Dragon Painter. VHS. Directed by William Worthington. Haworth Pictures Corporation, 1919.

Dyer, Richard. *The Matter with Images: Essays on Representations.* London: Routledge, 1993.

Eat a Bowl of Tea. DVD. Directed by Wayne Wang. American Playhouse, 1989.

Edelman, Lee. *No Future: Queer Theory and the Death Drive.* Durham, NC: Duke University Press, 2004.

Ellis, Havelock. *Studies in the Psychology of Sex.* Charleston, SC: BiblioBazaar, 2007.

Eng, David. *The Feeling of Kinship: Queer Liberalism and the Racialization of Intimacy.* Durham, NC: Duke University Press, 2010.

———. *Racial Castration: Managing Masculinity in Asian America.* Durham, NC: Duke University Press, 2001.

———, and Shinhee Han. "A Dialogue on Racial Melancholia." *Psychoanalytic Dialogues* 10 (2000): 667–700.

Eng, David, and Alice Hom, eds. *Q & A: Queer in Asian America.* Philadelphia: Temple University Press, 1999.

Enter the Dragon. DVD. Directed by Robert Clouse. Golden Harvest. 1973.

Espiritu, Yen Le. "'We Don't Sleep Around Like White Girls Do': Family, Culture, and Gender in Filipina American Lives." *Signs: Journal of Women, Culture, and Society* 26, no. 2 (Winter 2001): 415–440.

Ethan Mao. DVD. Directed by Quentin Lee. Margin Films, 2004.

Feng, Peter X. "Recuperating Suzie Wong: A Fan's Nancy Kwan-Dary." In Pp. 40–56 in Hamamoto and Liu, *Countervisions.*

Ferris Bueller's Day Off. DVD. Directed by John Hughes. Paramount Pictures, 1986.

Fighting Chance. DVD. Directed by Richard Fung. Video Data Bank, 1991.

Finishing the Game: The Search for a New Bruce Lee. DVD. Directed by Justin Lin. Barnstorm Pictures, Cherry Sky Films, Trailing Johnson Productions. 2007.

Flow. VHS. Directed by Quentin Lee. Tapeworm Video, 1997.

Flower Drum Song. DVD. Directed by Henry Koster. Universal Studios, 1961.

Forever Bottom! VHS. Directed by Hoang T. Nguyen. USA Video, 1999.

Foucault, Michel. *Ethics: Subjectivity and Truth (Essential Works of Foucault, 1954–1984, Vol. 1).* New York: New Press, 2006.

Freud, Sigmund. "Fetishism." Pp. 198–204 in *Miscellaneous Papers, 1888–1938.* Vol. 5 of *Collected Papers.* 5 vols. London: Hogarth and Institute of Psycho-Analysis, 1924–1950.

———. "Mourning and Melancholia" (1917). Pp. 237–258 in *The Standard Edition of the Complete Psychological Works of Sigmund Freud,* Volume 14 (1914–1916): On the History of the Psycho-Analytic Movement, Papers on Metapsychology and Other Works.* London: Hogarth Press, 1953–1974.

———. *On Narcissism: An Introduction.* New Haven, CT: Yale University Press, 1991.

Fujino, Diane. *Heartbeat of Struggle: The Revolutionary Life of Yuri Kochiyama.* Minneapolis: University of Minnesota Press, 2005

Fung, Richard. "Looking For My Penis: The Eroticized Asian in Gay Video Porn." Pp. 145–168 in *How Do I Look?*

Gabriel, Teshome. "Teaching Third World Cinema." *Screen* 24 (March–April 1983): 60–65.

Game of Death. DVD. Directed by Robert Clouse. Concord Productions, Inc., and Golden Harvest Company, 1978.

Game of Death 2. DVD. Directed by See-Yuen Ng. Seasonal Film Corporation, 1981.

Gran Torino. DVD. Directed by Clint Eastwood. Warner Brothers, 2008.

The Green Hornet. TV Series. DVD. Directed by William Beaudine and Darrel Hallenbeck. VCI Entertainment, 1966–1967.

Hagedorn, Jessica. "Asian Women in Film: No Joy, No Luck." *Ms. Magazine* 4, no. 4 (Jan.–Feb. 1994): 74–79.

Halberstam, Judith. *Female Masculinity.* Durham, NC: Duke University Press, 1998.

Hamamoto, Darrell Y. "The Joy Fuck Club: Prolegomenon to an Asian American Porno Practice." *New Political Science* 20, no. 3 (1998): 323–345.

———. "The Joy Fuck Club: Prolegomenon to an Asian American Porno Practice." Pp. 59–89 in Hamamoto and Liu, *Countervisions.*

———,and Sandra Liu, eds. *Countervisions: Asian American Film Criticism.* Philadelphia: Temple University Press, 2000.

Harold and Kumar Go to White Castle. DVD. Directed by Danny Leiner. New Line Cinema, 2004.

Harper, Phillip Brian. *Are We Not Men? Masculine Anxiety and the Problem of African American Identity.* New York: Oxford University Press, 1998

hooks, bell. *Black Looks: Race and Representation.* Boston: South End Press, 1999.

———. *Outlaw Culture: Resisting Representations.* New York: Routledge, 1994.

How Do I Look? Queer Film and Video. Edited by Bad Object-Choices. Seattle: Bay Press, 1991.

Huang, Yunte. *Charlie Chan: The Untold Story of the Honorable Detective and His Rendezvous with American History.* New York: W. W. Norton, 2010.

Hulk. DVD. Directed by Ang Lee. Universal Pictures. 2003.

Hunt, Darnell. "Prime Time in Black and White." University of California at Los Angeles, Ralph J. Bunche Center for African American Studies. Study released June 24, 2003.

Ingraham, Chrys. *White Weddings: Romancing Heterosexuality in Popular Culture.* New York: Routledge, 2008.

JJ Chinois. Directed by Lynne Chan. www.freewaves.org/archive/index. php?film=5624&search, 2002.

Joy Luck Club. DVD. Directed by Wayne Wang. Hollywood Pictures, 1993.

The Jungle Book. DVD. Directed by Stephen Sommers. Walt Disney Co., 1994.

Katz, Jonathan Ned. *The Invention of Heterosexuality.* Chicago: University of Chicago Press, 2007.

Kelsky, Karen. *Women on the Verge: Japanese Women, Western Dreams.* Asia-Pacific Series. Durham, NC: Duke University Press, 2001.

Kim, Daniel Y. "Once More, With Feeling: Cold War Masculinity and the Sentiment of Patriotism in John Okada's *No-No Boy.*" *Criticism* 47, no. 1 (Winter 2005): 65–83.

———. *Writing Manhood in Black and Yellow: Ralph Ellison, Frank Chin, and the Literary Politics of Identity.* Stanford, CA: Stanford University Press, 2005.

Kim, Elaine H. *Asian American Literature.* Philadelphia: Temple University Press, 1984.

Kimmel, Michael. *Manhood in America: A Cultural History.* New York: Oxford University Press, 1997.

The King and I. DVD. Directed by Walter Lang. 20th Century Fox, 1956.

Kingston, Maxine Hong. *Woman Warrior: Memoirs of a Girlhood among Ghosts.* New York: Vintage Books, 1989.

Klein, Christina. *Cold War Orientalism: Asia in the Middlebrow Imagination, 1945–1961.* Berkeley: University of California Press, 2003.

Koshy, Susan. "The Fiction of Asian American Literature." *Yale Journal of Criticism* 9, no. 2 (Fall 1996): 315–346.

Lee, Bruce. *Letters of the Dragon.* North Clarendon, VT: Tuttle, 1998.

Lee, Haiyan. "Enemy Under My Skin: Eileen Chang's *Lust, Caution* and the Politics of Transcendence." *PMLA* 125, no. 3 (May 2010): 640–656.

Lee, Joon Oluchi. "The Joy of the Castrated Boy." *Social Text* 23 (Fall–Winter 2005): 35–56.

Lee, Linda. *Bruce Lee: The Man Only I Knew.* New York: Warner Books, 1975.

Lee, Robert G. *Orientals: Asian Americans in Popular Culture.* Philadelphia: Temple University Press, 1999.

Legend of the Fist: The Return of Chen Zhen. DVD. Directed by Wai-keung Lau. Media Asia Films, Enlight Pictures, and Shanghai Film Media Asia, 2010.

Leong, Russell. *Asian American Sexualities: Dimensions of the Gay and Lesbian Experience.* New York: Routledge, 1995.

Levinas, Emmanuel. *Basic Philosophical Writings.* Edited by Adriaan T. Peperzak, Simon Critchley, and Robert Bernasconi. Bloomington: Indiana University Press, 1996.

———. *Humanism of the Other.* Translated by Nidra Poller. Chicago: University of Illinois Press, 2006.

———. *On Escape.* Translated by Bettina Bergo. Stanford, CA: Stanford University Press, 2003.

———. *Otherwise Than Being, or, Beyond Essence.* Translated by Alphonso Lingis. Pittsburgh: Duquesne University Press, 1998.

———. *Time and the Other.* Translated by Richard A. Cohen. Pittsburgh: Duquesne University Press, 1990.

———. *Totality and Infinity.* Translated by Alphonso Lingis. Pittsburgh: Duquesne University Press, 1959.

Little, John, and Bruce Lee. *Letters of the Dragon.* North Clarendon, VT: Tuttle, 1998.

———. *Words of the Dragon: Interviews with Bruce Lee, 1958–1973.* North Clarendon, VT: Tuttle, 1997.

Liu, Sandra. "Negotiating the Meaning of Access." Pp. 90–111 in Hamamoto and Liu, *Countervisions.*

Locke, Brian. *Racial Stigma on the Hollywood Screen from World War II to the Present: The Orientalist Buddy Film.* New York: Palgrave Macmillan, 2009.

Love Ltd. DVD. Directed by Jennifer Phang. CAAM, 2000.

The Lover. DVD. Directed by Jean-Jacques Annaud. MGM, 1992.

Lowe, Lisa. *Immigrant Acts: On Asian American Cultural Politics.* Durham, NC: Duke University Press, 1996.

Lukacs, Georg. *Ontology of Social Being, Vol. 3: Labour.* New York: Merlin, 1980.

Lust, Caution. DVD. Directed by Ang Lee. Universal Studios, 2007.

Macho Dancer. DVD. Directed by Lino Brocka. Strand Releasing, 1988.

Maid in Manhattan. DVD. Directed by Wayne Wang. Revolution Studios, Red Om Films, and Hughes Entertainment, 2002.

Map of the Human Heart. DVD. Directed by Vincent Ward. Australian Film Finance Corporation (AFFC), Les Films Ariane, Map Films, 1993.

Marchetti, Gina. *Romance and the "Yellow Peril": Race, Sex, and Discursive Strategies in Hollywood Fiction.* Berkeley: University of California Press, 1994.

Marriott, David. *On Black Men.* New York: Columbia University Press, 2000.

The Masseur. DVD. Directed by Brillante Mendoza. Picture this, 2005.

Masters of the Pillow. DVD. Directed by James Hou. Avenue Films, 2003.

May, Elaine Tyler. *Homeward Bound: American Families in the Cold War Era.* New York: Basic Books, 2008.

Miyao, Daisuke. *Sessue Hayakawa: Silent Cinema and Transnational Stardom.* Durham, NC: Duke University Press, 2007.

Modleski, Tania. *Loving With a Vengeance: Mass Produced Fantasies for Women.* New York: Routledge, 2007.

Moraga, Cherríe. "La Dulce Culpa." Pp. 417–424 in Vance, *Pleasure and Danger.*

Muñoz, José Esteban. *Cruising Utopia: The Then and There of Queer Futurity.* New York: New York University Press, 2009.

———. *Disidentifications: Queers of Color and the Performance of Politics.* Minneapolis: University of Minnesota Press, 1999.

Mura, David. *The Colors of Desire.* New York: Anchor, 1995.

———. *A Male Grief: Notes on Pornography and Addiction.* Minneapolis: Milkweed Editions, 1987.

———. *Where the Body Meets Memory: An Odyssey of Race, Sexuality and Identity.* New York: Anchor, 1997.

Neal, Mark Anthony. *New Black Man.* New York: Routledge, 2006.

Nemoto, Kumiko. *Racing Romance: Love, Power, and Desire Among Asian American/White Couples.* New Brunswick, NJ: Rutgers University Press, 2009.

Nguyen, Hoang Tan. "The Resurrection of Brandon Lee: The Making of a Gay Asian American Porn Star." Pp. 223–270 in *Porn Studies,* edited by Linda Williams. Durham, NC: Duke University Press, 2004.

Nguyen, Viet Thanh. "The Remasculinization of Chinese America: Race, Violence, and the Novel." *American Literary History* 12, nos. 1–2 (2000): 130–157.

Nomad: The Warrior. DVD. Directed by Sergey Bodrov and Ivan Passer. Ibrus. 2005.

Oishi, Eve. "Bad Asians: New Media by Queer Asian American Artists." Pp. 221–242 in Hamamoto and Liu, *Countervisions.*

Okada, John. *No-No Boy.* Seattle: University of Washington Press, 1981.

Okada, Jun. "The PBS and NAATA Connection: Comparing the Public Spheres of Asian American Film and Video." *Velvet Light Trap* 55 (2005): 39–51.

Ono, Kent. "Re/membering Spectators: Meditations on Japanese American Cinema." Pp. 129–149 in Hamamoto and Liu, *Countervisions.*

———,and Vincent Pham. *Asian Americans and the Media.* Cambridge, UK: Polity, 2008.

Oren, Tasha G. "Secret Asian Man: Angry Asians and the Politics of Cultural Visibility." Pp. 337–360 in *East Main Street: Asian American Popular Culture,* edited by Shilpa Davé, LeiLane Nishime, and Tasha G. Oren. New York: New York University Press, 2005.

Palumbo-Liu, David. *Asian/American: Historical Crossings of A Racial Frontier.* Stanford, CA: Stanford University Press, 1999.

Parikh, Crystal. *An Ethics of Betrayal: The Politics of Otherness in Emergent U.S. Literature and Culture.* New York: Fordham University Press, 2009.

———. "The Most Outrageous Masquerade: Queering Asian-American Masculinity." *Modern Fiction Studies* 48 (Winter 2002): 858–98.

Pascoe, Peggy. *What Comes Naturally: Miscegenation Law and the Making of Race in America.* New York: Oxford University Press, 2009.

Prashad, Vijay. "Bruce Lee and the Anti-Imperialism of Kung Fu: A Polycultural Adventure." *positions: east asia cultures critique* 11, no. 1 (2003): 51–90.

———. *Everybody Was Kung Fu Fighting: Afro-Asian Connections and the Myth of Cultural Purity.* New York: Beacon, 2002.

Pretty in Pink. DVD. Directed by John Hughes. Paramount Pictures, 1986.

Rapa Nui. DVD. Directed by Kevin Reynolds. Majestic Films International, 1994.

Rich, Adrienne. "Compulsory Heterosexuality and Lesbian Existence." In idem, *Blood, Bread, and Poetry.* New York: Norton Paperback, 1980.

Robot Stories. VHS. Directed by Greg Pak. Kino Video, 2005.

Rubin, Gayle. "Thinking Sex: Notes for a Radical Theory of the Politics of Sexuality." Pp. 3–44 in *The Gay and Lesbian Studies Reader.*, edited by Henry Abelove, Michèle Aina Barale, and David M. Halperin. New York: Routledge, 1993.

Schein, Louisa, and Va-Megn Thoj, "*Gran Torino*'s Boys and Men with Guns: Hmong Perspectives." *Hmong Studies Journal* 10 (2009). www.hmongstudies .org/HmongStudiesJournal.html.

Sea in the Blood. VHS. Directed by Richard Fung. Fungus Productions, 2000.

Sedgwick, Eve Kosofsky. *Between Men: English Literature and Male Homosocial Desire.* New York: Columbia University Press, 1985.

———. *Epistemology of the Closet.* 2nd ed. Berkeley: University of California Press, 2008.

———. *Touching Feeling: Affect, Pedagogy, Performativity.* Durham, NC: Duke University Press, 2003.

See, Lisa. *Snow Flower and the Secret Fan.* New York: Random House, 2006.

Shah, Sonia. *Dragon Ladies: Asian American Feminists Breathe Fire.* Boston: South End Press, 1999.

Sheen, Erica, and Annette Davison. *The Cinema of David Lynch: American Dreams, Nightmare Visions.* Brighton, UK: Wallflower Press, 2004.

Shibusawa, Naoko. *America's Geisha Ally.* Cambridge, MA: Harvard University Press, 2006.

Shimizu, Celine Parreñas. *The Hypersexuality of Race: Performing Asian/American Women on Screen and Scene.* Durham, NC: Duke University Press, 2007.

———. "Master-Slave Sex Acts." Pp. 218–232 in *The Persistence of Whiteness,* edited by Daniel Bernardi. New York: Routledge, 2007.

Shu, Yuan. "Reading the Kung-Fu Film in an American Context: From Bruce Lee to Jackie Chan." *Journal of Popular Film and Television* 31, no. 2 (Summer 2003): 50–59.

Silverman, Kaja. *Male Subjectivity at the Margins.* New York: Routledge, 1992.

———. *Threshold of the Visible World.* New York: Routledge, 1995.

Sisterhood of the Traveling Pants. DVD. Directed by Ken Kwapis. Warner Home Video, 2008.

Sixteen Candles. DVD. Directed by John Hughes. Universal Pictures, 1984.

Skin on Skin. DVD. Directed by Darrell Hamamoto. Avenue Films, 2004.

The Slanted Screen. DVD. Directed by Jeff Adachi. Passion River, 2006.

Slaying the Dragon. DVD. Directed by Deborah Gee. San Francisco: Center for Asian American Media. 1988.

Smoke. DVD. Directed by Wayne Wang. Miramax Home Entertainment, 1995.

Snow Flower and the Secret Fan. Directed by Wayne Wang. IDG China Media, 2011.

Sohn, Stephen H. "Introduction: Alien/Asian: Imagining the Racialized Future." *MELUS* 33, no. 4 (Winter 2008): 5–22.

Some Questions for 28 Kisses. VHS. Directed by Kip Fulbeck. Electronic Arts Intermix, 1994.

Son of the Gods. VHS. Directed by Frank Lloyd. First National Pictures, 1930.

Stockton, Kathryn Bond. *Beautiful Bottom, Beautiful Shame: Where "Black" Meets "Queer".* Durham, NC: Duke University Press, 2006.

Strossen, Nadine. *Defending Pornography: Free Speech, Sex and the Fight For Women's Rights*. New York: NYU Press, 2000.

Sueyoshi, Amy. "InnovAsian in Pornography? Asian American Masculinity and the 'Porno Revolution.'" Pp. 78–80 in *21st Century Sexualities: Contemporary Issues in Health, Education, and Rights*, edited by Gilbert Herdt and Cymene Howe. New York: Taylor & Francis, 2007.

Takaki, Ron. *Strangers from a Different Shore*. New York: Little, Brown, 1998.

Thomas, Bruce. *Bruce Lee: Fighting Spirit*. Berkeley: Frog Books, 1994.

Ting, Jennifer. "Bachelor Society: Deviant Heterosexuality and Asian American Historiography." Pp. 271–280 in *Privileging Positions: The Sites of Asian American Studies*, edited by Gary Y. Okihiro et al. Pullman: Washington State University Press, 1995.

———. "The Power of Sexuality." *Journal of Asian American Studies* 1, no. 1 (Feb. 1998): 65–82.

The Tong Man. VHS. Directed by William Worthington. Haworth Pictures Corporation, 1919.

Transgressions. DVD. Directed by Stuart Gaffney. Red Production Company, 2002.

Vance, Carole S., ed. *Pleasure and Danger: Exploring Female Sexuality*. Boston: Routledge and Kegan Paul, 1984.

Vang, Bee. "*Gran Torino*'s Hmong Lead Bee Vang on Film, Race, and Masculinity: Conversations with Louisa Schein." *Hmong Studies Journal* 11 (Spring 2010): 1–11.

Von Eschen, Penny. "Globalizing Popular Culture in the 'American Century' and Beyond." *OAH Magazine of History* 20, no. 4 (July 2006): 56–63.

Walk Like a Dragon. VHS. Directed by James Clavell. James Clavell Productions, 1960.

Wallace, Michele. *Black Macho and the Myth of the Super Woman*. London: Verso, 1999.

Warner, Michael. *Fear of a Queer Planet: Queer Politics and Social Theory*. Minneapolis: University of Minnesota Press, 1993.

Waugh, Thomas. "Good Clean Fung." *Wide Angle* 20, no. 2 (1998): 164–175.

The Way of the Dragon. DVD. Directed by Bruce Lee. Concord Productions and Golden Harvest Company, 1972.

The Wedding Banquet. DVD. Directed by Ang Lee. Ang Lee Productions, Central Motion Pictures Corporation, and Good Machine, 1993.

Weird Science. DVD. Directed by John Hughes. Universal Pictures, 1985.

Wong, Sau-ling. "Denationalization Reconsidered: Asian American Cultural Criticism at a Theoretical Crossroads."

World's Biggest Gang Bang. DVD. Directed by John T. Bone. Fantastic Pictures, 1990.

Xing, Jun. *Asian America through the Lens: History, Representations, and Identities.* Walnut Creek, CA: AltaMira, 1998.

Yellow Fever. Directed by Phillip Wang. Wong Fu Productions, 2006. www.youtube .com/watch?v=vC_ycDO66bw.

Yellowcaust: A Patriot Act. VHS. Directed by Darrell Y. Hamamoto. San Francisco International Asian American Film Festival, Hawaii International Film Festival, and San Diego Asian Film Festival, 2003.

Zia, Helen. *Asian American Dreams.* New York: Farrar, Straus and Giroux, 2001.

Index

Note: Page numbers in italic type refer to illustrations.